*Personal Identity
in Theological Perspective*

Personal Identity
in Theological Perspective

Edited by

Richard Lints,

Michael S. Horton,

&

Mark R. Talbot

WILLIAM B. EERDMANS PUBLISHING COMPANY
GRAND RAPIDS, MICHIGAN / CAMBRIDGE, U.K.

Wm. B. Eerdmans Publishing Co.
255 Jefferson Ave. S.E., Grand Rapids, Michigan 49503 /
P.O. Box 163, Cambridge CB3 9PU U.K.

Printed in the United States of America

10 09 08 07 06   7 6 5 4 3 2 1

Library of Congress Cataloging-in-Publication Data

Personal identity in theological perspective / edited by Richard Lints,
Michael Horton & Mark R. Talbot.

    p.   cm.

   ISBN-10: 0-8028-2893-0 / ISBN-13: 978-0-8028-2893-4 (pbk.: alk. paper)

   1. Theological anthropology — Christianity.   2. Image of God.

   I. Lints, Richard. II. Horton, Michael Scott. III. Talbot, Mark R.

BT701.3.P46 2006
233'.5 — dc22

                  2005032085

www.eerdmans.com

Contents

Contents

Section II: Signficant Challenges

Section III: Suggestive Proposals

Richard Lints | **Introduction**
Theological Anthropology
in Context

When I consider your heavens, the work of your fingers, the moon and the stars, which you have set in place, what is man that you are mindful of him, the son of man that you care for him? You made him a little lower than the heavenly beings and crowned him with glory and honor.

PSALM 8:3-5

This oft-quoted passage from the Psalms reminds both of the frailty of our humanity and also of its glory. We are merely creatures, whose very createdness is a pungent reminder that we are not God. Our existence is limited. And yet as the psalmist also writes, our dignity resides in this very act of being created by God. The Godness of God is reflected supremely in our humanity. There is something fundamentally ennobling about being in relationship to the God whose glory extends throughout the earth and above heaven itself (Ps. 8:1, 9). The greatness of God is reflected in the human creature. Human significance is attached to the One who has no beginning and has no end. Any consideration, then, of human identity must consider the God who created humans in his image or suffer the consequences of denying that linkage.

Poetically Psalm 8 suggests that the vastness of the universe is subtly magnified, for the heavens are the "work of God's fingers"! The heavens are prodded into shape by divine fingers. They are tiny by comparison to the immensity of God. This is in stark contrast to our perspective, from which the heavens seem so vast and immense. Do most of us not have a spontaneous reaction on warm summer evenings when we perceive the fullness of the night sky lit up? We become aware of our own insignificance by comparison to the immensity of the universe, a realization interwoven with the sense that this cannot all be an accident. Against that backdrop — the immensity of the heavens with dimensions beyond comprehension, and a God who fashions them with his proverbial fingers — our humanity appears insignificant indeed. The psalmist cannot help but ask, who are we? In the face of such immensity the intuitive answer is, Nothing! The psalmist deliberately wants us to experience this sense of despair. But the very asking of the question signals an ironic answer. Having a consciousness to ponder such profundities, the psalmist recognizes his attachment to the God whose glory fills the earth. He (and we) slowly comes to recognize that the inference of vastness is not God's remoteness but God's eye for detail. This is no cold and heartless world. It is designed to be a mirror of the divine character. The light of God's glory illuminates the whole earth. Is it any accident, then, that in the midst of the trials and tribulations of life, the mirror often seems distorted if not broken? On too many occasions it seems perfectly reasonable to ask not, "Who are we?" but, "Where is God?"

In the last century, after declaring that God was dead, Friedrich Nietzsche prophesied that the "convalescent society" would not be far off. Without a notion of transcendence from which to judge ourselves, the only two values left would be internally driven: health and happiness. The twentieth century has borne out Nietzsche's prophecy. Absorbed by concerns for health and happiness, Western culture created whole new industries devoted to crafting our self-image on the basis of good looks and a life-style of the rich and famous. The so-called "postmodern turn" has too often celebrated this ever-transient construct of self-image. And yet the radical confusion about what it means to be human has also brought an opportunity for renewed reflection on the nature of human identity. By now there appears good reason to be deeply suspicious of that nineteenth-century naturalism which Nietzsche had so thoroughly embraced. The dangers of reductionist and naturalistic accounts of human identity and dignity have become all too readily apparent as the third millennium begins. If the twentieth century brought convalescent cultures, it also brought unspeakable and heretofore unimaginable genocidal brutalities. Those brutalities now serve as potent reminders that there must be something more than mere animal instinct that drives human action and purpose.

It seems to some of us that the strange times in which we now live present new openings to retrieve the ancient biblical account of human identity as beings created in the image of God. The turbulence of our day provides ample motivation to ask the big questions of life anew. We must also be reminded, though, that there are dangers of retrieving that account in an age that does not much like fixed narratives of human identity. Any account of our humanity rooted in ultimate realities may appear woefully out of place in a time such as ours. In other words, hard work surely lies ahead in clearing the underbrush as a prelude to the rebuilding project. The present collection of essays is intended as one attempt at clearing some of that underbrush in the reconstruction project. Or to change metaphors, this volume is intended as an extended archaeological dig in order to retrieve important reminders of where we've come from and therefore who we are.

The doctrine of God looms ever present behind every one of the essays in this volume, the obvious point being that God creates and consummates human identity. It is therefore entirely pertinent to think about God when we think about ourselves. But what is it more particularly about God that illuminates the questions of human identity? Is it something that God has said or that God has done that reveals the essential elements of the human character? Or is it something about God's own nature that is the critical window into human purpose and meaning? What is the relationship between humans as creatures and the rest of God's creation? These and a host of related questions animate the discussion that follows. Bringing God into the picture may be the first step in the "archeological dig," but it raises a number of significant questions even as it answers a number of challenges in the wake of the conceptual disaster of the twentieth century, which was naturalism.

The Christian tradition has often begun the analysis of human identity with an exegetical treatment of Genesis 1:26-27:

> Then God said, "Let us make man in our image, in our likeness, and let them rule over the fish of the sea and the birds of the air, over the livestock, over all the earth, and over all the creatures that move along the ground." So God created man in his own image, in the image of God he created him; male and female he created them.

The importance attached to this fundamental text pervades most theological treatments of human identity. Consequently, the resultant framework normally was built around the concept of the *imago dei* (the image of God) as the controlling concept of human nature. From that point forward, it is not uncommon to find in theological texts the outlines of the history of redemption as a means to frame the development or devolution of the *imago dei*. The theological outline goes something like this: created in God's image, distorted by the fall, redeemed by Christ, and finally consummated by God. Within this framework, subtopics often occupying a central stage include the nature of sin, the nature of freedom, redemption or restoration of the image, the Perfect Image (Christ), and finally the ultimate end or purpose of human existence. This framework attached the meaning of human existence to the unfolding of the Divine Drama recorded in Scripture. The four "acts" in the drama were reflected in the fourfold state of humankind.

It was also not uncommon to find theological treatments of human nature pay close attention to the relationship of the *imago dei* to the rest of creation. The relationship between nature and human nature was of special interest. In these theological treatments questions such as the following were raised: What is it that humans have in common with the rest of nature and in what consist their differences? Underneath this larger umbrella fell subtopics such as the relation of body and soul, the rational faculties of humankind, the distinctiveness of human spirituality, the nature of gender, and the character of the moral life.

Prior to the nineteenth century, theological discussions of human nature almost always had a practical bent to them. In theological texts, they were often lodged under the section of what we might now call pastoral theology. Understanding human nature was of interest primarily to improve it in some fashion, whether to take its temptations more seriously or to encourage the harvest of moral fruit from it. Remnants of that tradition of moral anthropology have reappeared in our day, often as an antidote to the secular and commercial individualism of the twentieth century. Thus, it is not an accident that a renewed interest in communal and relational understandings of human identity has also reappeared in our time.

It is also not surprising to find in the history of Christian theology significant differences about human identity among the diverse traditions of Christendom. The organizing principles of any particular theological system and tradition were bound to be reflected in their expression of human identity. Traditions that have more strongly stressed the analogies between the divine and the human inevitably speak more constructively about human nature. Those traditions that more clearly emphasize the radical difference between the divine and the human often speak of the grave danger attendant upon human nature in its fallen condition. Those in Wesleyan and Arminian traditions often affirm the centrality of human freedom and human response as the central identifying marks of human nature. The Augustinian and early Protestant traditions often assert the limitations of human liberty and the corruptions of the will. Our differences about the differences which make a difference do indeed matter.

It should also be said that we should find our theological differences neither surprising nor disturbing. Most points of theological conviction and confession are interwoven with other points of theological conviction and confession. It has become incumbent upon us to bring the diverse theological traditions into dialogue with each other without supposing that this dialogue is an end in itself. The dialogue, rather, is a means to more fruitfully and faithfully harvest the richness of the biblical account. So it is with most normal human relationships — the more we genuinely engage others, the more likely it is that we will understand ourselves constructively and critically. It is also possible that we will understand our own (hidden) assumptions better as a result of the conversation.

The essays which follow were originally written as papers for a theological colloquium in Colorado Springs in the summer of 2002. This colloquium grew out of a collaborative conversation among several Evangelical, Reformed, Lutheran, and other confessionally oriented theologians who saw the need to constructively address the classic theological loci using the resources and insights from across significant theological traditions. It was the intention to have enough common interest to address the issues constructively and enough breadth to address them critically. It was our belief that theology had been addressed in predominantly defensive fashion by confessional Protestants over the last half century, and that as a result much theological dialogue never got beyond examining fundamental assumptions. As a part of a larger series of colloquia, there was an intention to move beyond that mode of theological reflection and engage our diverse traditions seriously and constructively on the major topics of theology.

The topic of the colloquium in the summer of 2002 was simply, "theological anthropology." This was the third in a planned series of ten colloquia. The first colloquium was held in the summer of 1998 on the topic of theological prolegomena. The second, held in the summer of 2000, addressed issues surrounding the doctrine of God. The colloquia were designed as small and intimate gatherings of serious scholars and clergy prepared to think deeply about the issues at hand. There was no design to construct as large a theological tent as possible to make sure no one was excluded. In other places and other times, that is a perfectly appropriate concern. Our concern was to make the theological tent small enough to actually engage our differences seriously and forge theological connections where possible. It was also an opportunity to speak faithfully within and across confessional traditions. No apologies needed here nor offered.

The papers were themselves followed by ample time for roundtable discussions, with each evening given over to an extended amount of free-flowing theological conversation. That rich theological discourse is in the background of each of the present redactions of the papers, as we have given opportunity to each of the essayists to revise their papers in light of the conversations. Unfortunately, we cannot capture the richness of the conversation itself in these pages. For the editors, there is certain sadness attached to that absence. But to most readers, it is surely a blessing that we have not tried to re-create spontaneous conversation — it normally makes for lousy reading!

The organization of the colloquium fell into three natural divisions. The first set of papers was written to retrieve significant historical discussions on the nature of human identity and to place them squarely in their confessional and ecumenical contexts. The second set of papers presented important contemporary challenges to the recovery of a distinctively Christian anthropology. The final set of papers offered constructive proposals toward a richer understanding of human identity. The essays in this volume follow roughly the order of the papers presented at the colloquium with two notable exceptions.

Mark Talbot prepared a paper that originally served as the introduction to the colloquium itself and to the possibility of doing Christian anthropology today. We have decided to place that paper in the section of suggestive proposals, believing that it nicely establishes the fruitfulness of the entire enterprise of the colloquium by bringing ordinary insights about human behavior and interaction to bear upon the larger theological justification of the Christian claims about human nature. It is, in this sense, a prolegomena to the proposals, but it is also a proposal about anthropological prolegomena.

The second change from the colloquium is the addition of an essay by Stanley Grenz not originally delivered as a paper at the colloquium. Grenz is an important voice in the recent movement to link Trinitarian discussions with anthropological discourse. He was also an ever-present voice throughout the conversation at the colloquium and offered a set of provocative summary comments at its end. Rather than including those summary comments we thought it would be better for this volume if Grenz were to offer a summary of his own work in theological anthropology. He agreed to do this, and the fruits are found in his essay, "The Social God and the Relational Self: Toward a Theology of the *Imago Dei* in the Postmodern Context."

The first section includes, then, four essays, by Robert Wilken, William Weinrich, Michael Horton, and Stanley Grenz. Wilken's essay places the anthropological discussion in its original patristic context. The influential voices of Irenaeus, the Cappodocians, and Augustine are used to examine the foundational Christian text of Genesis 1:26-27. Wilken effectively highlights the central threads that held the doctrine of anthropology together in the period from the middle of the fourth to the middle of the fifth centuries. Of particular interest is the manner in which Wilken brings Gregory of Nyssa and Augustine into conversation with each other over the significant consequences of the *imago dei*. Rebuking one modern and common misunderstanding of this Western theological tradition is Wilken's argument that the "body" formed an integral element of human nature.

Weinrich and Horton address the contrasting sides of the Magisterial Reformation traditions, Weinrich the Lutheran and Horton the Reformed/Calvinistic. Both essays remind that the Reformers were not much interested in the philosophical description of humanity as such. Most important was the fact that human identity was rooted in its creation by God and in the incarnation and redemption of Christ. For Lutherans, the law/Gospel distinction serves as the most adequate framework to discuss the relationship between humans as created and humans as redeemed. As a result, christology serves as the locus under which anthropology fits. Christ is the sum total of all that humans are supposed to be. Christ is the paradigmatic man in this sense, not simply an exemplar; Christ genuinely and radically unites his person to our humanity and thereby restores us in his person. The Reformed tradition, by contrast, viewed the covenant as the central theological construct around which the theological loci were organized. Horton goes to some length to suggest that the continuity of the Reformed tradition lies in part with the affirmation that God deals with humankind through a series of successive (and progressive) covenants. These covenants are entire arrangements of the divine/human relationship. The covenants draw primary emphasis to the history of redemption and to its impact upon human nature. As in Lutheran teaching, redemption is a gift from God which in part restores the *imago dei* in humans. In contrast to the Lutherans, however, the Reformed have emphasized those natural capacities in every human by which civil societies are to be organized. Horton draws attention to the fact that Lutherans have generally recognized these natural capacities but have given them relatively little importance. He closes by affirming that this difference of emphasis belies not two different theological anthropologies but simply two different ways of organizing the material. Undoubtedly there is some food for ecumenical thought here.

The two essays in the "Challenges" section, those by Nancey Murphy and Stanton Jones and Mark Yarhouse, look quite different from each other but address significant challenges of theological anthropology in the contemporary context. Murphy takes up the question of whether the traditional commitment to mind/body dualism ought to be affirmed in light of developments in neuroscience and in light of Christian belief. In her essay in this volume she continues her long-standing (and provocative) project of defending what she calls "evangelical physicalism" (the conviction that there is no extra-physical entity called the soul over and above the body and that this is a perfectly good Christian conviction) by answering common objections to it. Most especially she is concerned to answer the reductionist charge, namely, "if it is the brain that does the work once attributed to the mind or soul, then how can it *not* be the case that all human thought and behavior are simply determined by the laws of neurobiology?" Along the way, Murphy presses Christians to think more seriously about the relation of science to religion on questions of human identity and significance.

Stanton Jones and Mark Yarhouse take up a different challenge. They address the connection between recent discussions of sexual identity and of human identity. They are both psychologists deeply embedded in the wider academic discussion of sexual behavior and sexual identity. They take up the challenge of thinking about human identity against the backdrop of contemporary discussions of sexuality identity, affirming both the positive construals of sexual relationships within the Christian framework and also the restraints placed on sexual activity that are often repugnant to a wider secular audience. They are keen to root these in a larger (and positive) theological framework that takes seriously divine/human relationships.

Four essays follow in the "Suggestive Proposals" section, by David Kelsey, Mark Talbot, Michael Horton, and Richard Lints. Kelsey's essay takes up his long-standing concern to address anthropology in distinctively Christian and theological terms. He defends the claim that an anthropological description is distinctively theological precisely when it sees God relating to human creatures as central to the account. An anthropological description is distinctively Christian because it claims God relates to human creatures in three different but interwoven ways: creating, reconciling, and consummating. He suggests provocatively that these three ways of relating are interconnected, but that each has its own integrity in the canonical Scriptures.

Talbot's essay is linked with Kelsey's in its conceptual concerns, though Talbot begins his argument from ordinary discourse and works toward a distinctively Christian anthropology rather than, as in Kelsey, from distinctively Christian material toward a wider theological anthropology. The differences are important, as are the overlaps. At stake is the possibility of an account of humankind that is both distinctively Christian and also plausible to a wider secular audience.

Horton (in his second essay of the collection) and Lints both take up the traditional theological concern of the *imago dei*. Horton argues that in contrast to traditional theological anthropologies, which were essentialist, the *imago dei* is better understood in its covenantal context. The *imago dei* is not simply attributable to humans by virtue of some set of essential attributes. Rather, the *imago dei* functions as a term to illuminate the covenantal relationship with God. In this, it is a part of a larger narrative of God's actions toward humans, not reducible to philosophical description or to the "minimal self" of modern cultural experience. Lints addresses the oft noted omission of *imago dei* language after Genesis 9 in the Scriptures. He argues that the theological dynamic of imaging is analogous to the dynamic of idolatry. Both concepts carry a sense of worshipping something outside the self as well as being influenced by that object of worship. This then explains in part the continuous concern of the biblical writers with idolatry as the natural devolution of persons who chase after gods they've created in their own image. It also opens the door to a fresh examination of Jesus Christ as the perfect image.

It is our hope that the essays offered here, united by a common commitment to think in distinctively Christian ways about the nature of persons, succeed in retrieving important discussions from the past as well as in addressing the questions of the contemporary context. We also trust that the common commitment to speak in distinctively Christian ways does not preclude genuine conversations with those who are not Christian. But likewise, it is the firm commitment of those here represented that the wider conversation not preclude those with a distinctive Christian confession from speaking in ways faithful to those confessions. As with all theology, so here, the final commitment is not to the wider audience, but to the God who created us and reconciled us in Jesus Christ.

SECTION I | **Setting the Context**

Robert Louis Wilken | **Biblical Humanism**
The Patristic Convictions

Any discussion of the resources offered by the patristic tradition on Christian anthropology must begin with Genesis 1:26, "made in the image and likeness of God." This foundational text is quoted again and again by early Christian thinkers in many different contexts. In the *Confessions* St. Augustine reports that the Manichees had ridiculed the Catholics for believing that man was made in God's image. When he was under their influence he took the passage to mean that God had the "shape of a human figure" and like human beings was circumscribed, a belief he gave up only after being instructed by Ambrose, bishop of Milan, that "image" in the text referred to the soul and not to the body.[1] Genesis 1:26 is the backdrop for Irenaeus' understanding of redemption as "recapitulation," the summing up of all things in Christ, and he ends his *Against Heresies* with the affirmation that the God who made man will bring all things to perfection by remaking him in the "image and likeness of God."[2] But perhaps the best place to begin is with Gregory of Nyssa, who wrote a theological and philosophical exposition of the text.

Basil the Great, Gregory's older brother, had delivered a beautiful and, from a homiletical perspective, elegant series of homilies on the *Hexaemeron* (the making of the world in six days) shortly before his death. After Basil's death, Gregory, a more acute thinker than his brother, supplemented Basil's work with his own analysis of the creation of the world. But shortly after he had finished that work he be-

1. Augustine, *Confessions* 5.10.19; 6.3.4.
2. Irenaeus, *Against Heresies* 5.36.3.

gan another essay on Genesis 1:26. His ostensible reason for writing the book was that Basil's homilies had not reached verse twenty-six and as a consequence had not offered an "investigation of man." Gregory, however, was not one to be content with completing someone else's work. As in his treatise on the *Hexaemeron* Gregory had a larger agenda in mind. He thought it was time for a thorough presentation of the church's teaching on man. Earlier Christian thinkers had dealt with occasional questions concerning human beings, most notably freedom of the will and the soul, but Gregory was the first to deal systematically with the Christian doctrine of man in its fullness.

Like Basil, indeed like all thinkers in the early church, Gregory assumes that his discussion will proceed on the basis of an "interpretation of Scripture." Hence his treatise takes the form of a commentary on the biblical verse, "Let us make man in our image and likeness" (Gen. 1:26). But Gregory has a quite different sense of commentary than we do today. For him interpreting Genesis 1:26 meant treating the text theologically (not simply literally or historically) in relation to what is said elsewhere in the Scriptures and what can be known from philosophy and science about man. His aim, as he puts it, is to "fit together" what he learns from the Scripture with "conceptions that are drawn from arguments based on reason."[3]

In dealing with the person of Christ or the Holy Spirit, Christian thinkers drew primarily on the Scriptures and the knowledge of Christ and the Spirit gained by participating in the church's life and worship. But in addressing the creation of the world and the nature of man they could not appeal to the Scriptures alone; they had to give a hearing to Greek and Roman philosophers who had written on man and to the scientific and medical knowledge that was at their disposal.[4] Gregory's discussion will be based on arguments from reason and science as well as on passages from the Holy Scriptures. He draws, for example, on Aristotle's idea of the threefold distinction of the soul into the vegetative, animal, and intellectual faculty.[5] At the same time he shows that the Bi-

---

3. Gregory of Nyssa, Introductory letter to his brother Peter; PG 44:128b.

4. See Robin Darling Young, "On Gregory of Nyssa's Use of Theology and Science in Constructing Theological Anthropology," *Pro Ecclesia* 2 (1993): 345-63. See also Gerhart Ladner, "The Concept of the Image in the Greek Fathers and the Byzantine Iconoclastic Controversy," *Dumbarton Oaks Papers* 7 (1953): 1-34.

5. *Making of Man* 8 (145c). See Aristotle, *De Anima* 2.3; 414a.

ble speaks of a threefold faculty in man, and refers specifically to the words of St. Paul, "body, soul, and spirit" (1 Thess. 5:23). In discussing the relation between mind and body in human beings he draws directly on the thought of the physician and philosopher Galen.

Gregory does not, however, set up reason as an independent source of truth. In his view reason's role is to aid in understanding what is revealed in the Scriptures. His goal is to arrive at an understanding of man that is "coherent" and fits what "appears contrary" to the Scriptures into a unified conception.[6] The truth about man is not a private dogma of Christians, it is a truth for all reasonable persons.

To introduce his discussion Gregory says that the creation of the world set the stage for the creation of man. After a royal dwelling has been prepared (he has in mind the world and all its creatures), man is welcomed into the world. Only after God has adorned the world with beauties of every kind does God create man to "enjoy" what he has created. The use of the term "enjoy" is noteworthy. Gregory first uses it to speak about enjoying the things of this world, as in 1 Timothy 6:17, "God who richly furnishes us with every good thing to enjoy." But then he says that what is unique about human beings is that they are not only able to "enjoy" the good things of the earth, they are able to "enjoy God." Here was a theme so large in its proportions and so cumulative in its effect that it lurks behind everything the church fathers have to say about human nature, about sin, about redemption, about hope, about human destiny. "What food and drink are to the body, the means by which natural life is preserved, that for the soul is to gaze upon God," writes Gregory. Several centuries later Gregory the Great echoes the same theme: "The vision of God alone is our mind's true repast."[7] Everything else in nature finds its completion in things that have been made, but human beings find their fulfillment in God. In Augustine's unforgettable words, "You have made us for yourself, and our heart is restless until it rests in you."[8]

Of course, "enjoy" *(frui)* is an important term in Augustine. In his early writing he distinguished between "use" and "enjoy" and gradually worked out a complementary understanding of the two terms. Use re-

6. Gregory of Nyssa, Introductory letter to Peter; PG 44:128a-b.
7. Gregory the Great, *Moralia* 31.99.
8. Augustine, *Confessions* 1.1.

ferred to purpose, the reason for which we employ things — a hammer to nail, a roof to cover, a fire for heat, and so on. Use has to do with instrumentality, with an end that is not found in the thing itself, and wisdom is to know to what end something is to be used. Enjoy, on the other hand, refers to something "used" without relation to some other end; that is, it is employed for its own sake. Hence Augustine says that one does not "use" God; the proper term for God is "enjoy." In *De Doctrina Christiana* Augustine puts it this way: "To enjoy is to cling to something lovingly for its own sake";[9] that is to say, the term "enjoy" befits only God. Gregory does not develop the distinction but he is thinking along the same lines. Hence to say that human beings are made to enjoy God means that human life is directed toward God as its end. God is the final good, that good for which other goods are desired, the end that leads to fulfillment and perfection. Because man is made in the image of God, human life can never find fulfillment within itself; it is oriented to a reality that transcends itself.

It should be observed that the church fathers make very clear that the term "image of God" applies equally to women as to men. In Augustine's words, "In the original creation of man, inasmuch as woman was a human being, she certainly has a mind, and a rational mind, and therefore she also was made to the image of God."[10]

Now the Christian understanding of man has much in common with earlier Greek ideas, that human beings have free choice (a fundamental point in early Christian thinking), that reason and speech set them apart from animals, that they are social beings. But the biblical doctrine of the image of God set Christian thinking on a different course, as critics of Christianity recognized. Celsus had censured Christians for their belief that man was made in the image of God. "God," he wrote, "does not resemble any other form at all." For the Greeks man was a "microcosm," a "little world . . . composed of the same elements as the cosmos." Gregory had no quarrel with this, but he believed it was the wrong place to begin, for it misses what is distinctive about human life. What is so great, he asks, about being "an imprint and likeness of the world, i.e., of the heavens that go round and round, of the earth that changes, of all the things that they contain which are doomed to

9. Augustine, *De Doctrina Christiana* 1.22.20.
10. Augustine, *Literal Commentary on Genesis* 3.22.34; *The Trinity* 12.7.10.

pass when that which embraces them is gone"? If human beings are like the things of this world, they are as ephemeral as the grass that flourishes in the morning and in the evening withers. "Remember how much more you are honored by the creator than the rest of creation. He did not make the heavens in his image, nor the moon, sun, the beauty of the stars, nor anything else you see in creation. You alone are made in the likeness of that nature which surpasses all understanding. . . . Nothing in creation can compare to your greatness."[11]

According to the "Church's teaching," writes Gregory, what is distinctive about human beings is not that they are "like" the created world, but that they are made in the "likeness of the one who formed the world." We know ourselves by looking at the face of God. Though human beings have life as plants do and sensory activity like animals, they also have the capacity to know God.

> When you hear that the Divine Majesty is exalted above the heavens, that its glory is inexpressible, its beauty ineffable, and its nature inaccessible, do not despair of ever beholding what you desire. It is indeed within your reach, for your Maker has endowed your nature with this wonderful quality. God has imprinted on it traces of the good things of his own nature, as one impresses a design on wax.

The likeness to God makes man mysteriously different from all other things that are.[12]

My first point, then, is that patristic thinking on the nature of man seeks to establish, on the basis of Genesis 1:26, that human beings, though part of the natural world, are unique among all created things. Gregory says that it was only when God came to create man that he deliberated, "Let us make man. . . ." In the case of everything else he simply said, "let it be." Human beings participate in a spiritual world that transcends the world of matter and things. Call it soul, or spirit, or mind, it is that unique quality that gives rise to language, produces

---

11. Gregory of Nyssa, *Against Celsus* 6.63; Gregory of Nyssa, *Making of Man* 16 (PG 44:180a). The expression "microcosm" first occurs in Democritus, a pre-Socratic philosopher (Fragment 34 in H. Diels, *Die Fragmente der Vorsokratiker* [Berlin: 1922], 2:72). Gregory of Nyssa, *Homilies on the Song of Songs* 2 (Gregorii Nysseni Opera [GNO] 6:68).

12. Gregory of Nyssa, *Psalm Inscriptions* 1.3 (GNO 5:32, 18-19), and *The Beatitudes* 6 (GNO 7, 2:143).

works of art, establishes communities with memory (evident in the keeping of records and writing of history), and sets human life off from all other forms of life. It is a point worth pondering. We live in a culture that seeks to commodify everything — to divide up, weigh, measure, assign value — and we are perilously close to doing that with human beings, to identifying human nature so closely with the natural world that "human" loses its uniqueness. In a recent e-mail the sender included the following message, apparently sent to all correspondents as a truism: "Do not argue with the forces of nature. For you are small, insignificant, and BIODEGRADABLE!"

Of course, human beings do have bodies and are part of the natural world, and we shall see that another feature of patristic thinking on man is that human beings are not just souls, but souls with bodies. But Christian tradition insists that man cannot be reduced to the material, that what makes human being unique is spirit, the capacity to know and love God.

Second point: Because human beings are made in the image of God, the human self is a mystery. It was axiomatic that God is ineffable, beyond our powers of comprehension and understanding. "Who has known the mind of the Lord?" asked St. Paul (Rom. 11:34). God's thoughts are not our thoughts, God's ways are beyond our comprehending. But, "who has understood his own mind"? asks Gregory. Let those who reflect on the nature of God ask themselves whether they "know the nature of their own mind." Basil wrote, "We are more likely to understand the heavens than ourselves." We do not know ourselves, said Augustine, for "there is something of the human person that is unknown even to the 'spirit of man which is in him.'" For Gregory, the mystery of the human self is evidence human beings are created in the image of God: "Because our mind is made in the likeness of the one who created us, it escapes our knowledge. That is why it is reasonable to think that the human mind accurately resembles God's superior nature, portraying by its very unknowability that nature that is beyond our comprehension."[13]

Although the Cappadocians recognize that the human person is a

---

13. Gregory of Nyssa, *On the Making of Man* 11 (PG 44:153d-156b); also Basil: "We are more likely to understand the heavens than to understand ourselves" (*Hexaemeron* 10.2); Augustine, *Confessions* 10.5.7.

mystery like the mystery of God, it was Augustine who explored this theme most fully. In book 10 of the *Confessions,* in his discussion of memory, Augustine wrote, "I find my own self hard to grasp." For Augustine this applied to both the conscious and unconscious workings of the human mind, the mind present to itself, the mind remembering what it has experienced, and the mind "recalling" what it did not itself experience. For the mind relates not only to the world, and to itself, but also to God. He speaks of the "vast recesses of my mind" and "memory's huge cavern, with its mysterious secret, and indescribable nooks and crannies. . . ." Augustine found that as the mind turned inward it was drawn every more surely to God.[14] That is to say, the turn to the self is at the same time a turn to God, as the philosopher Charles Taylor has reminded us in recent times (drawing on Augustine).[15]

This godlike quality of the human mind, given at creation, made it possible for Augustine to explore the Holy Trinity through analogies with the human mind. Tertullian had begun such an attempt in his early work on the Trinity, *Against Praxeas,* but it was Augustine's *The Trinity* that examined the topic in depth. As his argument is coming to its conclusion in book 14 he writes,

> But now we have come to the point of discussing the chief capacity of the human mind, with which it knows God or can know him, and we have undertaken to consider it in order to discover in it the image of God. For although the human mind is not of the same nature as God, still the image of that nature than which no nature is better is to be sought and found in that part of us than which our nature also has nothing better.[16]

Augustine took the daring step of finding an analogy to the Trinity in the threefold activity of human remembering, understanding, and loving. He recognized that Romans 1:20, "Ever since the creation of the world [God's] eternal power and divine nature, invisible though they are, have been understood and seen through the things he has made," suggested that one might find traces of the Trinity in nature, but after

14. Augustine, *Confessions* 10.15.25; 8.14; 8.13; 10.16.

15. See Charles Taylor, *Sources of the Self: The Making of the Modern Identity* (Cambridge, Mass.: Harvard University Press, 1989), pp. 129-32.

16. Augustine, *The Trinity* 14.11.

examining the matter he returns to the mind of man as the only analogy to the Trinity.[17]

The mystery of the human person is not found in the human race, in mankind as a species, but in the individual person, as is evident from Augustine's exploration of memory in book 10 of the *Confessions*. Memory even when it is social or communal is always my memory. Though the inner life of a human being, like one's thoughts, is formed by language, and hence by society, the self that knows and the self that experiences is singular and unique. Hence the mystery of the self leads naturally to an affirmation of the uniqueness and dignity of the person. A human being cannot be made an instrument of some other end.

Third point: freedom. Among the divine qualities the maker impressed on our nature, the most important, says Gregory, is freedom. The measure of man's uniqueness is the "gift of liberty and free will." In an almost Jeffersonian phrase Gregory says that human beings are "free by nature," and in another place, "by nature equal." Gregory was one of the few church fathers to condemn slavery explicitly. It is a betrayal of human nature, he writes, "for man whose nature is free and possesses free will . . . to be condemned to slavery." Society's laws on slavery "overturn God's law for human beings," by "dividing human nature into slavery and ownership and making human nature at the same time slave to itself and master of itself."[18]

It might be observed that it was an early Christian writer, Lactantius, the Latin apologist, who first set forth a doctrine of religious freedom. In Lactantius' view, freedom of religion is necessary because of the nature of God. Religion, says Lactantius, has to do with love of God and purity of mind, neither of which can be compelled. "Why should a god love a person who does not feel love in return?" he asks. Religion cannot be imposed on someone, it can only be promoted by "words," that is, by persuasion, for it has to do with an interior disposition, and must be "voluntary." "Nothing," he writes, "requires freedom of will as religion."[19]

More often, however, Gregory speaks of human freedom as moral

---

17. Augustine, *The Trinity* 1.1-13.

18. Gregory of Nyssa, *Greater Catechism* 5 (GNO 3.4:19, 20; 20, 4); *Homilies on Ecclesiastes* 4 (GNO 5:335, 5-8; 336, 4-5).

19. On Lactantius' significance and for literature on the topic see Robert Louis Wilken, "In Defense of Constantine," *First Things* (April 2001).

freedom, the freedom to become what we were made to be. Freedom, as he puts it, is the "royal exercise of the will," but will is much more than choice, more than deciding to do one thing in preference to another. It is an affair of ordering one's life in terms of its end, freedom oriented toward excellence (the original meaning of virtue) and human flourishing. As we grow in virtue we delight in the good that is God. Hence freedom is never set forth in its own terms, it is always seen in relation to God. Because human beings were made in the image of God our lives will be fully human only as our face is turned toward God and our actions formed by his love. Freedom is as much a matter of seeing, of vision, as it is of doing. We know ourselves as we transcend ourselves, and we find ourselves as we find fellowship with God. Happiness, the happiness that gives fullness to life, will be ours only as our will conforms to God's will.[20]

Fourth point: Although human beings were made in the image of God, they sinned and the image was tarnished and disfigured. Thus the reality of human life is quite different from what "made in the image of God" suggests. Whatever may be the original state of man, something has gone terribly wrong. Human beings, as our daily experience bears witness, are most unlike God and show few signs that they are made in God's image. For Gregory the inexplicable contrast between what the Scriptures say about man in Genesis and the stubborn facts of human life was the starting point for talking about sin. How is it, he asks, that the man we know, someone who is "mortal, driven by unruly passions, soon to die," can be the image of a "nature that is uncontaminated, pure and exists forever"? What a contrast between the "misery and wretchedness of human nature" and the "happiness of the divine life"! While God dwells in bliss man is miserable. So different is the life of a human being from God that it seems what is made in the image of God must be "one thing" and what we experience in life "something else."[21] Even the Scriptures, he once mused, seem to contradict what is written in Genesis, for the words "all things are futile" in the book of Ecclesiastes seem an "indictment of creation."[22] How can God be the creator of futility?

---

20. Gregory of Nyssa, *Making of Man* 4 (PG 44:136b-c), 16 (PG 44:184b), and *On Infants' Early Deaths* (PG 46:173c).

21. Gregory of Nyssa, *Making of Man* 16 (PG 44:181a-b); ET, p. 405.

22. Gregory of Nyssa, *Homily 1 on Ecclesiastes* (GNO 5:283, 18).

Any full account of the "making of man" had to deal with man's unmaking, the fall and the intractability of evil in human life. Midway in the treatise Gregory turns his attention to man's experience in light of his origin, and discusses, albeit briefly, the misery of human life. Gregory can speak about the consequences of sin in language no less vivid than that of St. Augustine.

> Because of the guile of him who sowed in us the weeds of disobedi-ence, our nature no longer preserves the stamp of the divine image; it has been transformed and made ugly by sin. Our nature freely chose to act in accord with the evil one. For this reason human nature has become a member of the evil family of the father of sin.

Human nature is "enfeebled" and "enervated by evil" and man does not "return from evil to good as easily as he turns towards evil." Human be-ings are "prone to sin," and sin is "present in us when we are born, for it is written, 'in sin my mother conceived me.'"[23]

Like other early Christian thinkers Gregory was fascinated by the enigmatic reference to "garments of skins" at the very end of the narra-tive of creation in Genesis: "And the Lord God made for Adam and for his wife garments of skins, and clothed them" (Gen. 3:21). Moses is speaking, says Gregory, with veiled language, and the word "skins" should not be taken in its plain sense. When Adam and Eve were "stripped of happi-ness," they were clothed in garments of skins, that is, subject to death and at the mercy of "unruly passions." All who follow Adam wear the gar-ments of skin. "Adam is, as it were, living in us," says Gregory, and "after being stripped of our magnificent garments" we have been clothed in garments of skin. Among human beings no one can be found who "is able to live one day without stain." All human beings "share a common nature with Adam and participate in his fall. For, as the apostle says, 'in Adam we all die'. Therefore, the words that are suited for Adam's repen-tance are appropriate to all who have died with him." So pervasive is "sin" that "it arises when we come into existence," and "grows with us."[24]

23. Gregory of Nyssa, *Against Eunomius* 2.10 (GNO 2:293), *Lord's Prayer* 4 (GNO 7, 1:47, 17-18), *Life of Moses* (GNO 7, 1:42, 20), *On the Sixth Psalm* (PG 44:609d).

24. Gregory of Nyssa, *Greater Catechism* 8 (GNO 3, 4:30, 9-11), *Soul and Resurrection* (PG 46:148c), *Lord's Prayer* 5 (GNO 7, 2:64, 18-19; 65, 2-4; 66, 10-15), *Beatitudes* 6 (GNO 7, 2:145, 10-13).

Sin is always positioned between two certain truths, that man, on the one hand, is created in the image of God and, on the other, is destined for life with God. In the thinking of the church fathers, the reality of sin does not eradicate the image that lies hidden beneath the filth that obscures it. Hence when speaking about sin, they preferred metaphors that had to do with defacing or damaging or tarnishing the image: scraping off what was impressed on a coin, disfiguring the beauty of the image, making the image ineffective, becoming diseased. After the fall certain aspects of the image remained, for example, reason and freedom, though reason was darkened by sin and human freedom was captive to the passions. The image is "always there," says Augustine, "even if it be worn away almost to nothing."[25]

Fifth point: Image of God, even in the creation account in Genesis, cannot be understood without reference to Christ, the perfect image of God. In one place in *Making of Man* Gregory presents human nature in light of what it becomes in Christ: "The man who was shown forth at the first creation and the one who will be at the completion of things, are the same. For they equally carry the divine image." Even in an essay dealing with the creation of human beings Gregory discovered that he could not discuss the nature of man independent of its transformation in Christ. Again and again in his writings Gregory stresses that the archetypal image of God is the one "born of the virgin." In an Easter sermon he said, "On this day was created the true man, who is according to the image and likeness of God."[26] For Christian anthropology it is a matter of capital importance that in Christ human nature appeared in its original and authentic form.

In the interpretation of the church fathers the restoration of the image was also adumbrated in Genesis 1:26. Recall that there are two terms in the text, "image" and "likeness." Modern scholarship is inclined to take them as synonymous or at least complementary. But the church fathers, at least most of them, took the terms to refer to two moments in human life. "Image" refers to the gift received at creation, and "likeness" points to the re-creation and return to God. "Image" referred to man as

25. Gregory of Nyssa, *Lord's Prayer* 5 (GNO 7, 2:63), *Beatitudes* 1 (GNO 7, 2:81, 3-4); Basil, *Ascetic Discourse* 1.1 (PG 31:869d); *Lord's Prayer* 4 (GNO 7, 2:45, 23); Augustine, *The Trinity* 14.4.6.

26. *Making of Man* 16 (PG 44:183c-d); *Perfection* (GNO 9:288, 1-2); *The Triduum* (GNO 9:280, 1-2).

created, and "likeness" to man as re-created, renewed, restored, made again *like* the God who made them. The biblical text often paired with Genesis 1:26 was 1 John 3:2: "Beloved, we are God's children now; it does not yet appear what we shall be, but we know that when he appears *we shall be like him,* for we shall see him as he is." In commenting on Genesis 1:26, "Let us make man according to our image and likeness," Didymus the Blind, a contemporary of Gregory who lived in Alexandria, observed that "like" in 1 John echoes the word "likeness" in Genesis. "In the passage, 'Let us make man according to our image and likeness,'" he wrote,

> God speaks of two kinds of becoming. We are first made in God's image, and only later are we made in his "likeness." By advancing to perfection the image becomes the likeness of God which St. John sets forth when he writes: "Beloved, we are God's children now; it does not yet appear what we shall be, but we know that when he appears we shall be *like* him" (1 John 3:2). We are already made according to the image of God and we hope to become God's likeness.[27]

The words of Genesis encompass the entire mystery of salvation.

The term used by the church fathers to refer to the process of becoming "like God" is "divinization" or "deification," *theōsis* in Greek. In Athanasius' words, "The Word of God became man that we might become divine."[28] Or Gregory the Theologian: "In so far as he became man I become God." There are of course much misunderstanding and some suspicion of the idea of *theōsis,* and it is sometimes said that at the core it is a thoroughly Greek notion that stealthily made its way into Christian thinking. But the idea is biblical, and rests on the doctrine of the image of God. If human beings are made in the image of God, then the goal, the end, of human life is fellowship with God, sharing in the divine life, and that can take place only if we are fit to share God's life, that is, if we have become godlike. And that is what divinization means, becoming what we were made to be through the redemption in Christ and the gift of the Holy Spirit. There is no suggestion that human beings stop being human and become gods — the line between creator and creature is never crossed. Human nature becomes divine by participation, that is,

27. Didymus the Blind, *Didyme l'Aveugle. Sur La Genèse,* ed. Pierre Nautin and Louis Doutreleau, *Sources Chrétiennes,* no. 233 (Paris, 1976), 1:146-50.
28. Athanasius, *On the Incarnation* 54.

by grace; *theōsis* means *sharing* in the life of God, kinship with God made possible because of the endowment received at creation.

It is sometimes assumed that divinization is an Eastern notion found chiefly in the Greek fathers. But it is also found in the West. In a sermon, Augustine, for example, said, *Deos facturus qui homines erant, homo factus est qui Deus erat* ("He became man who was God that he might make gods those who were men").[29] For Augustine deification is very close to the Pauline notion of adoption, being made children of God.

> It is clear that he calls men gods being deified by his grace and not born of his substance. For he justifies, who is just of himself and not from another, and he deifies, who is God of himself and not by participation in another. But he who justifies himself deifies, because he makes sons of God by justifying. "For to them gave he power to become sons of God" (John 1:12). If we have been made sons of God, we have been made gods; but this is by grace of adoption and not of the nature of our begetter.[30]

One of Augustine's favorite texts was Psalm 73:28, *mihi adhaerere Deo bonum est*, for me to cleave to God is good. Here the term "cleave" expresses the fundamental idea of deification, fellowship with God, sharing in God's life through love that has been poured into our hearts by the gift of the Holy Spirit (Rom. 5:5).

Sixth and final point: Human beings have bodies, and in his treatise Gregory addresses the relation between the physical and spiritual aspects of human life, between the soul and the body. He realizes, of course, that "image of God" does not refer to the body. Yet he thinks it significant that man is not bent to the ground like other animals but stands upright "looking to heaven and to things above." At the same time he rejects any notion that the soul had a life of its own before its life in the flesh. The soul and body were formed together and have a "common" or "single beginning" in the "will of God."[31] It is a theme repeated again and again in early Christian literature. In the words of Maximus the Confessor, "Soul and body are indissolubly parts of the whole human species." To drive home his point he wrote, "The body,

---

29. Augustine, *Sermon* 192.1.1.
30. Augustine, *Enarrationes* in Ps. 49.1.2.
31. Gregory of Nyssa, *Making of Man* 29 (PG 44:233d).

after its separation from the soul [at death], is not simply called body, but the body of a man, indeed the body of a certain man. . . ."[32]

Although Christian thinking on the body is formed by the account in Genesis, of equal if not greater importance are Christ's resurrection and belief in the resurrection of the body. In the Nicene Creed adopted at the Council of Constantinople, the final clauses read: "We look forward to the resurrection of the dead and the life of the world to come." Christian thinking about human beings oscillates between the beginning and the end, origin and goal. The hope of resurrection led inevitably to the question whether the body was part of the definition of the self. The bodily resurrection of Jesus was of course a matter of biblical history, but it took time for Christian thinkers to draw out the full implications of the resurrection for Christian anthropology. For one thing there were texts such as 2 Corinthians 5:8, "away from the body and at home with the Lord." The story in Luke in which Jesus' body passed through walls also seemed to suggest a different view. And then there was that puzzling chapter 15 of 1 Corinthians. The metaphor of the seed implied that the raised body would be transformed into something as different as the plant is from the seed. Furthermore, bodies were always changing and subject to decay. Which body would be raised? The body of the youth, the middle-aged, or the old? In spite of very real intellectual challenges, Christian thinkers affirmed without qualification that without a body a soul is not a person.

The question of the body was not simply a matter of theological debate. It touched on that most sacred of human tasks, how one is to care for the bodies of those who have died. One of Augustine's least known, yet most fascinating, writings is a treatise entitled *On Caring for the Dead*. It was written in response to a letter he had received from Paulinus, bishop of Nola in southern Italy, concerning a widow who wanted to bury her son at a shrine where the famous St. Felix was buried. Would it benefit her son, Paulinus asked, to be buried next to St. Felix? Augustine answers her question in the negative, but as one reads into the treatise it is apparent that Augustine recognized there was something to the widow's wish. For the body is not simply an external or incidental covering for the soul, something that can be disposed of and forgotten. Gregory of Nyssa had the relics of martyrs buried alongside his parents.

---

32. Maximus the Confessor, *Ambiguum* 7 (PG 90:1101b).

When one sees the bones of a holy person it is as though the person "were fully present." As the ring or garment of a loved one is treated with love and affection, so we should care for the bodies of our loved ones as though they are the person. Bodies are not "ornaments," says Augustine, that are "fitted from without." The body belongs to the "very nature of man." Why is this so? "Care for the bodies of our dead is an affirmation of our firm belief in the resurrection."[33]

In an enigmatic passage in his *Literal Commentary on Genesis,* Augustine suggested that there could be no full vision of God without the body. Some had apparently claimed that the beatific vision would be given only to the soul, but Augustine asks, "If the spirits of the departed can be admitted to the highest blessedness without the body, why must they be reunited with their bodies in the resurrection?" Augustine acknowledges that the angels are able to behold God without bodies, but that is not the case with human beings. "For some mysterious reason," he writes, or "simply because it possesses a kind of natural appetite for managing the body," the soul needs the body. "As long as it is not joined to the body," it is not fully itself and it yearns to be united with its body. "Only when the soul . . . again receives this body . . . will it have the perfect measure of its being."[34] The direction Christian thought would take on the relation between the soul and body first appears in antiquity, but the view that the beatific vision was possible only when the soul rejoined the body was more fully explored in medieval times. St. Bonaventure, a contemporary of Thomas Aquinas in the thirteenth century, put it this way: "The person is not the soul; the person is a composite of soul and body . . . and unless there is soul and body there can be no perfect joy."[35]

The Christian doctrine of the resurrection shaped Christian understanding of the human person and in turn formed the culture of the West. What Christian tradition bequeathed to our civilization was not, as some suppose, gnosticism or shame over the body, but the psychosomatic unity of the human being. There is no self that is not embodied.

These, then, are six aspects of the early Christian understanding of

33. Augustine, *Homily on the Forty Martyrs* (GNO 10, 1:166, 10-12), *Homily on St. Theodore* (GNO 10, 1:63, 25-26), *On Caring for the Dead* 3.5.

34. Augustine, *Literal Commentary on Genesis* 12.35.68.

35. St. Bonaventure, *Sermon on the Assumption of the Blessed Virgin Mary* 1, 2, *Bonaventurae Opera Omnia,* vol. 9 (Quaracchi, 1901), p. 690.

the human person: (1) human beings are capable of knowing and enjoying God, hence of self-transcendence; (2) mystery of the human person; (3) freedom; (4) sin; (5) redemption as the restoration of the image of God (in the language of the church fathers, becoming divinized); (6) unity of body and soul.

Taken as a whole the thinking of the early church provides resources to develop a distinctly Christian humanism. The church has as great a stake in the question "What is man?" as it does in "Who is God?" The two are complementary, and there can be no full presentation of the one without the other. A profound humanism lies at the heart of the biblical tradition. "What is man that you are mindful of him, the son of man that you care for him? You have made him a little lower than God, and crowned him with glory and honor" (Ps. 8:4-5).

There are of course many ways to speak about the human person, but for Christians the most familiar, the most biblical, and the most comprehensive is, "made in the image of God." This truth about man underlies the church's moral witness on current social issues — for example, abortion, physician-assisted suicide, and now cloning. But it also grounds human freedom, artistic creativity, the life of the mind, the work of the imagination, the hopes and dreams of humankind. In the present cultural climate there is an urgency to the church's moral witness in our society, but the church's teaching on the human person cannot be reduced to ethics. If so it can easily be perceived as a narrow and restrictive moralism. Against any and all efforts to dehumanize man the doctrine of the image of God insists that the uniqueness of the human person is also found in man's love of beauty, awe before creation, and capacity for transcendence, in the wonder of a child learning language, a musician imagining the notes of a symphony, the giving of the self in love. These are divine works, hence distinctly human works. Unlike an animal, the course of whose life is set at birth, the lives of human beings are free, open, inventive.

At the opening of his *Letter to Artists* John Paul II cites Genesis 1:26. In fashioning of words and sounds, colors and shapes, the work of the artist is an "echo of the mystery of creation." The craftsman and artist, the Pope wrote, mirror God as creator. In calling human beings into existence God committed to them the work of making and creating, for through artistic creativity "man appears more than ever 'in the image of God.'"[36]

36. John Paul II, *Letter to Artists*, Vatican, 4 April 1999, Easter Sunday.

William C. Weinrich | ***Homo theologicus***
Aspects of a Lutheran
Doctrine of Man

The creeds of the early church correspond to the narrative structure of
the Holy Scriptures. They speak of God the creator; of the incarnation,
life, death, and resurrection of Christ; and of the work of the Holy
Spirit in the forgiveness of sins, the church, and the resurrection of the
dead. Yet, neither in the creeds nor in the Scriptures is there any interest in man as such. Statements concerning the natural capacities of
man — reason, will, creativity, and the like — are at best scattered and
isolated in the Bible. Nowhere is man considered in isolation as an autonomous and independent creature. Nonetheless, man lies at the center of interest both in the Scriptures and in the creeds. The Scriptures
begin with the creation of the world, which finds its culmination in the
making of Adam and Eve. The Scriptures end with the resurrection of
the body from the dead and the gift of eternal life. Central and determinative for this scriptural narrative is the man, Jesus, the Son and
Word of the Father, through whom all things are made and unto
whom all things tend (Col. 1:15-16). Similarly, in the Nicene Creed (to
take the most universally well-known and used), the summary of the

---

The use of the term "man" in the title of this essay is intended to be inclusive with reference to humankind. The Scriptures and ecclesiastical writers such as Luther thought of
humankind as a class which possessed a constitutive commonality of origin and destiny
and personal attributes. The term "man" allows us to speak generically, of humankind,
rather than referring to us only as individuals. At the same time, the term "man" suggests particularity, that humankind is a personal reality. "Humankind" is an abstraction
and does not suggest the personal character of man.

divine activities finds its determinative center in the words, "who for us and for our salvation came down from heaven and was made man."[1] In both the Scriptures and the creeds, man is defined by the works of God upon him and for him.[2]

Similarly in Luther and the Lutheran tradition, the mystery of man is most truthfully to be perceived in terms of his creation by God, his fall from God, and his restoration to God.[3] To be sure, Luther knew of the definition of man which emphasized his greatest and highest capacities. Traditionally, the fathers of the church and the medieval scholastics defined man, especially as the image of God, in psychological terms — memory, intellect or reason, and free will.[4] Luther is wholly respectful of this way of defining man. In his *Disputatio de homine* (1536), Luther begins with the philosophical definition of man: "Philosophy or human wisdom defines man as an animal having reason, sensation, and body."[5] He continues: "It is certainly true that reason is the most important and the highest in rank among all things

1. It seems to me preferable to render *enanthrōpēsanta* with "was made man." This allows both for the claim that Jesus was a man and that, as the New Adam, he represented in himself, as the head, all of humanity, both male and female.

2. Perhaps it is not insignificant that the early creeds had their context in baptism, whereby the sinner was "born from above of water and the Spirit" and made a "new man," that is, he received a new identity as a "child of God" (cf. John 1:12-13; 3:5; Rom. 8:15; Titus 3:5).

3. For example, John Andrew Quenstedt (†1688): "The subject of Theology is man, who fell into misery from his original happy state, and who is to be brought back to God and eternal salvation." Quoted in Heinrich Schmid, *The Doctrinal Theology of the Evangelical Lutheran Church*, third ed., trans. Charles A. Hay and Henry E. Jacobs (Minneapolis: Augsburg, 1961), p. 219.

4. For example, Gregory of Nyssa, *On the Making of Man* 16.11: "Thus there is in us the principle of all excellence, all virtue and wisdom, and every higher thing that we conceive; but pre-eminent among all is the fact that we are free from necessity, and not in bondage to any natural power, but have decision in our own power as we please; for virtue is a voluntary thing, subject to no dominion; that which is the result of compulsion and force cannot be virtue" (NPNF, second series, 5:405).

5. *Disputatio de homine,* thesis 1: Philosophia, sapientia humana, definit hominem esse animal rationale, sensitivum, corporeum. For the Latin text and commentary, see Gerhard Ebeling, *Disputatio de homine*, Part One: *Text und Traditionshintergrund* (Tübingen: J. C. B. Mohr, 1977); Part Two: *Die philosophische Definition des Menschen, Kommentar zu These 1-19* (Tübingen: J. C. B. Mohr, 1982). Here, Ebeling, 1.15. For the English translation, *Luther's Works* (Philadelphia: Muhlenberg; Saint Louis: Concordia, 1960), 34.137 (hereafter *LW*).

and, in comparison with other things of this life, the best and something divine."[6] Reason is "the inventor and mentor of all the arts, medicines, laws, and of whatever wisdom, power, virtue, and glory men possess in this life."[7] Indeed, reason is the "essential difference" which distinguishes human beings from the animals and all other things. Nor did God remove "this majesty of reason" after the fall of Adam, but confirmed it.[8]

Nonetheless, this philosophical consideration of man is, in the end, incapable of defining man as he truly and foundationally is: "But this must be known, that this definition describes man only as a mortal and in relation to this life."[9] Defined by his innate powers and capacities, man is in bondage to the devil and is destined to death: "But after the fall of Adam, certainly, he was subject to the power of the devil, sin, and death, a twofold evil for his powers, unconquerable and eternal."[10] For Luther, man cannot be adequately defined in terms of his own reality considered as an autonomous and independent being, or as a being whose reality lies, as it were, within himself. Nor can man be defined in reference to other, lesser creatures. Thus considered, man has his end in death. Man is, however, a more excellent creature who can be defined only in terms of realities which are beyond him and above him and outside of him. Therefore, the philosophical definition which knows only man's "material cause" renders virtually no certain

6. *Disputatio,* thesis 4: Et sane verum est, quod ratio omnium rerum res et caput et prae ceteris rebus huius vitae optimum et divinum quiddam sit (Ebeling, 1.16). English, *LW* 34.137.

7. *Disputatio,* thesis 5: Quae est inventrix et gubernatrix omnium artium, medicinarum, iurium, et quidquid in hac vita sapientiae, potentiae, virtutis et gloriae ab hominibus possidetur (Ebeling, 1.16). English, *LW* 34.137.

8. See *Disputatio,* theses 6, 9 (Ebeling, 1.16, 17). In his *Commentary on Genesis,* Luther begins his discussion of the image of God by giving a brief summary of Augustine's Trinitarian understanding, namely, that the Trinity is imaged in man's memory, intellect, and will. "I do not condemn or find fault with that effort and those thoughts by which everything is brought into relationship with the Trinity," writes Luther (*LW* 1.60). Nevertheless, typically Luther does not think such speculation "useful," since it does not relate man to the story of his fall and his restoration.

9. *Disputatio,* thesis 3: Sed hoc sciendum est, quod haec definitio tantum mortalem et huius vitae hominem definit (Ebeling, 1.15). English, *LW* 34.137.

10. *Disputatio,* thesis 22: Post lapsum vero Adae subiecta potestati diaboli, peccato et morti, utroque malo suis viribus insuperabili et aeterno (Ebeling, 1.19f). English, *LW* 34.138.

knowledge of man. For "philosophy does not know the efficient cause for certain, nor likewise the final cause [of man]." Philosophy is wholly ignorant of the fact that the efficient cause of man is "God the creator," and philosophy can find no other "final cause than the peace of this life."[11] Theology alone knows to define man according to his efficient and final causes, namely, that man is a creature of God and is destined to eternal life: "Theology to be sure from the fulness of its wisdom defines man as whole and perfect, namely, that man is a creature of God consisting of body and a living soul, made in the beginning after the image of God, without sin, so that he should procreate and rule over the created things, and never die."[12]

The distinction between man considered in relation to this world (philosophy) and man considered in relation to his efficient and final causes (God and eternal life: theology) was central to Luther's anthropological thinking. In his *Annotations on Ecclesiastes,* Luther raises the question of the special place man occupies within the world. Commenting on Ecclesiastes 3:18-19 — "I said in my heart with regard to the sons of men that God is testing them to show them that they are but beasts. For the fate of the sons of men and the fate of beasts is the same; as one dies, so dies the other" — Luther notes that the common view that Solomon is speaking of the wicked is false. On the contrary, Solomon is speaking of all persons, for all die, and so it seems as though Solomon is simply equating the life of every human person with that of the animals and bringing all things under the judgment of vanity. But, writes Luther, in keeping with the intent of the book, Solomon describes man as he is "under the sun," that is, "in the world," "in appearance." Considered in this way, man is like unto the beasts, for "being made of the same dust, [man and beast] also return to the same dust," and so they seem to be similar. But this is so only because "the

---

11. *Disputatio,* thesis 13: Nam philosophia efficientem certe non novit, similiter nec finalem (Ebeling, 1.17). Thesis 14: Quia finalem nullam ponit aliam quam pacem huius vitae et efficientem nescit esse creatorem Deum. English, *LW* 34.138.

12. *Disputatio,* thesis 20: Theologia vero de plenitudine sapientiae suae hominem totum et perfectum definit; thesis 21: Scilicet quod homo est creatura Dei carne et anima spirante constans, ab initio ad imaginem Dei facta sine peccato, ut generaret et rebus dominaretur nec unquam moreretur (Ebeling, 1.19). English, *LW* 34.138. Note also thesis 17: "Nor is there any hope that man in this principal part can himself know what he is until he sees himself in his origin which is God" (*LW* 34.138).

world, which judges on the basis of appearance and their common outcome, thinks this way and cannot think otherwise, since believing otherwise requires something more sublime than the world."[13] What is "more sublime than the world" is the gift of the Holy Spirit, who teaches us that he is from "beyond the sun" and, therefore, the life of godliness is to be distinguished from the life of the world: "To have a happy heart and to rejoice in present things with the fear of God is not a thing of the world but a gift of God. It comes from heaven, from beyond the sun."[14] The gift of immortality is neither understood nor fully believed by the world, for it is "not a thing 'under the sun'." Man is to be defined from *ultra solem,* from "beyond the sun," that is, as one destined by his creator for immortality and eternal life. And so, man lives in two arenas, the one destined to death and the one destined to life with God.

As one might expect, it is in his commentary on Genesis, begun in 1535, that Luther most thoroughly expounds the special place that man has in creation and draws the anthropological consequences from it.[15] To be sure, Adam was given a physical life that entailed eating, drinking, labor, and procreation, and this Adam would have done "even if our nature had remained unimpaired." This life is similar to that of the beasts, who also eat, drink, sleep: "Therefore, if you take into account their way of life, their food, and their support, the similarity is great."[16] Moses teaches, however, that there is an "outstanding difference" between the beasts and human persons. The words "Let us make" (Gen.

13. *Ecclesiastes of Solomon with Annotations* 3:18ff. (*LW* 15.57-61).

14. *LW* 15.58, 60.

15. Luther presented his lectures on Genesis during the years 1535 to 1545. That the commencement of these lectures in 1535/1536 coincides with his disputation on man in 1536 indicates the central place which the question of man was occupying in Luther's mind at the time.

16. *LW* 1.56. Had our nature remained unimpaired, our physical life would not have ended in death. Luther quotes approvingly "the scholars" who claim that "even if Adam had not fallen through his sin, still, after the appointed number of saints had been attained, God would have translated them from this animal life to spiritual life." Luther adds: "This would have surely been a pleasant and delightful life, a life about which we may indeed think but which we may not attain in this life" (*LW* 1.56f.). The entry of death into the life of man through sin now causes this life to end, not in a translation to the spiritual life, but in death. The animals, who were never created for eternal life, were always consigned to mortality.

1:26) show that "when He wanted to create man, God summons Himself to a council and announces some sort of deliberation." Man was created by "the special plan and providence of God." Moreover, God also created man "in the image of God." Both of these assertions indicate "that man is a creature far superior to the rest of the living beings that live a physical life," and that, indeed, man was created "for a better life in the future than this physical life would have been, even if our nature had remained unimpaired."[17] Man was created to inherit eternal life, immortality, and this is that which denotes man's excellence, namely, that he is "fit for immortality."[18]

That God by a special deliberation made man in his own image for eternal life, corresponds to the definition of man according to the efficient and final causes, which we noted also in the *Disputatio de homine*. Man *is* from God; man *is* for life with God (immortality). Moreover, it is in view of this claim that Luther also interprets the "image of God" in which man was made. The "image of God" indicates that we were created by God for a better life, namely, for a life with God. The "image of God," therefore, does not pertain to this physical life, nor to those special capacities of man by which he rules in this life (intellect, will, and so on). Indeed, Luther argues that were the image of God to consist of such powers as memory, will, and mind, Satan himself would have been created according to the image, for "he surely has these natural endowments, such as memory and a very superior intellect and a most determined will, to a far higher degree than we have them."[19] The image of God is "something far more distinguished and excellent." It is a "unique work of God" which is a much more encompassing reality than reason or will or any other natural capacity. This is indicated by the fact that "when we speak about the image, we are speaking about something unknown. Not only have we had no experience of it, but we continually experience the opposite."[20] Before sin, both Adam's "inner and outer sensations were all of the purest kind." He possessed not only the clearest intellect and the purest will, but also the keenest of eyesight and strength beyond that

17. *LW* 1.56f.; also 1.65, 83ff.
18. *LW* 1.84 *(capax immortalitatis)*.
19. *LW* 1.61.
20. *LW* 1.63.

of the bear. Nonetheless, we experience none of that, for in us all of that is "most depraved and most seriously weakened, yes, to put it more clearly, they are utterly leprous and unclean."[21] Our intellect, our will, our memory, our physical capacities are deformed by the loss of the image, and this suggests that the image of God, which man in Adam was, consists in none of these, but rather consists in that life which man freely receives from God and which is directed toward eternal life. In the *Disputatio de homine*, Luther had already in the third thesis claimed that the philosophical definition of man as "having reason, sensation, and body" describes man "only as a mortal and in relation to this life."[22] This point now receives its due emphasis: "After the Fall death crept into our life and came as a leprosy into all our perceptive powers, so that with our intellect we cannot even understand that image." As a creature living freely from God and unto eternal life with God, man was made in the image of God. With sin came the loss of the image, that is, with sin came death:

> Therefore my understanding of the image of God is this: that Adam had it in his being and that he not only knew God and believed that He was good, but that he also lived in a life that was wholly godly; that is, he was without the fear of death or of any other danger, and was content with God's favor. In this form it reveals itself in the instance of Eve, who speaks with the serpent without any fear, as we do with a lamb or dog. For this reason, too, if they should transgress His command, God announces the punishment: "On whatever day you eat from this tree, you will die by death," as though He said: "Adam and Eve, now you are living without fear; death you have not experienced, nor have you seen it. This is my image, by which you are living, just as God lives. But if you sin, you will lose this image, and you will die."[23]

Sin is, therefore, much more than a mere disobedient act. It encompasses man round about and destroys what man is according to his ef-

---

21. *LW* 1.61.

22. Ebeling, 1.15; *LW* 34.137.

23. *LW* 1.62f. Also *LW* 1.65: "Therefore that image of God was something most excellent, in which were included eternal life, everlasting freedom from fear, and everything that is good."

ficient and final causes. Sin redefines man. After the fall, man *is* Sinner, that is, sin places man in opposition to his creator and leads him to death as a judgment.[24] For, man was created *for* eternal life; that is essential to the definition of man. When man becomes subject to death, man ceases to be that man created for eternal life. Death is the sure sign that man has become cut off from his origin (God) and from his destiny (eternal life), from his efficient and final causes.

Man, whose life is from God and who is destined for life with God, exists always *coram Deo,* before God. As the image of God, man lived before God in faith, that is, in the belief that God was good and in contentment with God's favor. Man trusted God with an open receptivity grounded in this trust. Luther expresses this idea in his explanation of the first article of the Apostles' Creed in his *Small Catechism.* According to this explanation, to believe that God is the creator means that God gives and preserves all our natural endowments, that he daily provides all that we need to support our body and life, and that he does this "out of pure fatherly goodness and mercy without any merit or worthiness in me, for all which is my duty to thank and to praise Him, to serve and to obey Him." Faith is that foundational and defining posture of man before God in which man freely trusts God to be the giver and sustainer of his life.

From this it is clear why Luther was so adamant in rejecting works as the way of salvation, and insisted upon the justification of the sinner by way of faith. If man is defined in terms of his origin and his destiny, and these are from God and unto God, then there is nothing human works can accomplish. Either man *is* as the one who lives from God and unto life with God, or man *is* as the one who has himself against God and is subjected to death. Since man's life lies outside himself, both in terms of its origin and in terms of its destiny, man can, from himself, neither secure his life nor regain it again once this life is lost. For this life to be restored, that is, for the image of God to be restored in man, there is required another act of God by which he gives once again that life which was lost.

---

24. This does not mean that man is substantially a sinner. Luther thinks relationally, not substantially. In sin, man intends to establish himself in opposition to God. Man intends to be his own creator and to secure his own life. Man becomes, as it were, his own efficient and final causes.

This new act of God is the gospel by which God creates from sinful man that man originally intended for eternal life:

> But now the Gospel has brought about the restoration of that image. Intellect and will indeed have remained, but both very much impaired. And so the Gospel brings it about that we are formed once more according to that familiar and indeed better image, because we are born again into eternal life or rather into the hope of eternal life by faith, that we may live in God and with God and be one with Him, as Christ says. . . . In this manner this image of the new creature begins to be restored by the Gospel in this life, but it will not be finished in this life. But when it is finished in the kingdom of the Father, then the will will be truly free and good, the mind truly enlightened, and the memory persistent.[25]

In the *Disputatio de homine*, Luther had defined man by quoting the apostle Paul: "We hold that a man is justified by faith apart from works" (Rom. 3:28). Luther briefly comments: "[Paul] briefly sums up the definition of man, saying, 'Man is justified by faith'."[26] By God's justification of the sinner, man receives again, in faith, that life before God which will lead to eternal life with God. Significantly, Luther regards the justification of man as a definition of man. This anthropological character of God's justifying act is mostly clearly adumbrated in Luther's discussion of the "righteousness of Christ" in his great commentary on Galatians.

Through the fall into sin, Adam had brought death to man. As we have seen, with death, man lost the image of God, that is, man was now sinner, in rebellion against his creator and consigned to mortality. In his *Lectures on Galatians*, Luther adopts the classical christology of the early church and integrates the incarnation of Christ into the doctrine of justification of the sinner.[27] It was a common claim of the early Fathers that Christ became as we are, in order that we might become as he

---

25. *LW* 1.64f.

26. *Disputatio*, thesis 32: Paulus . . . breviter hominis definitionem colligit dicens: hominem iustificari fide (Ebeling, 1.22). English, *LW* 34.139.

27. For the following, see Tuomo Mannermaa, *Der im Glauben gegenwärtige Christus: Rechtfertigung und Vergottung. Zum oekumenischen Dialog* (Hannover: Lutherisches Verlagshaus, 1989), pp. 22-55. See also Bengt Haegglund, "Luthers Anthropologie," in *Leben und Werk Martin Luthers von 1526 bis 1546: Festgabe zu seinem 500. Geburtstag*, vol. 1, ed. Helmar Junghans (Göttingen: Vandenhoeck und Ruprecht, 1983), pp. 73-75.

is.[28] For a Greek Father such as Athanasius, this meant that the incorruptible, fully divine Son of the Father became corruptible as man, in order that we who are corruptible might become as he is, namely, incorruptible. Luther uses the same schema, but causes it to serve his doctrine of God's justification of the sinner: Christ, who is holy, righteous, and living, becomes as we are, sinful, unrighteous, and mortal, in order that we who are sinful, unrighteous, and mortal, might become as he is, holy, righteous, and living.

According to the Nicene Creed, the divine Son of God "for us and for our salvation came down from heaven, and was made man." In his comments on Galatians 3:13, "Christ redeemed us from the curse of the Law, having become a curse for us," Luther discusses this "man" that Christ became. This "man" that Christ became was not the neutral manhood of some abstract pure humanity. This "man" was Man the Sinner. Luther's discussion emphasizes the "for us" of Paul's statement. If "for us," then in our place as sinner. Christ became that man defined by sin and death. Christ became the greatest sinner *(maximus peccator)*. Luther makes this claim in a number of passages. For example:

> For Christ is innocent as far as His own Person is concerned. . . . But Christ took all our sins upon Himself, and for them He died on the cross. Therefore it was appropriate for Him to become a thief and, as Isaiah says, to be "numbered among thieves." And all the prophets saw this, that Christ was to become the greatest thief, murderer, adulterer, robber, desecrator, blasphemer, etc. there has ever been in the world. He is not acting in His own Person now. Now He is not the Son of God, born of the Virgin. But He is a sinner, who has and bears the sin of Paul, the former blasphemer, persecutor, and assaulter; of Peter, who denied Christ; of David, who was an adulterer and a murderer, and who caused the Gentiles to blaspheme the name of the Lord. In short, He has and bears all the sins of all men in His body — not in the sense that He has committed them, but in the sense that He took these sins, committed by us, upon His own body, in order to make satisfaction for them with His own blood.[29]

28. For example, see Irenaeus, *Adversus Haereses* 5.pref.; Marcellus of Ancyra, *De incarnatione et contra Arianos* 8 (the ascription to Marcellus is disputed).

29. *LW* 26.277. Also *LW* 26.278: "He is, of course, innocent, because He is the Lamb of God without spot or blemish. But because He bears the sins of the world, His inno-

Moreover, since Christ took the sins of all humans upon himself and therefore became the greatest sinner, it is also true that Christ became the only sinner *(solus peccator)*. He became the Man who is Sinner:

> [God] sent His Son into the world, heaped all the sins of all men upon Him, and said to Him: "Be Peter the denier; Paul the persecutor, blasphemer, and assaulter; David the adulterer; the sinner who ate the apple in Paradise; the thief on the cross. In short, be the person of all men, the one who has committed the sins of all men." . . . But because in the same Person, who is the highest, the greatest, and the only sinner, there is also eternal and invincible righteousness, therefore these two converge: the highest, the greatest, and the only sin; and the highest, the greatest, and the only righteousness.[30]

As we have noted, man has his efficient cause in God as the creator and his final cause in eternal life with God. Not surprisingly, therefore, precisely in this discussion of Christ becoming for us Man the Sinner, Luther also emphasizes that this Christ is also true God. In Colossians 2:15, Paul writes, "He disarmed the principalities and powers, triumphing over them in him." Luther comments on the phrase "in him":

> This circumstance, "in Himself," makes the duel more amazing and outstanding; for it shows that such great things were to be achieved in the one and only Person of Christ — namely, that the curse, sin, and death were to be destroyed, and that the blessing, righteousness, and life were to replace them — and that through Him the whole creation was to be renewed. If you look at this Person, therefore, you see sin, death, the wrath of God, hell, the devil, and all evils conquered and put to death. . . . Here you see how necessary it is to believe and confess the doctrine of the divinity of Christ. . . . For to conquer the

---

cence is pressed down with the sins and the guilt of the entire world. Whatever sins I, you, and all of us have committed or may commit in the future, they are as much Christ's own as if He Himself had committed them. In short, our sin must be Christ's own sin, or we shall perish eternally." And *LW* 26.280: "If the sins of the entire world are on that one man, Jesus Christ, then they are not on the world. But if they were not on Him, then they are still on the world. Again, if Christ Himself is made guilty of all the sins that we have committed, then we are absolved from all sins, not through ourselves or through our own works or merits but through Him."

30. *LW* 26.280f.

sin of the world, death, the curse, and the wrath of God in Himself — this is the work, not of any creature but of the divine power. Therefore it was necessary that He who was to conquer these in Himself should be true God by nature. . . . Since Scripture attributes all these things to Christ, therefore He Himself is Life, Righteousness, and Blessing, that is, God by nature and in essence.[31]

Christ, who for us has become the person of all sinners, is in his own person true God. No human work or merit can deserve or obtain this person; only faith receives and obtains this person who is God. That which faith obtains, however, is not merely an assurance of the forgiveness of sins and of salvation. Faith does not merely have as its object the fact that we are forgiven; nor is justifying faith only an abstract and verbal act. Faith is rather the receiving and possessing of the person of Christ. Against the scholastic notion that faith was formed by love, Luther insisted that faith receives its form from that which it receives and possesses, namely, Christ:

We say that faith takes hold of Christ and that He is the form that adorns and informs faith as color does the wall. Therefore Christian faith is not an idle quality or an empty husk in the heart, which may exist in a state of mortal sin until love comes along to make it alive. But if it is true faith, it is a sure trust and firm acceptance in the heart. It takes hold of Christ in such a way that Christ is the object of faith, or rather not the object but, so to speak, the One who is present in the faith itself. . . . Therefore faith justifies because it takes hold of and possesses this treasure, the present Christ. . . . Therefore the Christ who is grasped by faith and who lives in the heart is the true Christian righteousness, on account of which God counts us righteous and grants us eternal life.[32]

Faith, therefore, is participation in the person of Christ who is present in faith. This Christ, who for us became Man the Sinner, is also true God, himself our righteousness, on account of whom God grants us eternal life. In Christ, therefore, man receives anew and by grace his efficient and his final causes. In faith man possesses the man who is

31. *LW* 26.282.
32. *LW* 26.129f.

God and is given eternal life. Indeed, the new life which we are granted in Christ is Christ himself. In the person of Christ, man receives his new identity as man; man is one person with Christ.[33] In commenting on Galatians 2:20, "Nevertheless, I live, yet not I, but Christ lives in me," Luther writes:

> When he says: "Nevertheless, I live," this sounds rather personal, as though Paul were speaking of his own person. Therefore, he quickly corrects it and says: "Yet not I." That is, "I do not live in my own person now, but Christ lives in me." The person does indeed live, but not in itself or for its own person. But who is this "I" of whom he says: "Yet not I"? It is the one that has the Law and is obliged to do works, the one that is a person separate from Christ. This "I" Paul rejects; for "I," as a person distinct from Christ, belong to death and hell. This is why he says: "Not I, but Christ lives in me." . . . The life that I now live, He lives in me. Indeed, Christ Himself is the life that I now live. In this way, therefore, Christ and I are one. . . . But faith must be taught correctly, namely, that by it you are so cemented to Christ that He and you are as one person, which cannot be separated but remains attached to Him forever and declares: "I am as Christ." And Christ, in turn, says: "I am as that sinner who is attached to Me, and I to him. For by faith we are joined together into one flesh and one bone."[34]

Originally, man was created by God for eternal life. This was man's identity and definition. Through the fall into sin, man was redefined as sinner, one who opposed God and was consigned to death as judgment. Through his incarnation, the person of God the Son assumed the person of sinful man, and through the innocent suffering and death of the person of God the Son, the person of sinful man receives, in faith, the person of God the Son. By grasping hold of him who for us is greatest sinner, we receive, in faith, the life of God. Luther can be

33. That the Christian is and lives in another, namely, Christ, and not from and in himself is crucial for understanding Luther. The Christian lives extrinsically, *extra se*, by an alien righteousness. See Wilfried Joest, *Ontologie der Person bei Luther* (Göttingen: Vandenhoeck und Ruprecht, 1967), esp. pp. 233-74; more recently Daphne Hampson, *Christian Contradictions: The Structures of Lutheran and Catholic Thought* (Cambridge: Cambridge University Press, 2001), pp. 9-55.

34. *LW* 26.167f.

quite bold in the articulation of this: "Faith makes a man God."[35] This is the so-called "happy exchange" of which Luther also speaks in his sermon on the Magnificat:

> Just as God in the beginning of creation made the world out of nothing, whence He is called the Creator and the Almighty, so His manner of working continues unchanged. Even now and to the end of the world, all His works are such that out of that which is nothing, worthless, despised, wretched, and dead, He makes that which is something, precious, honorable, blessed, and living. On the other hand, whatever is something, precious, honorable, blessed, and living, He makes to be nothing, worthless, despised, wretched, and dying. In this manner no creature can work; no creature can produce anything out of nothing.[36]

From the foregoing we can see that such words as these present both an anthropological and soteriological program. Both anthropology and soteriology, however, are utterly determined by the economy of Christ in the flesh. That which is something, precious, honorable, blessed, and living — namely, the Son of God — is made to be nothing, worthless, despised, wretched, and dying — namely, the greatest sinner — while that which is nothing, worthless, despised, wretched, and dead — namely, sinful man — is made to be something, precious, honorable, blessed, and living — namely, one person with Christ.

The work of God in Christ is described as a *creatio ex nihilo,* which only God can do. It is precisely the sinner who in faith apprehends the deity of Christ, however, and so becomes like God.[37] For Luther, this means that man through faith is become, like God, a creator who from

---

35. *LW* 26.100.

36. *LW* 21.299; see also *LW* 26.314: "For God is the God of the humble, the miserable, the afflicted, the oppressed, the desperate, and of those who have been brought down to nothing at all. And it is the nature of God to exalt the humble, to feed the hungry, to enlighten the blind, to comfort the miserable and afflicted, to justify sinners, to give life to the dead, and to save those who are desperate and damned. For He is the almighty Creator, who makes everything out of nothing."

37. We recall the quotation in which Luther gives his understanding of the image of God (*LW* 1.62f.). It includes living a life "that was wholly godly," that is, a life such as God lives. When Luther speaks of the restoration of the image, the thought that man has become like God is not far away.

his fullness gives to those who have nothing. He who is lord is to become servant. The definition of man as "justified by faith" carries with it the definition of man as a "wonderful creator":

> And so it is very beneficial if we sometimes become aware of the evil of our nature and our flesh, because in this way we are aroused and stirred up to have faith and to call upon Christ. Through such an opportunity a Christian becomes a skillful artisan and a wonderful creator, who can make joy out of sadness, comfort out of terror, righteousness out of sin, and life out of death.[38]

It is as this "wonderful creator" that justified man is like God, who descends from heaven that he might cause the lowly to ascend through the bestowal of his good gifts. Luther can speak of the man of faith as "in heaven": "Christ and faith must be completely joined. We must simply take our place in heaven; and Christ must be, live, and work in us."[39] Gustav Wingren has pointed out Luther's way of using spatial terms when speaking of man's vocation of service to the neighbor. To perform one's vocation is to perform works "below," "down here."[40] It was in the condescension of Christ that he revealed himself to be the true creator who makes that which is nothing to be something. Justified by that faith which lays hold of Christ and possesses him, man now ascends into the heavens with Christ, so that he might descend to serve his neighbor with the works of love:

> When we have taught faith in Christ this way, then we also teach about good works. Because you have taken hold of Christ by faith, through whom you are righteous, you should now go and love God and your neighbor. Call upon God, give thanks to Him, preach Him, praise Him, confess Him. Do good to your neighbor, and serve him; do your duty. These are truly good works, which flow from this faith and joy conceived in the heart because we have the forgiveness of sins freely through Christ.[41]

38. *LW* 27.74 (on Gal. 5:17).

39. *LW* 26.357.

40. Gustav Wingren, *Luther on Vocation,* trans. Carl C. Rasmussen (Philadelphia: Muhlenberg, 1957), pp. 123-43, esp. 125-30.

41. *LW* 26.133.

"Therefore, we define a Christian as follows: A Christian is not someone who has no sin or feels no sin; he is someone to whom, because of his faith in Christ, God does not impute sin."[42] This is man as theology knows him.

---

42. *LW* 26.133.

Michael S. Horton | **Post-Reformation Reformed Anthropology**

According to Stanley Grenz, the Reformation in general and Calvin in particular represent "the birth of the relational imago."[1] While it was hardly their intention to prepare the ground for a wholly relational understanding of personhood, there can be little doubt that Calvin and his theological heirs have contributed significantly to the discussion before us and that they have done so with a willingness both to appropriate and to critique the tradition they had inherited from the patristic and medieval periods. In this essay I attempt to provide a somewhat general account of the principal themes in theological anthropology that found a distinctive emphasis among the Reformed, with special attention to the traditional dogmatics of the post-Reformation period.

---

1. Stanley J. Grenz, *The Social God and the Relational Self* (Louisville: Westminster John Knox, 2001), p. 162. He cites Paul Ramsey: "The image of God, according to this view, consists of man's position before God, or, rather, the image of God is reflected in man because of his position before him." But even more than Luther, Calvin stands out as the Reformer who gave "greater attention to the *imago dei* 'than any great theologian since Augustine' [David Cairns]." "Douglas Hall, in turn, cites Calvin as more important than Luther for the emergence of the relational understanding of the *imago dei*." Furthermore, Calvin develops an eschatological (future-anticipatory) approach.

Michael S. Horton

Creation and Covenant

John Calvin famously launched his *Institutes* with the recognition of the dialectical relationship of theology proper and anthropology. Calvin thought that the knowledge of God and humankind was complementary and dialectical: consideration of one leads us by the hand to the other and back again. For Calvin, neither topic can be abstracted from the other, which means, in the current discussion, that any so-called "Christian" anthropology that begins with general (that is to say, secular) notions of personhood is already a house built on sand.

Thus, the *Institutes,* for example, begins with God's revelation in creation and Scripture.[2] As T. F. Torrance observes of Calvin's approach, "This Biblical knowledge of man is gained: (a) Through the law, which enables man to see himself as he really is in comparison with his original truth which is the law of his being. . . . (b) Through the Gospel, which not only reveals to man what he actually is [in Christ], but brings him regeneration so that he may become what he is meant to be."[3] Thus, anthropology "has no independent status" for Calvin.[4] As we will see below, this is as true for the Reformed scholastics, upon whom we will draw at various points along the way.

With increasing emphasis, the Reformed tradition saw in the biblical motif of "covenant" a way of expressing the inherent unity of God's external works in creation, redemption, and consummation. A broad post-Reformation Reformed consensus emerged with respect to the existence in Scripture of three distinct covenants: the covenants of redemption *(pactum salutis)*, of creation *(foederus naturae)*, and of grace *(foederus gratiae)*.

The Covenant of Redemption

The covenant of redemption is distinguished from the covenants of creation and grace particularly as to its logical priority and its part-

2. Rightly rejecting the prevalent notion of a "central thesis" in Calvin's work (namely, predestination), Mary Potter Engel speaks of Calvin's thought generally as "a dynamic perspectival structure" (*John Calvin's Perspectival Anthropology* [Atlanta: Scholars Press, 1988], p. xi).

3. T. F. Torrance, *Calvin's Doctrine of Man* (Westport, Conn.: Greenwood, 1957; repr. 1977), p. 13.

4. Torrance, *Calvin's Doctrine of Man,* p. 14.

ners. As the eternal pact entered into by the members of the Trinity, it represents the close relationship of the *opera ab intra* and the *opera ad extra*, or of the immanent and economic Trinities. Beyond the textual evidence Scripture gives us concerning the reality of this intratrinitarian covenant, we cannot access it in its details. Believers are not to search out this secret decree, but to concentrate on the historical covenants that God has made with his creatures. While investigating God's secret council is both impossible and dangerous, God has revealed his will in creation, in Scripture and supremely in Christ.

This covenant of redemption is not merely a theological speculation, but has been regarded by the Reformed as the fruit of careful and detailed exegesis. In the ministry of Christ, for example, the Son is represented (particularly in the Fourth Gospel) as having been given a people by the Father (John 6:39; 10:29; 17:2, 6-10; Heb. 2:13, citing Isa. 8:18) who are called and kept by the Holy Spirit (Rom. 8:29-30; Eph. 1:11-13; Titus 3:5; I Pet. 1:5). In fact, to affirm the covenant of redemption was little more than affirming that the Son's self-giving and the Spirit's regenerative work were the execution of the Father's eternal plan. Consequently, while it is an intratrinitarian arrangement and each person is perichoretically involved in the action of the other, it all takes place "in Christ" — hence, the emphasis in covenant theology on the theme of "Christ the Mediator." Thus, even before creation and the fall, the elect are "in Christ" in terms of the divine *purpose* for history, though not yet *in history* itself.[5]

Given the hiddenness of God's eternal decree in Christ, most of the interest in covenant theology falls on the revealed purposes of God in the two historical covenants (creation and grace). One of the most succinct statements of this scheme of the two historical covenants is found in the seventh chapter of the Westminster Confession of Faith:

> The distance between God and the creature is so great, that although reasonable creatures do owe obedience unto him as their Creator, yet they could never have any fruition of him, as their blessedness and reward, but by some voluntary condescension on God's part, which he hath been pleased to express by way of covenant. The first cove-

5. For our purposes, we will leave to one side the variations within this concept between so-called infralapsarianism and supralapsarianism (either of the orthodox or Barthian varieties).

nant made with man was a covenant of works, wherein life was promised to Adam, and in him to his posterity, upon condition of perfect and personal obedience. Man, by his Fall, having made himself incapable of life by that covenant, the Lord was pleased to make a second, commonly called the covenant of grace: wherein he freely offered unto sinners life and salvation by Jesus Christ, requiring of them faith in him, that they may be saved, and promising to give unto all those that are ordained unto life, his Holy Spirit, to make them willing and able to believe.

The Covenant of Creation (Works)

The covenant of creation (also known as the covenant of nature/works, law of nature) represents the original stage in the temporal execution of God's eternal decree. Furthermore, it has as its partners the triune God and humanity in Adam. If the covenant of redemption remains controversial, the so-called covenant of creation *as a covenant of works* is more still, especially in contemporary Reformed theology. Ever mindful that this is supposed to be an exercise in *historical* theology, I will attempt to allow some of the tradition's most exemplary representatives to define the position.

Regarded by many, including Jürgen Moltmann and Wolfhart Pannenberg, as the virtual founder of the subdiscipline of biblical theology, Johannes Cocceius (1603-1669) remarks,

> Man who comes upon the stage of the world with the image of God, exists under a law and a covenant, and that a covenant of works. . . . When further we say that he who bears the image of God given in creation was established under God's covenant, we do not mean that he has a right to the communion and friendship of God, but that he is in that state in which he ought to ask the right to the communion and friendship of God and to make it stable and so to have the offer of God's friendship, if he obeys His law.[6]

---

6. Cocceius, *Summa Theologiae* XXII, 1, cited in Heinrich Heppe, *Reformed Dogmatics,* revised and ed. by Ernst Bizer; English trans. by G. T. Thompson (London: Wakeman Trust, from the 1950 Harper and Brothers edition), p. 281. Cf. Witsius, I, II, 1: "The covenant of works is the agreement between God and Adam created in God's image to be the

This covenantal arrangement is "God's pact with Adam in his integrity, as the head of the whole human race, by which God requiring of man the perfect obedience of the law of works promised him if obedient eternal life in heaven, but threatened him if he transgressed with eternal death; and on his part man promised perfect obedience to God's requirement."[7] This view reaches confessional status in the Westminster Confession, as we have mentioned, and is everywhere presupposed in the Canons of Dort. Although it becomes more hermeneutically significant for the Reformed scholastics, the exegesis of the relevant passages concerning the original state of humankind may be found in the ancient Christian writers, including Irenaeus and Augustine.

The cavils of Barth and many of his students notwithstanding, Calvin was a Calvinist. That is to say, the broad lines of his thought were refined and developed rather than distorted by his theological successors. In fact, the architects of federal theology clearly recognized that their covenant of works/grace scheme arose from their prior commitment to the distinction between law and Gospel. As early as the first page of his *Commentary on the Heidelberg Catechism,* Ursinus (primary author of the Heidelberg Catechism and formative federal theologian)

---

head and prince of the whole human race, by which God was promising him eternal life and felicity, should he obey all his precepts most perfectly, adding the threat of death, should he sin even in the least detail; while Adam was accepting this condition" (cited p. 283). The terms were that "he should by this natural holiness, righteousness and goodness possess a blessed state of life" (Eglin, *De foedere gratiae,* II, 10, cited p. 283). For a somewhat baroque explanation, cf.: "According to this the covenant of works retained the following four connections (Wyttenbach Tent. II, 571): 'The act by which a first party demands something from a second is called *stipulatio;* the act by which it assigns good to it, *promissio;* while the act by which the second party takes upon itself to supply what the first had demanded is called *adstipulatio* and where it asks for the promise, *restipulatio.* Thus in any covenant there are four acts, two belonging to the party initiating the covenant, and two to that which accepts the covenant offered. In God's covenant with the first man all four covenant acts are discernible. Whereas God has demanded of man perfect keeping of the law, we have discerned the *stipulatio* in it, and whereas He promised man life in heaven and has already conferred the greatest happiness in this world, we discern the *promissio.* On the other side as long as man studied to keep God's law, *adstipulatio* was being given by him to God's demand. Had he persisted therein vigorously and non-stop, he might in the end have asked a good promise of God and so *restipulatio* would have ensued'" (p. 295).

7. Cocceius, *Summa Theologiae* XXII, 1, cited in Heppe, *Reformed Dogmatics,* p. 283.

states, "The doctrine of the church is the entire and uncorrupted doctrine of the law and gospel concerning the true God, together with his will, works, and worship."[8]

> The doctrine of the church consists of two parts: the law, and the gospel; in which we have comprehended the sum and substance of the sacred Scriptures. . . . Therefore, the law and gospel are the chief and general divisions of holy scriptures, and comprise the entire doctrine comprehended therein . . . for the law is our schoolmaster, to bring us to Christ, constraining us to fly to him, and showing us what that righteousness is, which he has wrought out, and now offers unto us. But the gospel, professedly, treats of the person, office, and benefits of Christ. Therefore we have, in the law and gospel, the whole of the Scriptures comprehending the doctrine revealed from heaven for our salvation. . . . The law prescribes and enjoins what is to be done, and forbids what ought to be avoided: whilst the gospel announces the free remission of sin, through and for the sake of Christ. . . . The law is known from nature; the gospel is divinely revealed. . . . The law promises life upon the condition of perfect obedience; the gospel, on the condition of faith in Christ and the commencement of new obedience.[9]

Calvin's successor in Geneva, Theodore Beza, made precisely the same point in his *Confessio* — adding the warning that "ignorance of this distinction between Law and Gospel is one of the principal sources of the abuses which corrupted and still corrupt Christianity."[10] William Perkins, father of Elizabethan Puritanism, taught practical theology to generations of students through his *Art of Prophesying* (1592, 1606). In that work he asserts,

> The basic principle in application is to know whether the passage is a statement of the law or of the gospel. For when the Word is preached, the law and the gospel operate differently. The law exposes the disease of sin, and as a side-effect stimulates and stirs it up. But

---

8. Zacharius Ursinus, *Commentary on the Heidelberg Catechism,* trans. G. W. Williard (Phillipsburg, N.J.: P & R Publishing, from the 1852 Second American Edition), p. 1.

9. Zacharius Ursinus, *Commentary on the Heidelberg Catechism,* pp. 2-3.

10. Theodore Beza, *The Christian Faith, by Theodore Beza,* trans. James Clark (Lewes, England: Focus Christian Ministries Trust, 1992), pp. 41ff.

it provides no remedy for it. . . . The law is, therefore, first in the order of teaching; then comes the gospel.[11]

Continental and British Reformed traditions are agreed in their insistence upon this distinction, and it was strengthened rather than aban-
doned as federal theology became increasingly refined. This pattern of
rendering "law-gospel" and "covenant of works/covenant of grace" interchangeable continues all the way up to Louis Berkhof's *Systematic
Theology*, under the heading, "The Two Parts of the Word of God Considered as a Means of Grace."[12] While his work is hardly representative
of a fully developed federal theology, Calvin does assert the main features of the covenant of creation.[13]

Rejecting concupiscence as attributing weakness to created nature,
Calvin cautions restraint in speculating why Adam fell or why God did
not create him incapable of ruin.[14] In a number of places, Calvin refers
to Christ's having "merited" salvation for his people by his obedience,
once more emphasizing the satisfaction of law as a necessary prerequisite for everlasting life.[15] The basic elements of the covenant of works

11. William Perkins, *The Art of Prophesying* (Edinburgh: Banner of Truth, 1996), p. 54.

12. Louis Berkhof, *Systematic Theology* (Grand Rapids: Eerdmans, 1941): "The
Churches of the Reformation from the very beginning distinguished between the law
and the gospel as the two parts of the Word of God as a means of grace. . . . The law comprises everything in Scripture which is a revelation of God's will in the form of command or prohibition, while the gospel embraces everything, whether it be in the Old
Testament or the New, that pertains to the work of reconciliation and that proclaims
the seeking and redeeming love of God in Jesus Christ. And each one of these two parts
has its own proper function in the economy of grace" (p. 612).

13. John Calvin, *Institutes of the Christian Religion*, ed. John T. McNeill, trans. Ford
Lewis Battles (Philadelphia: Westminster, 1960), 1.15.8.

14. Calvin, *Institutes* 1.15.8.

15. John Calvin, *Institutes*, 1.15.8: "By his obedience, however, Christ *truly acquired
and merited* grace for us with his Father. Many passages of Scripture surely and firmly
attest this. *I take it to be commonplace* that if Christ made satisfaction for sins, if he paid
the penalty owed by us, if he appeased God by his obedience . . then he *acquired* salvation for us by his righteousness, which is tantamount to *deserving it*. . . . Hence it is *ab-
surd to set Christ's merit against God's mercy*" (2.17.1, 3, emphasis added). The Belgic Confession says that Adam "transgressed the commandment of life" (art. 14), terminology
that was used in the emerging covenant theology (especially by Bullinger and Martyr)
as interchangeable with "covenant of works." In Article 22, "We believe that for us to acquire the true knowledge of this great mystery the Holy Spirit kindles in our hearts a
true faith that embraces Jesus Christ with *all his merits*, and makes him its own, and no

can even be discerned in Augustine's claim, "The first covenant was this, unto Adam: 'Whensoever thou eatest thereof thou shalt die the death,'" and this is why all his children "are breakers of God's covenant made with Adam in paradise."[16]

The federal theologians founded this notion exegetically in two ways: first, by connecting the definition of a "covenant" (in its ancient Near Eastern background, as far as those conventions were known to them) with the admittedly sparse details of the Genesis narrative; second, by observing the references to such a natural arrangement in various subsequent texts. As to the first, it was argued, every covenant in Scripture is constituted by a series of formulae, most notably, oaths taken by both parties with stipulations and sanctions (blessing and curse). It would appear that these elements are present, albeit implicitly, in the creation narrative. Adam is created in a state of integrity with the ability to render God complete obedience, thus rendering a suitable human partner. Further, God commands such complete obedience, and promises, upon that condition, the *right* (not the *gift*) to eat from the Tree of Life.

As further confirmation, the presence of the Sabbath at the end of

---

longer looks for anything apart from him. . . . And therefore we justly say with Paul that we are justified 'by faith alone' or by faith *'apart from works.'* However, we do not mean, properly speaking, that it is faith itself that justifies us — for *faith is only the instrument by which we embrace Christ, our righteousness.* But Jesus Christ is our righteousness in making available to us *all his merits* and all *the holy works* he has done for us and in our place" (art. 23, emphasis added). It is Christ's merits, not our obedience — not even our faith — that is the ground of our salvation. "In fact, if we had to appear before God relying — no matter how little — on ourselves or some other creature, then, alas, we would be swallowed up" (art. 23).

16. Augustine, *City of God* (bk. 16, ch. 28), trans. Henry Bettenson, ed. David Knowles (New York: Penguin, 1972). He speaks of "the origin which is common to all mankind, since all have broken God's covenant in that one man in whom all sinned." There are various covenants, "But the first covenant, made with the first man, is certainly this: 'On the day you eat, you will surely die.' . . . For the covenant [curse] from the beginning is, 'You will surely die.' Now, seeing that a more explicit law was given later, and the Apostle says, 'Where there is no law, there is no law-breaking,' how can the psalm be true, where we read, 'I have counted all sinners on earth as law-breakers'? It can only be true on the assumption that those who are held bound by any sin are guilty of a breach of some law." Thus even infants are "recognized as breakers of the Law which was given in paradise." He goes on to clearly distinguish this covenant from that gracious covenant made with Abraham (pp. 688-89).

the "six-day" work-week (probation) holds out the promise of everlasting confirmation in blessedness. If Adam should default in this covenantal relationship, he would "surely die," and we learn from the subsequent failure of Adam that this curse brought in its wake not only spiritual but physical, inter-relational, and indeed environmental disaster. A canonical reading of this episode brings into still sharper focus the corporate and representational character of Adam's covenantal role. Not only was he in covenant with God; all of humanity was in covenant with God by virtue of participating federally in Adam. Indeed, all of creation was in some sense judged in Adam (Gen. 3:17-18; Rom. 8:20). It is with this simultaneously legal and relational background in mind that Paul makes his well-known statements on the imputation of Adam's sin as the corollary of the imputation of the Second Adam's righteousness (esp. Rom. 5).[17]

Thus, the elements of covenant-making seem to be present in the Genesis narrative, especially as interpreted by the rest of Scripture. Further, there are the texts that appear to take into account just such an arrangement. Mastricht, for example, quite typically appeals to Hosea 6:7, where it is said of Israel, "Like 'Adam, they have broken my covenant" (cf. Job 31:33). As a theocracy typological of the true Paradise of God, Israel's *national* existence was a repetition of the covenant of works — hence, the comparisons drawn by the biblical writers to Adam and the original creation.[18] Israel was called to see itself as a new theocratic garden of God's presence and as a new creation in the sense of representing humanity before God — all of this typological of the true Israel, the faithful 'Adam, who is also the true heavenly temple and everlasting Sabbath of God.

As with Adam, the Sinaitic covenant made with Moses is conditional. If Israel is faithful, the people "may dwell long in the land the Lord your God is giving you." Thus, Israel's tenure in the land, like

---

17. This approach also rejects the frequent opposition between "relational" and "legal" categories of the divine-human relationship. "Covenant" is an inherently legal relationship.

18. While this parallel is drawn by a number of writers, it is given a thorough description and analysis in Herman Witsius (1636-1708), *The Economy of the Covenants* (Escondido, Calif.: den Dulk Christian Foundation, 1990). For a more contemporary summary, see Charles Hodge, *Systematic Theology* (Grand Rapids: Eerdmans, 1946), pp. 117-22.

Adam's, is conditional. Precisely the same terms and sanctions apply. As with his appeal to the two Adams for double imputation, Paul draws on the analogy of two mountains and two mothers to contrast the covenant of works (law) and the covenant of grace (promise) (Gal. 3 and 4).

But for our purposes here, it is important to notice, as Mastricht points out, that the principle of works is strenuously maintained in Scripture. The "works of the law" demand "most punctilious obedience ('cursed is the man who does not do all the works therein')." Only in this context, says Mastricht, can we possibly understand the role of Jesus Christ as the "fulfiller of all righteousness."

> Heb. 2:14-15 (since the children are sharers in blood and flesh, he also in like manner partook of the same; that through death he might bring to nought him that hath the power of death, that is, the devil). . . . If you say the apostle is speaking of a covenant not in Paradise, but the covenant at Sinai, the answer is easy, that the Apostle is speaking of the covenant in Paradise so far as it is re-enacted and renewed with Israel at Sinai in the Decalogue, which contained the proof of the covenant of works.[19]

A further argument, says Mastricht, is the following:

> Synonyms of the covenant of works are extant in the NT Rom. 3:27 (where is the glory? It is excluded. By what manner of law? Of works? Nay: but by a law of faith) Gal. 2:16 (knowing that a man is not justified by the works of the law save through faith in Jesus Christ . . . because by the works of the law shall no flesh be justified).[20]

If one objects that these passages merely demonstrate the opposite conclusion — namely, that one cannot be justified in a covenant of works — these theologians reply that it is only humanity after the fall (humanity as sinful) that cannot be justified by works. Adam, however, was in a state of rectitude, perfectly capable of acceding to the divine mandate.

To refuse *in principle* the possibility of Adam's fulfillment of the covenant of works is to challenge the state of rectitude (not mere inno-

---

19. Cited by Heppe, *Reformed Dogmatics,* p. 290.
20. Cited by Heppe, *Reformed Dogmatics,* pp. 289-90.

cence) in which the race was created. The Lutherans and the Reformed were agreed in rejecting the "Socinian" view that the image consists only in dominion and moral innocence and not, rather, in wisdom, justice, and holiness.[21] And against Rome, they hold that man was created in a state of righteousness and not merely in a "neutral" state, and jointly affirm that this original state was natural and not a supernatural gift.[22]

In addition to the exegetical arguments, Mastricht adduces the intrasystematic importance of the doctrine:

> To very many heads of the Christian religion, e.g., the propagation of original corruption, the satisfaction of Christ and his subjection to divine law Rom. 8:3-4 (what the law could not do, in that it was weak through the flesh, God, sending his own Son in the likeness of sinful flesh and for sin, condemned sin in the flesh, that the requirement of the law might be fulfilled in us, who walk not after the flesh, but after the Spirit) Gal. 3:13 (Christ redeemed us from the curse of the law, having become a curse for us . . .), we can scarcely give suitable satisfaction, if the covenant of works be denied.[23]

Olevianus, co-author of the Heidelberg Catechism, sees in the original covenant's prohibition the essence of the whole law — love of God and neighbor.[24] And in this state Adam could expect — for himself and his covenant heirs — royal entrance into the consummation, the Sabbath rest of God himself, and everlasting confirmation in righteousness. In the words of the Formula Consensus Helvetica, "the promise annexed to the covenant of works was not just the continuation of earthly life and felicity," but a confirmation in righteousness and everlasting heavenly joy.[25]

A final argument in favor of the covenant of creation is supplied by Cocceius, in terms natural to one influenced by Calvin's thought:

21. See, for instance, Francis Turretin, *Institutes of Elenctic Theology,* trans. George Musgrave Giger, ed. James T. Dennison Jr., vol. 1: *First through Tenth Topics* (Phillipsburg, N.J.: P&R, 1992), p. 467.

22. See, for instance, John Theodore Mueller, *Christian Dogmatics* (St. Louis: Concordia, 1934), p. 206.

23. Cited by Heppe, *Reformed Dogmatics,* p. 290.

24. Heppe, *Reformed Dogmatics,* p. 294.

25. Cited by Heppe, *Reformed Dogmatics,* p. 295.

the argument from *conscience*. By nature human beings know that they have offended God's friendship and communion. All of this presupposes an original relationship that has been breached.[26] According to Cocceius, we know this is a real covenant from "(1) the conscience (Ro. 2:15), (2) the longing for eternal life, (3) the 'daily and continual benefits by which man is urged to seek his Creator and Benefactor and to love, glorify and thank Him.'"[27] Cocceius sharply rejects the nominalist covenant theology of the late Middle Ages. "A *debitum* on God's part only exists *ex pacto*. . . ." Heppe relates, "Cocceius is therefore (XXII, 39) zealous against the [medieval] Scholastics, who by an appeal to the 'absolute lordship of God' assert, that if He willed God could abandon even a perfectly obedient man and the holy angels to eternal damnation."[28] The covenant of works is an arrangement that is suited to the intelligence, wisdom, and virtue of the human creature.[29]

It is therefore premature to insert into the creation covenant an element of divine graciousness, strictly speaking. To be sure, God's decision and act to create is a "voluntary condescension" (Westminster Confession of Faith 7.1), as is his entrance into a covenantal relationship with his human creatures. Nevertheless, if "grace" is to retain its force as divine clemency toward those who deserve condemnation, we are wiser to speak of divine wisdom, goodness, justice, and righteousness as the governing characteristics of creation.

It is within this framework, then, that Reformed orthodoxy understood the active obedience of Jesus Christ, emphasizing the significance of his humanity in achieving redemption for his covenant heirs.[30] The priority of law in the covenant of creation establishes the fact that God cannot acquit the guilty; nor can he simply forgive sinners. In the context of the covenant of creation, the law must be perfectly satisfied, either personally or representatively. We see this ethical emphasis of the so-called *imago* in the fact that not only Adam and his progeny, male and female, as well as Christ and his progeny, male and female, in a special sense, are

26. Heppe, *Reformed Dogmatics*, p. 286.
27. Cited by Heppe, *Reformed Dogmatics*, p. 287.
28. Heppe, *Reformed Dogmatics*, p. 288.
29. Heppe, *Reformed Dogmatics*, p. 288.
30. The Fourth Gospel once again especially underscores the "fulfilling of all righteousness" that is central to Jesus' mission (John 5:19; 6:38; 17:4).

image-bearers, but that the law itself is a "mirror" of God's own essential righteousness. To reflect God as his image is therefore to be righteous, holy, obedient — a covenant servant, defined as such by the covenant charter (Hos. 6:7 and Isa. 22; Isa. 24:5; Jer. 33:20, 25; 31:35-37).[31]

Thus all humans are created in God's image — remain so, in fact, after the fall — precisely because they are *ex pacto* participants in the covenant of creation by their very existence. To be created in God's image is to be in covenant with God. Though vitiated by human rebellion, this covenant is still in effect. It was renewed in the Noah narrative and is repeatedly reaffirmed in the many biblical references to God's common providence; its lines were thickened by the extraordinary institution of the Mosaic theocracy, and its fulfillment is anticipated in the Servant and true Son of Adam, Son of Man, Son of God, who will be the true and faithful Adam-Israel. It is he who, in his royal entrance, brings captives in his train, claiming the reward for his obedience for himself and for his brethren. Thus, in him, law and gospel embrace without being confused; justice and grace are equally displayed without being synthesized.

This account provides the soil for a robust notion of the humanity of Christ. God the Father alone could not have saved us. Our savior had to be the second Adam. Throughout his relatively brief messianic career, Jesus recapitulated Adam's testing in the Garden and Israel's forty-year testing, in his own forty-day probation in the desert and, in fact, in the entirety of his life.

31. Moreover, in the light of recent studies of ancient Near Eastern treaties, we can affirm with Meredith Kline that the arrangement in the Genesis narrative has all the elements of a covenant. Not only are the formulaic stipulations and sanctions present, as the older theologians recognized; other elements now recognized as fixtures of such covenants, such as a preamble and a historical prologue, are present as well. See Meredith Kline, *Kingdom Prologue*, vols. 1, 13, 17. In fact, there can be little doubt that Genesis 1 and 2 constitute just such a preamble ("In the beginning God created the heavens and the earth") and narrative prologue both contextualizing and justifying the terms of the treaty that follow. This covenant is "produced through divine words and acts of commitment and it was subject to the sanctions of ultimate divine blessing and curse. . . . Described in terms of varieties of international covenants familiar at the time of the writing of the Book of Genesis, the Covenant of Creation was thus a suzerain-vassal covenant plus the proposal of a special grant to the vassal for loyal service." For the distinctive elements of treaty-making, see also Klaus Baltzer, *The Covenant Formulary* (Philadelphia: Fortress, 1971).

Michael S. Horton

The Covenant of Grace

The third covenant in the federal scheme is the covenant of grace. Once this Second Adam has successfully fulfilled this covenant ("For their sakes I sanctify myself that they may be truly sanctified," John 17:19), the benefits of this feat are dispersed by the Spirit according to a *gracious* covenant. Thus, the terms of the divine benediction here are reversed. Instead of acknowledging the inherent goodness, truth, and beauty of sinners, he pronounces them just on the basis of the inherent justice of another *(iustitia aliena)*. It is a true judgment rather than a legal fiction because the requisite covenantal righteousness is indeed fully present in the covenantal head (by the fulfilling of the creation covenant) and therefore belongs to his body by incorporation.

Like the covenant of creation, this covenant is made between God and human partners — in this case, fallen Adam, Seth, Abraham, and David. It is in this covenant that provisions are made for offenders, based on another's fulfillment of the legal covenant on their behalf. Thus, instead of it being a covenant based on law ("Do this and you shall live"), it is based on promise ("Live and you will do this").

It is precisely this contrast that, according to the Reformed theologians, energizes so much of Pauline theology in particular. Jesus is the faithful Israelite who fulfilled the covenant of works so that we could through his victory inherit the promises according to a covenant of grace. This gracious covenant is announced in Eden after the fall, as the so-called *protoeuangelion* (Gen. 3:15). Eventually, God will call Abram out of the city of alienation and establish his covenant of grace with him, along with a provisional and thoroughly conditional covenant of works. The former covenant establishes the basis for the everlasting inheritance of the heavenly Jerusalem, while the latter establishes the terms of the temporal inheritance of the earthly Jerusalem as a typological reunion of cult and culture pointing forward to the reign of God in Christ. Abraham himself was looking through the temporal promises to the "city with foundations whose builder and architect is God" (Heb. 11:10).

As far as the temporal land-grant, Israel ("like Adam," Hos. 6:7) defiled the land, transgressed this conditional covenant, leading to its eviction from the new temple-garden of God, and yet, once more, the covenant of grace provided the terms of rescue for those who looked to the promise rather than the law for their redemption. The Abrahamic covenant rather than the Mosaic covenant establishes the terms of this arrangement. It is in this context that we better understand such passages as Jeremiah 31:32 ("It will not be like the covenant I made with their fathers in the wilderness . . .") and Galatians 3:17-18: "My point is this: the law, which came four hundred thirty years later, does not annul a covenant previously ratified by God, so as to nullify the promise. For if the inheritance comes from the law, it no longer comes from the promise; but God granted it to Abraham through the promise."

Thus, in the covenant of grace God restores in his new creation what was lost in the old creation and could not be recovered according to the original principle that was established in nature. Because of the covenant of grace, and the Messiah's having fulfilled the covenant of works, "There still remains the promise of a Sabbath rest" (cf. Heb. 4:1, 9).

Covenant theology, therefore, has always been eschatologically oriented, convinced that creation was the beginning rather than the goal of human existence. Humankind was created to pass through the probationary period and attain the right to eat from the Tree of Life. Thus, the telos of human existence was not fully present in creation, but was held out as a future reward. Humankind would lead creation in triumphal procession into the consummation, represented by the Tree of Life. Adam was to imitate God's sovereign session and, as a creature, to climb the steps of eternal glory to claim his prize for himself and his posterity, and to take his place as vassal-king under the great Suzerain.[32] Only in the fulfillment of the covenant of creation by the second Adam is the destiny of the image-bearer finally attained and dispensed through the covenant of grace.

---

32. Drawing upon important features of covenant theology, Meredith Kline has written extensively on the remarkable strategy employed in the two creation narratives of Genesis 1 and 2 (*Kingdom Prologue*, vol. 1:26-31). Rather than attempting a report on the chronology of origins, these chapters pillage the pagan cosmogonic myth — the slaying of the dragon by the hero-god, followed by celebration of his glory in a royal residence built as a sequel to his victory. This interpretation, fortified by recent studies in ancient suzerainty treaties of the Near East, represents a powerful polemic against the idols of the nations that Israel must confront. This creation narrative, therefore, constitutes the treaty or covenantal charter that asserts Yahweh's sovereignty. It also exhibits the unmistakably covenantal character of creation itself.

We turn now from the delineation of the classical covenantal model to the application of this perspective to the questions of human personhood and the *imago dei*.

Imago Dei

Calvin

The dialectical thought of the Genevan Reformer is finally receiving deserved attention.[33] Calvin's dim view of fallen humanity must be measured against his sometimes astonishing respect for created humanity. Utterly essential for Calvin — and instructive for us — is the refusal to locate the slightest weakness or defect in humanity that might make the fall and consequent need for redemption necessary from the start. "For the depravity and malice both of man and of the devil, or the sins that arise therefrom, do not spring from nature, but rather from the corruption of nature."[34] This he distinguishes from the "Manichean error." "For if any defect were proved to inhere in nature, this would bring reproach upon [God]."[35] "Finally, we shall learn that in forming man and in adorning him with such goodly beauty, and with such great and numerous gifts, he put him forth as the most excellent example of his works."[36]

What then constitutes the "image"? First, its proper seat is the soul, but Calvin goes beyond the earlier tradition in attributing its glory to the whole person.[37] This image (Calvin judges ṣelem and demuth to be synonymous), seated in the soul, nevertheless "extends to the whole excellence by which man's nature towers over all kinds of living creatures." Consequently, "there was no part of man, not even the body itself, in which some sparks did not glow."[38] Second, the true nature of this image "can be nowhere better recognized than from the restoration of his corrupted nature." Adam was alienated from God.

33. See especially in this regard Kilian McDonnell, OSB, *John Calvin, the Church, and the Eucharist* (Princeton, N.J.: Princeton University Press, 1967).
34. Calvin, *Institutes* 1.14.3.
35. Calvin, *Institutes* 1.15.1.
36. Calvin, *Institutes* 1.14.20.
37. Calvin, *Institutes* 1.15.3.
38. Calvin, *Institutes* 1.15.3.

Therefore, even though we grant that God's image was not totally annihilated and destroyed in him, yet it was so corrupted that whatever remains is frightful deformity. Consequently, the beginning of our recovery of salvation is in that restoration that we obtain through Christ, who also is called the Second Adam for the reason that he restores us to true and complete integrity.[39]

The willful distortion of this image is a measure both of its ineradicable status and of human depravity. This is what is meant in the command to "Put on the new man, who has been created according to God" (Eph. 4:24).[40] "Now we see how Christ is the most perfect image of God; if we are conformed to it, we are so restored that with true piety, righteousness, purity and intelligence we bear God's image."[41] Calvin rejects both Augustinian speculations concerning a "trinity" of the soul and neoplatonic "emanation," "as if some portion of immeasurable divinity had flowed into man."[42]

Reformed Orthodoxy

Like Calvin, the Reformed scholastics appeal to the traditional (Aristotelian) identification of humanity as a sort of "microkosmos," displaying in a signal manner God's external works. God's likeness in humanity, according to Mastricht, is "that conformity of man whereby in his own way (i.e., as a creature) he reproduces the highest perfection of God."[43] "For

---

39. Calvin, *Institutes* 1.15.4.

40. Calvin, *Institutes* 1.15.4.

41. Calvin, *Institutes* 1.15.4.

42. Calvin, *Institutes* 1.15.5. Here Calvin challenges Osiander's "infusionist" perspective. Despite his training and his early interests (namely, his refutation of "soul-sleep" in his first theological treatise, *Psychopannychia*), Calvin has surprisingly little interest in subtle excursions into the nature of the soul with respect to the divine image: "It would be foolish to seek a definition of 'soul' from the philosophers . . ." (1.15.6). That is not to suggest that such philosophical discussion is to be utterly rejected. "But I leave it to the philosophers to discuss these faculties in their subtle way. For the upbuilding of godliness a simple definition will be enough for us" (1.15.6). Eschewing "useless questions," he says it is sufficient for our purposes to recognize that the human soul consists of "understanding and will" (1.15.7).

43. Cited in Heppe, *Reformed Dogmatics,* p. 232.

the understanding of the Reformed Church doctrine of the divine image in man it should be noted that it is thoroughly connected with man as such, indeed with the entire man, with his entire spirit-body being. . . ."[44]

Peter Martyr Vermigli, characteristic of the tradition, follows Calvin's analysis quite closely, insisting that the proper interpretation of the image will have to look to Christ and our renewal in him by the Spirit. It is not that we are no longer human after the fall, but that we abuse our office in self-interest. In our fallen condition, we no longer exercise proper dominion, but "exercise tyranny over things instead." "The image of God is the new man, who understands the truth of God and desires its righteousness. So Paul has taught us, when he writes to the Colossians: 'Put on the new nature, which is being renewed in the knowledge of God, after the image of its Creator.'"[45] We may be renewed in the image of Christ, but Christ is "the primary and true image" of God.[46]

The only reference that we find in the Heidelberg Catechism identifies the image with the "true righteousness and holiness" in which Adam was created (Q. 6).[47] And the Westminster Confession elaborates along the same lines:

> After God had made all other creatures, he created man, male and female, with reasonable and immortal souls, endued with knowledge, righteousness, and true holiness after his own image, having the law of God written in their hearts, and power to fulfill it; and yet under a possibility of transgressing, being left to the liberty of their own will, which was subject unto change. Besides this law written in their hearts, they received a command not to eat of the tree of the knowledge of good and evil; which while they kept they were happy in their communion with God, and had dominion over the creatures (Chapter 4).

According to Heinrich Heppe,

44. Cited in Heppe, *Reformed Dogmatics,* p. 232.
45. Cited in Heppe, *Reformed Dogmatics,* p. 232.
46. Cited in Heppe, *Reformed Dogmatics,* p. 44.
47. Heidelberg Catechism, Q. 6: "God created man good and in his image, that is, in true righteousness and holiness, so that he might rightly know God his Creator, love him with his whole heart, and live with him in true blessedness, praising and glorifying him."

Cocceius (*Sum. theol.* XVII) finds the divine image not in the "substance of the soul," nor yet in the "faculties of the soul," nor yet in the "*imperium* which man had over the living," but in the *rectitudo* which he explains (para. 22) as moral reciprocity with God in all a man's parts, in the soul of course as the *hegemonikon* and in the body and limbs as the *skeuos*. Similarly Heidegger (VI, 19), Braun (I, ii, 15), Riissen (VI, 60), etc.[48]

Others see the *imago* in the *dominio*. According to Vermigli, it renders man "a kind of representative (vicar) of God."[49] Those in "Melanchthon's school" are, according to Heppe, more likely to locate the *imago* in the incorporeal substance of the soul.[50]

As we will see below in our concluding interaction with Lutheran dogmatics, the *definition* of the image is all-important in deciding whether it has been wholly abolished after the fall. Ursinus speaks for the Reformed in carefully distinguishing the sense in which this image is lost and retained: "But after the fall, man lost this glorious image of God, on account of sin, and became transformed into the hateful image of Satan."[51] He hastens to add, "There were, however, some remains and sparks of the image of God still left in man, after his fall, and which even yet continue in those who are unregenerated," which include the rational soul and will, knowledge of the arts and sciences,

---

48. Heppe, *Reformed Dogmatics,* p. 44.

49. Cited in Heppe, *Reformed Dogmatics,* p. 233. But the view that came to dominate (via Melanchthon) was a distinction between the substance (in the personal nature of man) and the actual endowments (original righteousness). Despite a formal rejection of the semantic difference between "image" and "likeness," this approximates the patristic distinction.

50. For example, Ursinus argues, "It will have to be estimated not by the state in which men began to be after the entry of sin, but by the reparation made through Christ, i.e., from the nature of man born again," and hence explains that "further, the image of God is not to be sought in the sole substance of the soul, but particularly in the virtues and gifts with which it was adorned by God in creation" (cited in Heppe, *Reformed Dogmatics,* p. 233). Compare with the nineteenth-century Lutheran dogmatician J. T. Mueller: "The seat of the divine image was not the body, but the soul of man; for the knowledge of God together with holiness and righteousness inheres properly in the soul. Nevertheless also the body shared in the divine image, since it is the organ of the soul" (Mueller, *Christian Dogmatics,* p. 207) — not that, in most instances, Mueller would want to have been identified with "Melanchthon's school"!

51. Ursinus, *Commentary on the Heidelberg Catechism,* p. 32.

"traces and remains of civic virtue," "the enjoyment of many temporal blessings," and some measure of dominion over other creatures. What is lost, however, are the most important things belonging to the image, namely, true knowledge of God, his will, and his works; the regulation of affections and actions in accordance with God's law; a genuine stewardship over creation; and a true happiness in this life and the next.

In spite of this breach of the covenant of creation, however, God has (explains Ursinus) promulgated the covenant of grace:

> God the Father restores this image through the Son; because he has 'made him unto us wisdom, righteousness, sanctification, and redemption' (1 Cor. 1:30). The Son, through the Holy Spirit, 'changes us into the same image, from glory to glory, as by the Spirit of the Lord' (2 Cor. 3:18). And the Holy Ghost carries forward and completes what is begun by the Word and the use of the Sacraments.[52]

Polanus makes a similar argument.[53] From these writers we learn that the image is chiefly rectitude, the law written on the conscience. The law of God and image of God are therefore two sides of the same coin. Even Christ can be said to be the incarnate law of God as the archetypal divine image, since he perfectly *represents* this will as God and *fulfills* this will as human. It is not, therefore, a question of some inner faculty or quality in the soul or mind, "as though it were an essential part of his nature" (Heppe), nor a matter of a supernatural gift, since only the restoration of the image by grace qualifies as such. This original rectitude is lost, but not the knowledge of God's law entirely. Nevertheless, this is not a saving knowledge for human beings. As Vermigli notes, "Knowledge of natural law did not make them better, because even if the law is known it cannot change us nor give us strength to act rightly; therefore, we must run to Christ."[54]

Not surprisingly, these theologians included the covenantal dimension of the *imago:*

> Mastricht (III, ix, 33): "Original righteousness was conferred on Adam not as a private but as a public person, or what is the same

---

52. Ursinus, *Commentary on the Heidelberg Catechism,* pp. 32-33.
53. Cited in Heppe, *Reformed Dogmatics,* pp. 234-35.
54. Vermigli, cited in Heppe, *Reformed Dogmatics,* p. 24.

thing, in Adam on the whole of human nature, whence it would have been transmitted to all his posterity. But this original righteousness is not a substance as Illyricus used to rave, but a quality diffused as it were through all the substance, and so common to body and soul, to the mind, also to the will and the affections."[55]

So despite some lingering affects of the more neoplatonic bent of the patristic and medieval tradition, Calvin and his theological colleagues and successors came to clearly affirm the psychosomatic unity of the image. More recently, John Murray has reflected this abiding emphasis:

> Man is bodily, and, therefore, the scriptural way of expressing this truth is not that man has a body but that man *is* body. . . . Scripture does not represent the soul or spirit of man as created first and then put into a body. . . . The bodily is not an appendage.[56]

Perhaps the last great scholastic theologian, Francis Turretin defines the image, which is "the principal glory of man," in fourfold terms:

> The first is of the Son of God who is called "the image of the invisible God" (*eikon tou Theou aoratou,* Col. 1:15); the second of Adam who was made in the image of God; the third of the renewed who are said to be "renewed in knowledge after the image of him that created them" (Col. 3:10); the fourth of man who in a peculiar manner is called "the image of God" above the woman, who is "the image of the man" (1 Cor. 11:7). The Son of God is the essential image of most perfect equality, having the same numerical essence with the Father. Adam is the accidental and analogical image of inadequate and imperfect similitude (as to nature, gifts and state). The renewed are the spiritual image (as to supernatural gifts). Man compared with woman is the image of authority (as to the power he has over his wife).[57]

With Calvin, Turretin argues that the soul is the seat of the image, but that its rays "glitter" in the body as well. After all, says Turretin, the

---

55. Cited in Heppe, *Reformed Dogmatics,* p. 240.

56. John Murray, *Collected Writings of John Murray,* vol. 2 (Edinburgh: Banner of Truth, 1977), p. 14.

57. Francis Turretin, *Institutes of Elenctic Theology,* vol. 1, p. 465.

body participates in the immortality bestowed upon the saints.[58] He also, as is typical of these writers ever since Calvin, invokes Ovid: "Whilst other animals look downwards upon the earth, he gave man a lofty face, and ordered him to look at heaven, and lift his countenance upwards towards the stars" (*Metamorphoses* 1.85 [Loeb, 3:8-9]."[59] Even unbelievers are in some sense in God's image "by reason of spirituality and incorruptibility," and he takes exception to Flacius' contention that the fall "injured the essence of the soul."[60]

It is noteworthy that although the Reformed scholastics follow the older tradition in distinguishing the soul as the proper seat of the image, their emphasis on the goodness of nature as nature and humanness as human keeps them from the nature-grace dualism that marks and mars so much of the medieval synthesis. "As flesh and spirit (taken physically) are *disparates, not contraries*," explains Turretin, "so also are the appetites, inclinations and habits of both in themselves. The repugnancy now found in them arises accidentally from sin."[61]

Conclusion: The Perpetuity of the Image

As mentioned above, the decision concerning the presence of the image in humankind after the fall rests on definitions. This becomes essential in the one point that is said to be of obvious contention between Lutheran and Reformed anthropologies, with the former said to deny the post-fall image while the latter affirm its perpetuity. It is worth observing that the two traditions do not appear to make very much of this difference — despite the fact that the scholastics were hardly shy in pointing out cleavages. One would expect, at least later in the tradition,

---

58. Turretin, *Institutes of Elenctic Theology,* vol. 1, p. 465.

59. Turretin, *Institutes of Elenctic Theology,* vol. 1, p. 465.

60. Turretin, *Institutes of Elenctic Theology,* vol. 1, p. 465.

61. Turretin, *Institutes of Elenctic Theology,* vol. 1, p. 468, emphasis added. This echoes Peter Martyr Vermigli: On the basis of Genesis 9:4, he argues that "the blood is the soul." This represents a metonymy: "Since the blood is a sign of the soul's presence, it may be called the soul itself. . . . I do not offer this as if I accept it as the reason why God gave that commandment [against eating the blood of animals], but to indicate the communion of man's soul with the body" (*The Peter Martyr Library,* vol. 4: *Philosophical Works,* trans. and ed. Joseph C. McLelland [Kirksville, Mo.: Thomas Jefferson University Press, 1996], p. 42).

something along the lines of the following hypothetical proposition: "That all human beings, even after the fall, continue to be created in the image of God. This we affirm; our opponents deny." But I have not yet come across such a statement in our systems.

The Lutheran position is formally embodied in the following statement from the Formula of Concord, Solid Declaration Article 1: "Furthermore, that original sin is the complete lack or absence of the original concreated righteousness of paradise or of the image of God according to which man was originally created in truth, holiness, and righteousness, together with a disability and ineptitude as far as the things of God are concerned."[62] Similarly, the Apology of the Augsburg Confession (Article II) declares, "What else is this [image of God] than that a wisdom and righteousness was implanted in man that would grasp God and reflect him, that is, that man received gifts like the knowledge of God, fear of God, and trust in God?"[63]

Clearly, the Lutheran view turns on the identification of the image of God with "original righteousness," an equation that is further substantiated, for example, in Melanchthon's *Loci communes* (1543).[64] As we have seen from Calvin and his successors, to the extent that this equation is in view, the image is indeed abolished by the fall and is restored only in the new creation. The Reformed certainly share the Lutheran concern to assert the ethical character of the image and, consequently, the rectitude of the original state. Furthermore, they equally stress the depravity of the human condition as a result of the fall, insisting that thereby humans are rendered incapable of any true righteousness *coram Deo*. The human will is bound in sin, and actual sins arise out of an inherited sinfulness that is both imputed and imparted.

Both traditions insist that the law is natural to humankind, while the Gospel is foreign. Both reject the original righteousness as a supernatural gift or mere neutrality (Rome) and are equally wary of Eastern Orthodoxy's "ontological realism." The emphasis in Eastern Orthodoxy, writes G. C. Berkouwer, "is quite different from that in Lutheran or Reformed theology," and this necessarily affects the extent to which

---

62. *The Book of Concord: The Confessions of the Evangelical Lutheran Church*, trans. and ed. Theodore G. Tappert (Philadelphia: Fortress, 1959), p. 510.

63. *Book of Concord*, p. 102.

64. Philipp Melanchthon, *Loci Communes 1543*, trans. J. A. O. Preus (St. Louis: Concordia, 1992), p. 48.

one acknowledges the corruption of sin. "Thus the image of God," for Eastern Orthodoxy as opposed to Lutheran and Reformed orthodoxy, "is both ontic and actual, and it is viewed in a manner which relates it closely to a semi-Pelagian view of man's will."[65]

So how is it that these two traditions diverge on such a crucial question as the perpetuity of the divine image? I would argue that the differences are not material when Lutheran theology allows for a "wider" and "narrower" sense of the image. J. T. Mueller summarizes the Lutheran position:

> Though the image of God does not constitute the nature of man, since even after the Fall he is still a true man, yet the divine image belonged to the nature of the uncorrupt man or to the uncorrupt human nature. . . . Therefore we declare on the basis of Scripture that man through the Fall has entirely lost the image of God in its proper sense, that is, his concreate wisdom, righteousness, and holiness, so that his intellect now is veiled in spiritual darkness, 1 Cor. 2:14, and his will is opposed to God, Rom. 8:7.[66]

So what about James 3:9 and Genesis 9:6, where even unbelievers are apparently identified as image-bearers?

> Luther and other dogmaticians (Philippi, Hofmann) explain them as describing man as he was originally and as he should again become through faith in Christ Jesus (restoration of the divine image through regeneration). Melancthon, Baier, Quenstedt, and others regard them as teaching a divine image in a wider sense, namely, inasmuch as man, even after the Fall, is still an intelligent, self-determining rational being, who even now, though feebly, rules over the creatures of God.[67]

Although Mueller prefers the narrower definition, he acknowledges that the broader is not, properly speaking, contradictory. It seems that this is precisely where the Reformed tradition stands. While there is no doubt that the moral ability of human beings to fulfill their

---

65. G. C. Berkouwer, *Man: The Image of God* (Grand Rapids: Eerdmans, 1962), p. 50.

66. Mueller, *Christian Dogmatics,* p. 207.

67. Mueller, *Christian Dogmatics,* p. 207.

office as image-bearers has been unequivocally lost, Lutherans no more than the Reformed maintain that human beings are somehow no longer human. And the Reformed, for their part, do not deny any more than the Lutherans that whatever vestiges of the original image are left testify to God's work in creation and not to an inherent righteousness that could make them acceptable before God.

Berkouwer cites, for example, Johann Gerhard's suggestion that

> If the image could be thought of as man's essence, as will and intellect, then indeed it was not lost; but, he [Gerhard] argues, if we think of it supernaturally, as righteousness and holiness, then the image is radically and totally lost: the restoration of the image in Christ presupposes that it has been lost. But Gerhard then unexpectedly adds that there are indeed "remnants" *(reliquiae)* of the image even in fallen man. . . .[68]

Does it not appear, then, that it is because the Reformed tradition adopted the practice of defining the image in broader terms that it has been distinguished from Lutheranism on this point? Perhaps the more appropriate point of debate between the two traditions thus concerns the question as to whether there should be a significant place given to the broader concept of the image, to which the Reformed have a long history of offering a resounding affirmation.

---

68. Berkouwer, *Man: The Image of God,* pp. 46-47.

| Stanley J. Grenz | **The Social God**
| | **and the Relational Self**
| | Toward a Theology of the *Imago Dei*
| | in the Postmodern Context

In the mid 1990s, airwaves across North America were monopolized by Canadian pop diva Alanis Morissette's "All I Really Want." The lyrics ramble through a hodgepodge of seemingly disconnected preferences and competing desires that the singer finds present within and around her. Morissette bemoans life in a world populated by superficial people, and she desperately yearns for a soulmate, a kindred spirit, someone who truly understands. Sixteen-year-old Aminah McKinnie of Madison, Mississippi, like many others of her generation, spends many of her non-school waking hours on the Internet. She lives in a strangely paradoxical realm in which the opinions of peers and relationships are crucial, and yet social groups are fluid, friendships change over a period of months or even weeks, and the possibility of lifelong "best friends" is not even on the radar screen.[1] The fluidity characteristic of the contemporary ethos is epitomized by the Internet chat room. Here participants are able to be whomever they want, to try on new identities with ease, even to the point of becoming a different person with each foray into cyberspace.

Do the resources of Christian anthropology have anything to offer in the realm described by Alanis Morissette or inhabited by Internet devotees and chat-room dwellers? The answer to this question requires

---

1. For this report on the millennial generation, see Sharon Begley, "A World of Their Own," *Newsweek* (May 8, 2000): 54-55.

a theological conversation involving Scripture, read within a particular hermeneutical context, and the intellectual underpinnings of the postmodern condition. The goal of this essay is to indicate how such a conversation might proceed. The first section sets the context by surveying the intellectual trajectory that lies behind both the advent of the centered self and its dissipation. Part Two then introduces the central theological resource that Christian theology brings to the conversation, namely, the biblical concept of the *imago dei*, understood as God's intention for humankind from the beginning, embodied in Jesus Christ and finding its fullness in the eschatological new creation. The final, constructive section connects this understanding of the *imago dei* with contemporary developments in Trinitarian theological and relational philosophy to propose the ecclesial self constituted in relation to the triune God as the model for forming the self in the face of the fluidity endemic to the postmodern condition.

The Context: The Rise and Demise of the Self

No concept has been more important for the understanding of the human person in Western intellectual history than the "self." The idea that every human being is a self belongs to the standard vocabulary of Western society. The "self," however, is a modern invention, one that stands at the apex of a long intellectual process. Moreover, it is now under attack from a variety of quarters. The intellectual trajectory that includes both the rise and demise of the self provides the background and forms the context for a constructive theological conversation with the contemporary anthropological situation.

From Interiority to Psychotherapy: An Archeology of the Self

The trajectory that gave rise to the modern self begins with Augustine.[2] Building from the Greek dictum "Know thyself," Augustine transposed

2. See, for example, Charles Taylor, *Sources of the Self: The Making of the Modern Identity* (Cambridge, Mass.: Harvard University Press, 1989), p. 121. Christopher Kaiser asserts, "The inter-personal models used by the earlier fathers, which culminated in Basil's

71

the focus of the search for self to the realm within. In this manner, the church father opened the door to what Charles Taylor calls "the first-person standpoint."[3] Augustine's inward journey was at least in part motivated by the desire to overcome the fragmentation that he sensed in his own life and that characterized the times in which he was living.[4] He was convinced that without God providing its unity, the self could only remain scattered. Therefore, Augustine viewed the inward call as none other than God's own voice inviting him to cling to the divine unity and thereby to find the unity of his own life restored in God.[5] In short, he was convinced that the inward journey marks the pathway to God.[6]

The World-Mastering/Self-Mastering Rational Self Augustine's inward turn launched the process that led to the concept of the self as the stable, abiding reality that constitutes the individual human being. The modern self that stands at the end of this trajectory assumes several forms. Yet the mode of the self that has predominated in the Western philosophical tradition since the Enlightenment focuses on mastery. The "mastering self" takes charge of the world it inhabits in both the outer and the inner dimensions of that world, so as to constitute itself and determine its identity.

The Enlightenment linked the human person to the power of reason. This was not a new idea, of course. What was new in the Age of Reason was a particular understanding of the rationality that supposedly

---

distinction of the divine hypostases, led Augustine to postulate internal relations within the godhead, but the complete dissociation of these eternal intra-trinitarian relations from ordinary human relations forced him into a rather static concept of the deity, on the one hand, and an individualistic concept of humanity, on the other." Christopher B. Kaiser, *The Doctrine of God: An Historical Survey* (London: Marshall, Morgan and Scott, 1982), p. 81. Gunton goes so far as to claim that the development of the individualistic concept of person which emerged out of Augustine's approach "has had . . . disastrous effects on modern Western thought." Colin Gunton, *The Promise of Trinitarian Theology* (Edinburgh: T&T Clark, 1991), p. 95.

3. Taylor, *Sources of the Self,* p. 130.

4. Sandra Lee Dixon, *Augustine: The Scattered and Gathered Self* (St. Louis: Chalice, 1999), p. 37.

5. Dixon, *Augustine,* p. 199.

6. Augustine, *The Happy Life* 2.11, in the *Fathers of the Church,* ed. Ludwig Schopp (New York: CIMA, 1948), 5:58-59.

comprises the self. Rather than understanding reason as the ability to see the presence of the eternal within the material that typified the outlook of ancient philosophy, the thinkers of the Age of Reason equated reason with proper method. By hitching this human power to a mechanistic view of the world, they came to view reason as the means to objectify the world in the cause of gaining mastery and exercising instrumental control over it. Moreover, the Enlightenment philosophers conceived of the human person not as the static, contemplative soul of the medieval ideal, but rather as a restless, discontented transformer of the world.[7] The active agent in the task of world-mastery was assumed to be the rational self that establishes itself through the exercise of instrumental reason.

The new instrumental science found its religious parallel in the Puritan and Pietist movements, together with the eighteenth-century evangelical awakenings they spawned. The new religious consciousness abetted the fledgling instrumental stance toward the world by providing it with a spiritual purpose.[8] Yet even more significant was its elevation of the self as the agent in the task of self-mastery, which at least initially was viewed as a religious vocation. In shifting the focus in this manner, the religious stream from the Puritans to the revivalists developed the other side of mastery endemic to the Enlightenment, namely, the attempt to gain control over the self.[9]

The Self-Sufficient Self The impulse toward the self-mastering self opened the door to the self-sufficient, self-constructing self[10] of modern psychology. One important voice in this process was Abraham Maslow. Maslow spoke of the human ideal as "self-actualization" or "full-humanness,"[11] and he characterized his proposal as "a growth and self-actualization psychology,"[12] at the heart of which was his

7. Giorgio de Santillana, *The Age of Adventure* (New York: New American Library of World Literature, 1956), p. 46.

8. Taylor, *Sources of the Self,* p. 231.

9. For this view of the Enlightenment, see Louis Dupré, *Transcendent Selfhood: The Loss and Rediscovery of the Inner Life* (New York: Seabury, 1976), p. 4.

10. Robert N. Bellah et al., *Habits of the Heart: Individualism and Commitment in American Life,* Perennial Library edition (New York: Harper and Row, 1986), p. 127.

11. Abraham H. Maslow, *Toward a Psychology of Being,* second ed. (New York: D. Van Nostrand, 1968), pp. vi-vii.

12. Maslow, *Toward a Psychology of Being,* pp. 189-90.

widely known "hierarchy of needs."[13] Maslow was convinced that he had uncovered a morally neutral, essential human nature, the actualization of which led to health, whereas its thwarting was pathological.

The ascendancy of modern psychology marks what Philip Rieff aptly characterizes as "the triumph of the therapeutic." In this emergent kingdom of the self, the individual self is looked to as providing the "center" that is able to hold together even as the surrounding world disintegrates.[14] Moreover, the individual self assumes the role of being the arbiter and focal point of meaning, values, and even existence itself. The highest value that this self can posit is freedom, which, when understood as the flip side of self-consciousness or self-awareness, involves the capacity either to mold[15] or to actualize oneself.

From Autobiography to Preference: The Undermining of the Self

Although the self-mastering self became the dominant mode, the forays of other thinkers into the inner sanctum netted a particular rather than a universal self, a self-focused rather than an essence-focused self. In this alternative trajectory, the self does not emerge so much through self-mastery as through self-expression, that is, through the expression of the self's own uniqueness.

The Self-Focused Self Self-construction through self-expression requires self-exploration as a first step. Indeed, self-expression presupposes an awareness of one's unique self, which in turn arises by means of observing and cataloguing one's personal thoughts and feelings. The process of looking inward to find one's unique individuality gives rise to the "autobiographical self." This self was invented by the sixteenth-century French civil servant, Michel de Montaigne, who used the literary form of autobiography to discover the unique self within. Jean-Jacques Rousseau, in turn, engaged in writing autobiography to

13. Abraham H. Maslow, *Motivation and Personality* (New York: Harper and Row, 1954), pp. 80-92.

14. Philip Rieff, *The Triumph of the Therapeutic: Uses of Faith After Freud* (New York: Harper and Row, 1966), p. 5.

15. See, for example, Rollo May, *Man's Search for Himself,* Delta book edition (New York: Dell, 1973 [1953]), p. 160.

discover the particular nature that constituted him as a unique self, which he believed was at the same time the soul of humanity. In the process, Rousseau pronounced the self intrinsically good.[16]

The autobiographical self is not yet the complete self, however. Self-construction demands not only self-discovery but also self-expression. The development of the self-expressive self was the work of the heirs of Montaigne and Rousseau, whose writings coalesced in what is often designated the Romantic movement. The Romantic vision was driven by the belief that ultimate reality, viewed as the cosmic self, is intricately connected with the individual self and that the world is in some profound sense the creation of the self.[17]

The Demise of the Centered Self What happens when the concept of the infinite within the finite, upon which the self-expressive self depends for its sense of stability and for its ability to overcome its own particularity, proves to be an unstable center? The destabilizing of this Romantic self came on the heels of explorations into the world-constructing self, especially the self as will, charted by the nineteenth-century German idealists. The result was an intellectual crisis precipitated by the conclusion that the universal will was irrational and impersonal (Schopenhauer) and that human values were undergirded merely by the will to power (Nietzsche).

This crisis was especially felt by the turn-of-the-twentieth-century Vienna "modernists"[18] (including Freud), who sensed that an unhappy and unstable "psychological man" was emerging out of "the dissolution of the classical liberal view of man," to cite Carl Schorske's description.[19] By displacing interest in questions regarding the unity of personal identity-development in favor of an emphasis on the mechanism of the process, Freud effectively undercut the older concept of the unitary self characterized by permanence, continuity, and cohesion.

16. Robert C. Solomon, *Continental Philosophy Since 1750: The Rise and Fall of the Self* (Oxford: Oxford University Press, 1988), p. 1.

17. For a similar summary, see Solomon, *Continental Philosophy Since 1750*, p. 75.

18. For this designation, see Jacques Le Rider, *Modernity and Crises of Identity: Culture and Society in Fin-de-Siecle Vienna*, trans. Rosemary Morris (New York: Continuum, 1993), p. 11. See also Taylor, *Sources of the Self,* pp. 456-66.

19. Carl E. Schorske, *Fin-de-Siècle Vienna: Politics and Culture,* Vintage Books ed. (New York: Vintage, 1981), p. 22.

Only a short step led from Freudian psychoanalysis to the sense of a free-floating self without any semblance of a fixed identity, that is, to the sense that the self is — as Jacques Le Rider states — merely "an endless, unpredictable interplay of conscious and unconscious identities" and that the supposed "opposition between reality and fantasy is meaningless in any attempts to understand a personality."[20]

The modernists continued the quest to discover an inner "depth," even if this required that they cast aside the dream of the centered self. Yet the die was cast. What Irving Howe observes as the "demotion, even dispossession" of the self[21] soon followed. The conceptual tools for this final demolition were provided by Ferdinand de Saussure's structural linguistics[22] and the structuralism of such anthropologists as Claude Levi-Strauss, which dissolved the self into the structures of the social realm without and the brain within.

The Death and (Re)birth of the Self Yet structuralism was itself the last gasp of modernism. The postmodern turn was finally completed when Michel Foucault admonished his scholarly colleagues to leave behind all pretense of neutrality and declared that subjectivity is the product of the unconscious internalization of a host of social factors[23] that govern how people think, live, and speak.[24] In so doing, Foucault extended Nietzsche's metaphor of the death of God to encompass the death of the self as well.

The postmodern ethos is characterized not only by the loss of the self but by the *embrace* of its demise. As Louis Sass observes, postmodern thinkers "seem to take an inordinate delight in dancing

20. Le Rider, *Modernity and the Crises of Identity*, p. 43.

21. Irving Howe, "The Self in Literature," in *Constructions of the Self*, ed. George Levine (New Brunswick, N.J.: Rutgers University Press, 1992), p. 264.

22. On this, see Emile Benveniste, *Problems in General Linguistics*, trans. Mary Elizabeth Meek (Coral Gables, Fla.: University of Miami Press, 1971), pp. 5, 8. Because language is "a system that has its own arrangement," Saussure excludes "external linguistics." Ferdinand de Saussure, *Course in General Linguistics*, ed. Charles Bally, Albert Sechehaye, and Albert Riedlinger, trans. Wade Baskin (New York: Philosophical Library, 1959), pp. 20-23.

23. David Couzens Hoy, "Foucault: Modern or Postmodern?" in *After Foucault: Humanist Knowledge, Postmodern Challenges,* ed. Jonathan Arac (New Brunswick, N.J.: Rutgers University Press, 1988), p. 27.

24. Edward W. Said, "Michel Foucault, 1926-1984," reprinted in *After Foucault,* p. 10.

round [the self's] burning image."[25] Yet the postmodern turn away from the self does not mark the inauguration of pure selflessness. The postmodern condition retains a semblance of a "self" or, perhaps better stated, a trace of the now absent self. The postmodern "self" is the narrative self whose experience-organizing "plot" arises from one's social group (or community of reference). Postmodern thinkers routinely picture this socially constructed "self" as a position in a vast web, a nexus, a point of intersection,[26] a crossroad within a "web of interlocution."[27] The postmodern self, therefore, looks to relationships for identity.[28] In a fast-changing world, this results in a highly unstable, impermanent self that is little more than a bundle of fluctuating relations and momentary preferences, a situation that readily translates into "psychic fragmentation," to cite Fredric Jameson's designation.[29] The spiritual chaos occasioned by the postmodern condition does not necessarily lead to the celebration of the death of the self, however; it may also occasion a new quest for some semblance of meaning[30] in the face of the terrifying emptiness endemic to the postmodern condition.

The Theological Resource: The Concept of the *Imago Dei*

Throughout much of Christian history the link made in Scripture between humans and the divine image has served as the foundation for the task of constructing a Christian conception of the human person or the self. Theologians generally approached the biblical texts from the perspective of the prior concern for personal identity and, conse-

25. Louis A. Sass, "The Self and Its Vicissitudes in the Psychoanalytic Avant-Garde," reprinted in *Constructions of the Self*, p. 17.

26. Jean-François Lyotard, *The Postmodern Condition: A Report on Knowledge*, trans. Geoff Bennington and Brian Massumi (Minneapolis: University of Minnesota Press, 1984), p. 15.

27. Taylor, *Sources of the Self*, p. 36.

28. See, for example, George Herbert Mead, *Mind, Self and Society*, ed. Charles W. Morris (Chicago: University of Chicago Press, 1934, 1974), pp. 138-58.

29. Fredric Jameson, *Postmodernism, or the Cultural Logic of Late Capitalism* (Durham, N.C.: Duke University Press, 1995), p. 90.

30. Alasdair MacIntyre, *After Virtue*, second ed. (Notre Dame: University of Notre Dame Press, 1984), pp. 203-4.

quently, with the goal of finding in the texts the basis for a sense of self. Moreover, as the Christian tradition developed in conversation with Western philosophical trends, many thinkers came to read the *imago dei* passages through lenses that were increasingly colored by the concern for the construction of the individual self, a concern that mushroomed in the wake of Augustine's theological work. To a culture enamored with the inward turn that reigned from Augustine to Maslow, Christian theologians announced that each human is created in the divine image, understood either as a structure of human nature or the individual as standing before God.

Does the language of the *imago dei* continue to speak after the demise of the self that stands at the end of the intellectual trajectory running from Montaigne to Foucault? And how might a renewed understanding of the biblical concept of the *imago dei* foster the reconstruction of the self in the wake of its dissipation?

In recent years, cherished ideas regarding the nature of the *imago dei* have come under the scrutiny of biblical exegetes as well as constructive theologians. Bringing this theological concept into conversation with the contemporary demise of the self begins, therefore, with a return to the biblical texts that explicitly refer to the concept of the *imago dei*. The contemporary demise of the self occasions a reading of these texts that reveals the presence within them of an often overlooked perspective that sees the *imago dei* as the divinely given goal or destiny awaiting humankind in the eschatological future and toward which humans are directed "from the beginning." The concept of the *imago dei* as destiny, which views humans as a history or a narrative, provides the hermeneutical perspective for constructive theological engagement with the contemporary context.

From Humankind to the True Human: The Imago Dei *and Biblical Christo-Anthropology*

Although not a dominant motif within the Bible, the *imago dei* is central to biblical anthropology. This is evident, of course, in the first Genesis creation narrative. Claus Westermann goes so far as to assert that the "most striking statement" of the narrative, "over and above God being the creator, preserver and sustainer of creation, is that God created human beings in his image."[31] But references to *imago dei* do not end here. The concept reemerges as a crucial aspect of the New Testament reflection on the person and work of Christ. For this reason, the survey of the central texts best follows the flow of the salvation-historical narrative of the Bible itself, which moves from creation, through Christ, to new creation.

Humankind and the *Imago Dei* Despite its importance to biblical and Christian anthropology, the Hebrews likely did not invent the concept of humans as the divine image. Rather, the background for the idea lies in the kingship ideology of ancient Near Eastern cultures. In the ancient world, images were viewed as representatives of the entity they designated. The representational motif was especially strong when an image was designed to depict a deity. The god's spirit was believed actually to indwell the image (or idol).

Images were often thought to represent and even mediate the presence of one who is physically absent, whether this absent reality be the conquering king whose throne is in a distant city or a deity whose abode is on the remote mountain of the gods. By extension, the concept of the *imago dei* indicates that humankind somehow mediates within creation the immanence of the transcendent Creator. Viewed from this perspective, Genesis 1:26-27 stands at the pinnacle of the biblical creation narrative that posits a God who creates a world that is external to God's being and then places humankind within that creation as a creaturely representation of the transcendent deity.

The story of the creation of humankind as the *imago dei* was included in the Genesis narrative for the purpose of undermining the exclusivity of the royal ideology out of which the biblical concept emerged. By extending the divine image to humankind, the first creation narrative — in a manner akin to Psalm 8 — declared that humankind, and not merely the king, is the representation of, and witness to, God on earth. At the same time, neither the words nor the actions in Genesis 1:26-27 reference to individuals as individuals. Rather, both have in view humankind (as is evident by the use of the corporate term *adam*) or perhaps humans-in-relationship (suggested by the reference

---

31. Claus Westermann, *Genesis: An Introduction,* trans. John J. Scullion (Minneapolis: Fortress, 1992), p. 111.

to male and female in verse 27). Rather than embodying a "democratization" of the royal ideology, therefore, the first creation narrative effects a universalizing of the divine image.

Although the use of the two descriptive nouns, "image" and "likeness," suggests that as the divine image humans are to resemble their Creator, Genesis 1:26-28 only hints at the nature of this resemblance. The search for the full meaning of the *imago dei* — the quest to understand how humans are to fulfill the role of being the divine image — leads to the full sweep of the biblical narrative. Because this wider narrative centers on Jesus as Israel's Messiah, the open-ended character of Genesis 1:26-27 clears the way for a move from a creatio-centric to a christocentric anthropology. Three New Testament passages explicitly sound this theme.

The *Imago Dei* and the True Human   In 2 Corinthians 4:4-6, Paul links Christ as the *imago dei* with the glory-christology evident throughout the New Testament. For Paul, being the *imago dei* means that Christ radiates the very glory of God. Rather than offering some great philosophical or speculative conclusion about the ontological nature of Christ, however, Paul's statement evidences a narrative focus. It embodies an implicit allusion to the creation of humankind in the divine image narrated in Genesis 1:26-27 as understood through the lens of Christ as the Second Adam.

The centrality of narrative is even more pronounced in Colossians 1:15-20, in which Paul[32] incorporates what some scholars suggest is an edited version of a previously formed hymn, one which not only emphasizes Christ's preeminence over all things but extols his centrality in creation and redemption. Crucial for understanding the nature of the *imago dei* in the Colossian hymn is the twofold assertion that Christ is the "firstborn" *(prōtotokos),* a motif that brings together the themes of the two strophes into which the hymn is divided. The one who is the *eikōn theou* is the "firstborn of all creation" (v. 15) and, reiterating a theme found elsewhere in the New Testament, the "firstborn from the

---

32. The use of "Paul" in this context is not intended to take a position on the contentious issue of the authorship of Colossians. For a helpful discussion of this matter, see James D. G. Dunn, *The Epistles to the Colossians and to Philemon,* in the *New International Greek Testament Commentary,* ed. I. Howard Marshall and Donald A. Hagner (Grand Rapids: Eerdmans, 1996), pp. 35-39.

dead" (v. 18). The repetition of the term links the "beginning" with the "new beginning," and it draws the entire creation/salvation-historical narrative into its central focus, namely, Jesus, who as the center of God's actions is the preeminent one and the *imago dei*.

Similar to the great Johannine declaration, "the Word became flesh and lived among us" (John 1:14), Paul draws together into a single whole the entire life of Jesus as it centers on his resurrection as the prolepsis of the eschaton (v. 18) and on his death as God's great act in reconciling all creation (v. 20). The apostle's intent is to declare that this historical life is the dwelling place of the fullness of deity, understood in accordance with the wisdom tradition and as the fulfillment of the creation story. Or stated in the opposite manner, the entire narrative of the invisible God's self-disclosure though the divine wisdom, together with the Genesis story of humankind being created in the divine image, can be rightly understood only when viewed in the light of the narrative of Jesus who as the preeminent Christ is the *eikōn* of God.

The opening four verses of the epistle to the Hebrews, which comprise one sentence in the Greek, sound the theme of the entire book, the superiority of Jesus Christ. More specifically, by declaring that Jesus is the reflection of God's glory and the imprint of God's being (Heb. 1:3), the author fuses glory and image language (Heb. 1:3) to declare what it means to say that as the one who is "Son," Jesus Christ is the *imago dei,* even though the phrase is not explicitly used in the text. Jesus manifests who God is, but not by being a passive reflector of the divine reality, similar to a mirror that can only reflect the light issuing from another source. Rather, Jesus *is* this light. That is, he is the pattern according to whom those who are stamped with the divine image are conformed.

The high point toward which the author moves comes with the declaration of Jesus' historical work of making "purification for sins" (v. 3). Rather than merely ascribing to Christ the role in creation the wisdom tradition had reserved for the divine wisdom, the introduction to Hebrews finds the wisdom of God displayed preeminently in the passion and death of the crucified Jesus on behalf of sinful humankind. The point of Hebrews 1:1-3, therefore, is to declare that Jesus Christ, who as the Son is the visible manifestation of the divine reality, ultimately fulfills this role and therefore comes to possess this accolade only through his historical work in salvation history. In short, the point of this text — indeed, the point of New Testament christology in general — is that Jesus Christ fully reveals God, and thereby is the *imago dei* in fulfillment of Genesis 1:26-27, as he redeems humankind.

From Eschatological Hope to Ongoing Task:
The Imago Dei *and the New Humanity*

Not only is Jesus the divine image, he is also the head of the new humanity destined to be formed according to that image, in fulfillment of God's intent for humankind from the beginning. Consequently, the biblical narrative of the *imago dei* does not end with christology but finds its *telos* in the new creation.

The Image of God as Eschatological Goal In Romans 8:29, Paul articulates the point in christocentric language reminiscent of Genesis 1:26-27. According to the apostle, God's intention is that those who are in Christ participate in his destiny and thereby replicate his glorious image. The eschatological orientation of the text is confirmed by the prefix *sun-* in the word *summorphos,* which carries overtones of a central theme of Paul's theology, the idea of being "in Christ." In Romans 8:29 Paul declares that his readers will be caught up in the Christ event and become copies of God's Son. Above all, however, the eschatological focus is evident in the crucial phrase, the "image of his Son," with its overtones of the Son-christology found repeatedly in the pages of the New Testament. By declaring that they are destined for conformity to the *eikōn tou huiou autou,* Paul is reminding his readers of God's purpose to imprint them with the very qualities of Christ, who as the image of God is the divine Son.

The climax of the verse comes in the subordinate clause that follows, "that he might be the firstborn," which expresses the christological intent of God's foreordination, namely, the preeminence of Christ among those who participate in the eschatological resurrection. The designation of these as Christ's *adelphoi* indicates the communal interest of the text, which marks Romans 8:29 as the final exegesis of Genesis 1:26-27. Although in his risen glory Jesus Christ now radiates the fullness of humanness that constitutes God's design for humankind from the beginning, God's purpose has never been limited to this. God's goal is that as the Son, Jesus Christ be preeminent within a new humanity stamped with the divine image. Consequently, the human-kind created in the *imago dei* is none other than the new humanity con-formed to the *imago Christi,* and the *telos* toward which the Old Testa-ment creation narrative points is the eschatological community of glorified saints. In this manner, the narrative of the emergence of the new humanity provides the climax to the entire salvation-historical story and becomes the ultimate defining moment for the Genesis ac-count of the creation of humankind in the *imago dei.*

The question as to the exact nature of conformity to Christ leads beyond Romans 8:29 to its "essential commentary,"[33] 1 Corinthians 15:49. Here Paul connects the *imago Christi* with the resurrected new hu-manity by means of an Adam-Christ typology with its correlate last-Adam christology. Earlier in the chapter (vv. 20-28), Paul sets forth an Adam-Christ typology to present Christ's resurrection as the guarantee of the eschatological general resurrection. In Paul's second use of the Adam-Christ typology an eschatologically orientated, christologically determined anthropology comes explicitly to the fore. Paul sets forth Jesus' resurrected body as the paradigm for all who will bear his image.

To this end, the apostle introduces an antithesis between the *psychikon sōma* and the *pneumatikon sōma,* and then draws a contrast be-tween Adam and Christ as the representations of these two corporate realities. Involved here is a type of "midrashic" reflection on Genesis 2:7 in the light of the apostle's own experience of having seen the risen Je-sus. Paul's christological reading of this Old Testament text yields the conclusion that the advent of the spiritual body was in view at the cre-ation, yet not as an aspect that was inherent within human nature from the beginning but as the eschatological destiny of the new humanity in Christ. Paul's Adam-Christ typology, therefore, indicates that the cre-ation of Adam did not mark the fulfillment of God's intention for hu-mankind as the *imago dei.* Instead, this divinely given destiny comes only with the advent of the new humanity who participate in the *pneumatikon sōma* by means of their connection to the last Adam. In this manner, Paul paints Christ as the true image of God imparting his supernatural characteristics to his spiritual progeny in a manner simi-lar to Adam passing on his natural traits to his physical offspring.

---

33. Brendan Byrne, *Romans,* vol. 6 of *Sacra Pagina,* ed. Daniel J. Harrington (Collegeville, Minn.: Liturgical Press, 1996), p. 268.

The Image of God as a Present Reality The biblical narrative of the *imago dei* that climaxes with the glorified new humanity sharing in the divine image contains a present component as well. The new humanity already shares in the divine image through being "in Christ." This is explicitly stated in 2 Corinthians 3:18, which comes as the climax to Paul's midrash on Exodus 34:29-35. In this verse, the apostle provides a statement of his understanding of "the essence of the Christian life" viewed as unity with Christ.[34] At the heart of the verse is a contrast between believers who now see the Lord's glory, albeit indirectly, and Israelites who in Moses' time could not look upon God's splendor and who in Paul's day remained veiled. Reading the text in the light of 2 Corinthians 4:6 suggests that the apostle here asserts that believers see the reflected glory of God through Christ who is the image of God, yet who is likewise the divine glory seen as in a mirror. As in 2 Corinthians 4:6, Paul has in view the historic person of Jesus as the one in whom the invisible God becomes visible.

Paul does not simply equate the new humanity with the divine image, however, but declares that those who behold the divine glory are participants in a process of transformation into that image that is gradual and progressive. Margaret E. Thrall rightly notes that this "assimilation to Christ as the image of God produces a visibly Christ-like character, so that the divine image becomes visible in the believer's manner of life."[35] Moreover, this building of character occurs through the new narrative inaugurated at conversion and reaching its climax at the eschatological resurrection. Yet envisioned here is no mere private beholding, leading to an individualistic "me-and-Jesus" understanding of transformation. Rather, the metamorphosis involves the reformation of relationships and the creation of a new community of those who share together in the transforming presence of the Spirit and who thereby are, as A. M. Ramsey notes, "realizing the meaning of their original status as creatures in God's image."[36]

In Colossians and Ephesians, the apostolic author takes the matter a

34. Jan Lambrecht, "Transformation in 2 Cor 3,18," *Biblica* 64 (1983): 254.

35. Margaret E. Thrall, "A Critical and Exegetical Commentary on the Second Epistle to the Corinthians," in the *International Critical Commentary*, ed. J. A. Emerton, C. E. B. Cranfield, and G. N. Stanton, two vols. (Edinburgh: T&T Clark, 1996), 1:285.

36. A. M. Ramsey, *The Glory of God and the Transfiguration of Christ* (London: Longmans, Green and Co., 1949), p. 151.

step further. Those who are destined to be the new humanity and therefore are already in the process of being transformed into the divine image, carry the ethical responsibility to live out that reality in the present.

The declaration in Colossians 3:9-11 that through conversion/baptism into Christ, the Colossians have put off the "old human" and have put on the "new" evidences an underlying Adam-Christ typology. For Paul, being "in Adam" and being "in Christ" designate not only two orders of existence but also the way of living that characterizes each. In this text, the apostle uses the imagery of changing garments to signify an exchange of identities. The old and new human designate two frames of reference from which participants in each realm gain their identity, and out of which, on the basis of which, or in keeping with which they conduct their lives. Or stated in another manner, the old and new human bring into view two distinct narratives, which in believers coalesce into a composite story, namely, the narrative of being transferred from the sin-story into the grace-story. The text concludes with a grand declaration that the way of living that belongs to the realm in Christ is communal; it entails what is appropriate to life in the new community. The new humanity not only does not emerge from the distinctions that separate humans into competing communities, but that new humanity has no place whatsoever for such peculiarities,[37] and this because "Christ is all and in all."

The Colossians text finds echo in Ephesians 4:17-24. Although the *imago dei* is not explicitly mentioned here, it comes to the fore in the final infinitive of the passage, that is, the apostle's declaration that believers put on the "new human" (v. 24). In Ephesians 2:15, the writer declares that Christ has created in himself "one new human" out of the formerly warring groups of Jew and Gentile. In Ephesians 4:24, this corporate focus emerges again. Rather than referring to the new self in an individual sense, the term designates the new form of human life that results from redemption, namely, "life patterned after God's"[38] life (cf. Eph. 5:1). This new realm is characterized by righteousness and holiness, because these qualities reflect God's own character as it is revealed through the biblical narrative.

---

37. Dunn, *Colossians and Philemon*, p. 223.

38. Andrew T. Lincoln, *Ephesians*, vol. 42 of the *Word Biblical Commentary*, ed. David A. Hubbard, Glenn W. Barker, and Ralph P. Martin (Waco, Tex.: Word, 1990), p. 287.

Stanley J. Grenz

The Application: The *Imago Dei* and the Postmodern Context

The survey of biblical texts yields a christocentric, eschatologically focused anthropology in which the Old Testament idea of humankind as the *imago dei* is interpreted as reaching its fulfillment in the new humanity headed by Jesus Christ. Pursuing this salvation-historical trajectory leads inevitably back to Genesis 1:26-27, that is, to a hermeneutical journey from new creation back to creation. This, in turn, opens the way for the theological construction that can facilitate the reconstruction of the self-in-relationship in the wake of the demise of the centered self. At the heart of this construction is a Trinitarian ontology of the person-in-community that not only emerges from the biblical texts but also resonates with the postmodern sensitivities that stand at the apex of the intellectual trajectory from Montaigne to Foucault.

The Imago Dei *and Sexual Differentiation*

Two anthropological themes stand at the heart of Genesis 1:26-27 — the creation of humankind in the divine image and the creation of humans as sexually differentiated and hence relational creatures. The enumeration of these two themes sparks the query as to the connection between them, a query that can be answered only by reading this text together with the second creation story and ultimately within the biblical narrative as a whole.

Sexuality and the Creation Narratives   Claus Westermann points out that the central concern of the Genesis 2 narrative is not the creation of the woman as such, or even the origin of the mutual attraction of the sexes, but the creation of humankind. The making of woman completes the creation of humankind, and this because "God's creature is humankind only in community."[39] But why? The answer leads back to the perspective on sexuality suggested by the story. Adam's cry of delight as the presence of the woman rescues him from his debilitating

---

39. Claus Westermann, *Genesis 1–11: A Commentary,* trans. John J. Scullion (London: SPCK, 1984), p. 192.

solitude, with which the second creation story reaches its climax, suggests that individual existence as an embodied creature entails a fundamental incompleteness, or, stated positively, an innate yearning for completeness. Sexuality, in turn, is linked not only to the incompleteness each person senses as an embodied, sexual creature, but also to the potential for wholeness in relationship with others that parallels it.[40] Sexuality comprises the dynamic that forms the basis of the uniquely human drive toward bonding. For the narrator, the drive toward bonding finds expression in marriage, which in turn leads to the establishment of the broader human community.

Reading the Genesis creation accounts canonically suggests that the creation of sexual creatures in the image of God is most clearly seen in the light of the eschatological goal of God's creative work. When seen from the perspective of the new humanity as God's intent from the beginning, the ultimate goal of sexuality (and hence of the impulse toward bonding) is participation in the fullness of community, that is, life together as the new humanity in relationship with God and all creation. Although the anticipated fullness of community is a future reality, a partial — yet genuine — foretaste of the eschatological fullness may be enjoyed prior to the eschaton. The focus of the prolepsis of the future reality is the community of reconciled people in fellowship with God through Christ.

Human Sexuality and the Relational God The relational "self," therefore, is sexual. This "self" consists of the person-in-bonded-community. But how does sexuality relate to humankind as the *imago dei*, if at all?

This question takes us back to the plural address found in the first creation narrative: "Let us make humankind in our image" (Gen. 1:26). Although the narrator surely did not intend this as a reference to the Trinitarian persons, looking back at the account from the vantage point of the post-Cappadocian hermeneutical trajectory facilitates Christians in seeing the triune God at work in the creation of humankind as male and female. This, in turn, raises the possibility that cre-

---

40. James B. Nelson and Sandra P. Longfellow, "Introduction," in *Sexuality and the Sacred: Sources for Theological Reflection*, ed. James B. Nelson and Sandra P. Longfellow (Louisville: Westminster John Knox, 1993), p. xiv.

ation in the *imago dei* endows human sexual differentiation with significance as reflecting something about the Creator. But what about the Creator could the creation of humans as male and female represent? The most promising possibility is divine relationality.

Dietrich Bonhoeffer may have been the first theologian to propose that the image of God be interpreted by means of a relational analogy in which the duality of male and female is the defining human relationship.[41] Yet Karl Barth was responsible for the wide influence the idea has enjoyed.[42] In setting this forth, Barth draws from I-Thou relationality, which he claims is grounded in the triune God, was disclosed in Christ, and remains evident in both divine and human life. For Barth, sexuality is theologically crucial because of the I-Thou relationship that the creation of humans as male and female facilitates. According to his interpretation of the second creation narrative, the fashioning of the woman is crucial in that it facilitates in the created realm the kind of I-Thou relationality that characterizes the eternal Trinity.

Barth correctly finds in the story the idea that the male-female bond involves the recognition of sameness and difference. The man sees in the woman a creature like himself, in contrast to the animals who are unlike him, but acknowledges as well that the two are different, for he is male and she is female. For the narrator, this sameness and difference — this mutuality within a plurality — explains the mystery of the two forming the unity of "one flesh," for this unity is held together by the attraction they sense as male and female for each other. Read in the light of Genesis 2, Genesis 1 suggests that the interplay of sameness and difference is present in a prior way in the triune God.

Barth goes astray, however, when he exchanges the dynamic of sexuality, understood as the sense of incompleteness that gives rise to the drive toward bonding, for the paradigm of I-Thou relationality. In spite of his concern to draw deeply from the creation of humankind as male and female, in the end Barth leaves human sexuality behind. Sexuality, however, simply cannot be left behind. Marriage and genital sexual expression are limited to this penultimate age, of course. But sexuality is not. To leave sexuality behind is to undercut the significance of the res-

---

41. Phyllis A. Bird, "'Male and Female He Created Them': Genesis 1:27b in the Context of the Priestly Account of Creation," *Harvard Theological Review* 74 (1981): 132 n. 8.

42. Bird, "Male and Female He Created Them," p. 132 n. 8.

urrection. This central Christian doctrine indicates that sexuality is not eradicated en route to eternity. Instead, after the manner of the risen Jesus, humans participate in the transforming event of resurrection as the embodied persons — male or female — they are.[43] Above all, however, to relegate sexuality to the temporal is to undermine the basis for community in eternity. Even though genital sexual expression is left behind, the dynamic of bonding continues to be operative beyond the eschatological culmination, for this dynamic is at work in constituting humans as the community of the new humanity within the new creation in relationship with the triune God.

The reminder that the human destiny as the *imago dei* is linked to the new humanity leads to the other debilitating difficulty posed by the appropriation of I-Thou relationality. This approach leads theologians like Barth to move directly from the male-female relationship to the divine prototype. Reading the Genesis creation narratives in the light of the *telos* of the *imago dei* which is the establishment of the new humanity indicates, however, that an intermediate step is required.

The New Testament writers declare that ultimately the *imago dei* is Christ and, by extension, the new humanity, consisting of those who through union with Christ share in Christ's relationship to God and consequently are being transformed into the image of God in Christ. For this reason the church emerges in the New Testament as an even more foundational exemplar of the *imago dei* in this penultimate age. In the final analysis, then, the *imago dei* is not simply the I-Thou relationship of two persons standing face-to-face. Instead, it is ultimately communal. It is the eschatological destiny of the new humanity as the representation of God within creation. For this reason, the pathway between humankind as male and female and the *imago dei* leads inevitably through the church as the prolepsis of the new humanity, and the relational self is ultimately the ecclesial self.

The Relational Self as the Ecclesial Self

The image of God does not lie in the individual per se, but in the relationality of persons in community. This assertion calls for a rela-

---

43. For a fuller explication of this view, see Stanley J. Grenz, *Sexual Ethics: An Evangelical Perspective,* second ed. (Louisville: Westminster John Knox, 1997), pp. 24-27.

tional ontology that can bring the divine prototype and the human antitype together.

The philosophical genesis of the contemporary idea of the social self begins with William James's distinction between the "me" (the objective, empirical person, the "empirical self") and the "I" (the subjective consciousness of the *me* as continuing in time). Although James is sometimes credited with introducing the social self,[44] the American social psychologist[45] George Herbert Mead set the development in motion with his postulate that the individual experiences himself or herself only indirectly by means of the reflected standpoints of the social group.[46] The "me" emerges within a dialogue, as it were, between the "I" and the social context. In so doing, Mead also opened the door to viewing the self as an ongoing process — rather than as a given that exists prior to social relationships[47] — which may be said to have both a past and a future that taken as a whole forms a "narrative."

The trajectory of social psychology inaugurated by Mead opens the way for a reintroduction of the *perichoretic* understanding of the construction of the self in relationship that enjoys a long pedigree within the Christian tradition but was overshadowed by the Augustinian inward turn. Beginning with John of Damascus, the patristic thinkers appropriated the christological concept of *perichoresis* to express the dynamic of the divine life. This term, which had been invoked to speak about the interdependence of Christ's deity and humanity,[48] provided a ready way of describing the relations among the Trinitarian persons. The three persons "mutually inhere in one another, draw life from one another, 'are' what they are by relation to one another," to cite

44. For James's own position, see William James, *The Principles of Psychology*, 2 vols. (New York: Dover, 1950 [1890]), 1:293-96.

45. For this descriptor, see Charles W. Morris, "Introduction: George Herbert Mead as Social Psychologist and Social Philosopher," in Mead's *Mind, Self and Society*, pp. xi-xii. For a discussion of the genesis of Mead's move to social psychology, see Gary A. Cook, *George Herbert Mead: The Making of a Social Pragmatist* (Urbana, Ill.: University of Illinois Press, 1993), pp. 43-47.

46. Mead, *Mind, Self, and Society*, p. 138. For a similar characterization of Mead's position, see Paul E. Pfuetze, *The Social Self* (New York: Bookman Associates, 1954), p. 79.

47. Mead, *Mind, Self, and Society*, pp. 222-26.

48. For what may have been the initial use of this term as a christological descriptor, see Gregory of Nazianzus, Epistle 101 in the *Nicene and Post-Nicene Fathers*, Second Series, ed. Philip Schaff (Peabody, Mass.: Hendrickson, 1995 [1894]), 7:439-43.

Catherine LaCugna's insightful description of *perichoresis*.[49] Hence, the word indicates that the personhood of the three is relationally determined; each is a person-in-relationship to the other two. By avoiding any hint of dividing God into three and yet maintaining the personal distinctions within God, the appeal to *perichoresis* preserved both the unity of the one God and the individuality of the Trinitarian persons.

The corresponding linking of the insight of social psychology regarding the formation of the self to the human person emerges by means of the idea of "in Christ" that lies at the heart of the New Testament conception of spirituality. The thread that unites the two is the shared conclusion that personal identity arises *extra se*. Social psychology relates the *extra se* character of the construction of the self to the dynamic of self-consciousness, in which one's sense of self is dependent on the "generalized other." When understood in the context of the social character of the self articulated by Mead and other social psychologists, being "in Christ" describes the genesis of the ecclesial self. The self emerges *extra se* in that participation "in Christ" constitutes the identity of participants in the new humanity.

Yet this connection between being "in Christ" and the ecclesial self must be given its full Trinitarian-theological cast. The pneumatological foundation of the ecclesial self emerges from the Pauline understanding of the role of the Spirit in believers' lives. Paul links the prerogative of addressing God as "Abba" explicitly to the presence of the indwelling Spirit, whom the apostle identifies as "the Spirit of [God's] Son." Furthermore, according to Paul, the Spirit who leads those who are "in Christ" to address God as "Abba" likewise constitutes them as "heirs of God and joint heirs with Christ" (Rom. 8:17). Taken together, these Pauline observations imply that by incorporating the new humanity into Christ, the Spirit gathers them into the dynamic of the divine life. Yet the Spirit does so in a particular manner, namely, specifically and solely "in the Son." Through the Spirit, those who are "in Christ" come to share the eternal relationship that the Son enjoys with the one whom he called "Father." Because participants in this new community are by the Spirit's work co-heirs with Christ, the Father of Jesus bestows on them by virtue of their being "in Christ" what he eter-

---

49. Catherine Mowry LaCugna, *God for Us: The Trinity and Christian Life* (San Francisco: HarperSanFrancisco, 1992), pp. 270-71.

nally lavishes on the Son. Being "in Christ" by the Spirit means as well that in the Son they participate in the Son's act of eternal response to his Father. In this manner, those who by the Spirit are in the Son participate in the very *perichoretic* dynamic that characterizes the eternal divine life. This participation constitutes the self-in-community of all who are "in Christ," thereby transforming the relational self into the ecclesial self.

Personhood, then, is bound up with relationality, and the fullness of relationality lies ultimately in relationship with the triune God. Creating this relational fullness is the work of the Spirit, who places humans "in Christ" and thereby effects human participation in the dynamic of the divine life. Moreover, being "in Christ" entails participating in the narrative of Jesus, with its focus on the cross and the resurrection (cf. Rom. 6:1-14), an identity-constituting narrative, I would add, that is a shared story — a communal narrative. Consequently, being-in-relationship with the triune God not only inherently includes, but is even comprised by, being-in-relationship with those who participate together in the Jesus-narrative and thereby are the ecclesial new humanity. As the indwelling Spirit proleptically comprises the new humanity as the *imago dei* after the pattern of the *perichoretic* life of the triune God, the Spirit constitutes continually the "self" of the participants in Christ's ecclesial community and, by extension, the "self" of the world. And this self, whose identity and longevity emerge from its centeredness in Christ in whom all things find their interconnectedness, offers hope in the face of the loss of self articulated in Alanis Morissette's poignant song and experienced by sixteen-year-olds such as Aminah McKinnie.

SECTION II | **Significant Challenges**

Nancey Murphy | **Nonreductive Physicalism**
Philosophical Challenges

Introduction

One thing we have in common with the first Christians is this: We have available to us a wealth of conflicting ideas of what a human being, most basically, is. It is important to be aware of this fact since whatever each of us believes on this subject will influence how we think about a number of other issues — for example, what happens after we die? Is an embryo a person? But ordinarily we do not talk about our theories of human nature, so these disagreements are kept largely below the surface of our discussions. Here's an example: When Dolly the sheep was cloned I got calls from media people looking for a Christian reaction. I recall one reporter who seemed frustrated that I had no strong condemnation of the idea of cloning humans. After the reporter made repeated attempts to provoke me to express some sort of horror at the prospect, light dawned for me. I asked him, "Do you read a lot of science fiction?" "Well, some." "Are you imagining that if we try to clone a human we'll clone a body but it won't have a soul? It will be like the zombies in science fiction?" "Yes, something like that." "Well," I said, "Don't worry. None of us has a soul and we get along perfectly well!"

Because we do not ordinarily talk about our theories of human nature it is difficult to know what others think. I have had to resort to informal polling whenever I get the chance. I ask students in various classes and often ask my audiences when I lecture. Let me lay out some of the options. The first option can be called either physicalism or materialism. This is the view that humans are composed of only one "part," a physical body. The terms "physicalism" and "materialism" are pretty much interchangeable in philosophy, but "physicalism" is more fashionable now, and it is more appealing to Christians because "materialism" has long been used to refer to a *worldview* that excludes the divine. So even though a materialist account of the person is perfectly compatible with belief in God, "materialism" does carry those unhappy connotations for Christians.

The second option is dualism, and we recognize two sorts these days, body-soul and body-mind dualism. The terms "mind" and "soul" were once interchangeable, but in recent years "soul" has taken on religious connotations that "mind" has not.

A third theory regarding the composition of human beings is called trichotomism. This view comes from Paul's blessing in 1 Thessalonians 5:23: "May the God of peace sanctify you entirely; and may your spirit and soul and body be kept blameless at the coming of the Lord Jesus Christ." So trichotomists hold that humans are composed of three parts: body, soul, and spirit.

Here are the results I usually get. Among my students and a general audience, trichotomism is usually the favorite, followed closely by dualism. There are usually only one or two physicalists. In groups of specialists the numbers are different. If I were to ask scientists, I am sure I would find that most biologists and neuroscientists are physicalists. It is not so easy to predict what chemists or physicists will say, however. If I ask philosophers, their answer will depend largely on whether they are Christians or not. Secular philosophers are almost all physicalists — I know only one exception. Christian philosophers are divided between dualism and physicalism. When I speak at seminaries on the liberal end of the spectrum all but incoming students are physicalists.

I assumed when writing this essay that my audience would include both dualists and physicalists. My own position is physicalism, and I suppose I should say that I am an evangelical physicalist, since I believe it is very important to get the word out that physicalism is an acceptable position for Christians. Several years ago my colleague Warren Brown at Fuller Seminary's School of Psychology predicted that growing interest in the cognitive neurosciences would lead to public focus on the issue of human nature. Given that the majority of conservative Christians are dualists (or trichotomists) he further predicted that this would become a focus of controversy. Wanting to do our bit to forestall a new science-religion conflict, we organized a conference involving scientists from several fields along with theological educators of an evangelical stripe. Our goal was to explore a concept of human nature consistent with science and to argue for its biblical and theological acceptability.[1]

I do not intend to argue directly for physicalism here. I just mention in passing what I take to be the most pressing problems with dualism. First, it may be conceptually impossible to give an account of mind-body interaction — how can something nonmaterial interact causally with material entities?[2] Second, while neuroscience can never prove that there is no mind or soul, it is increasingly clear that, to quote Laplace out of context, we have no need of that hypothesis. Finally, in addition to being *unnecessary* on biblical or theological grounds, I take dualism to be theologically *undesirable* because of its penchant for distorting Christian priorities. That is, it has given Christians something to be concerned about — the soul and its final destiny — in place of Jesus' concern with the kingdom of God.[3]

What I *am* going to do in this essay is to discuss what I take to be the main philosophical challenges facing a physicalist account of human nature. I acknowledge that there are challenges of other sorts. For example, there are biblical texts that are hard to square with physicalism, as well as theological problems such as the Catholics' and Calvinists' doctrine of the intermediate state. My plan is not to attempt to solve any of the philosophical problems — that is work in progress for me and I'm not ready to go to press with it. Rather, I shall simply describe what I take to be the main challenges and then indicate promising directions to look for solutions.

1. See Warren S. Brown, Nancey Murphy, and H. Newton Malony, *Whatever Happened to the Soul?: Scientific and Theological Portraits of Human Nature* (Minneapolis: Fortress, 1998).

2. There is also a problem in explaining how God interacts with physical creation, but this is a problem Christians have to come to terms with, while the problem of body-mind interaction is not. For a discussion of the problem of divine action see my "Divine Action in the Natural Order: Buridan's Ass and Schrödinger's Cat," in *Chaos and Complexity: Scientific Perspectives on Divine Action,* ed. Robert J. Russell, Nancey Murphy, and Arthur R. Peacocke (Vatican City State: Vatican Observatory Publications, 1995), pp. 325-58, and other essays in that volume.

3. Nicholas Lash argues along these lines in a number of his works. See, for example, *Easter in Ordinary: Reflections on Human Experience and the Knowledge of God* (Charlottesville, Va.: University Press of Virginia, 1986).

Here are the main issues, as I see them. First, there is an epistemological question — what are the grounds for thinking that physicalism is true? Second, if humans have no souls, what accounts for traditional views that humans have a special place among the animals — in what does human distinctiveness lie? Third, if there is no soul, what accounts for personal identity over time? This topic is a difficult one in any case, but Christian expectation of bodily resurrection adds complications — we have to ask what accounts for pre- and post-resurrection identity.

I believe that these three issues can be dealt with relatively easily. Two more issues, however, are less tractable. Both of these have to do with the problem of reductionism. If humans are purely physical — that is, if it is the brain that does the work once attributed to the mind or soul — then how can it *not* be the case that all human thought and behavior are simply determined by the laws of neurobiology? This is the general problem, but I'll distinguish two subtopics. One is the problem that philosophers address under the heading of mental causation: how does reason get its grip on the brain? The other is a version of the problem of free will.

The Epistemological Issue

Philosophical arguments for dualism and against dualism, for physicalism and against, seem to be interminable. I mentioned earlier that recent successes of the neurosciences in studying mental capacities as brain functions has provided strong motivation for physicalism. Science , however, can never *prove* that there is no soul, a soul whose capacities are simply well *correlated* with brain functions.[4]

I have argued (elsewhere) that the best way to view the contest between dualism and physicalism is to treat each position not merely as a philosophical thesis but as the "hard core" of a scientific research program.[5] This argument is based on the philosophy of science of Imre

4. For a recent example of such an account, see Richard Swinburne, *The Evolution of the Soul,* revised ed. (Oxford: Clarendon, 1997).

5. See my "Nonreductive Physicalism: Philosophical Issues," in *Whatever Happened to the Soul?* by Brown et al., pp. 127-48, esp. 139-42.

Lakatos, who argued that research programs in science are unified by metaphysical theses about the essential nature of the subject-matter under investigation. So, for example, atomism is the philosophical thesis behind modern physics and chemistry.[6] In this light, it is clear that the physicalist program is doing extremely well: all recent advances in neurobiological understanding of cognition, emotion, and action, as well as progress in certain forms of cognitive science, are the product of a physicalist understanding of human nature. In contrast, scarcely any research follows from a dualist theory; Sir John Eccles has been the only noted scientist whose research was based on body-mind dualism. He believed that the mind could influence physical processes at the quantum level in the brain and so solve the mind-brain interaction problem. Nothing, finally, has come of his project. Thus, however inconclusive the philosophical arguments may be, we can say that *science* provides as much evidence as could be desired for the physicalist thesis.

Human Distinctiveness

Here is my second question for the physicalist: if humans are, as evolutionists tell us, closely related to other animals, then what makes us distinctively human? It has been common for Christians to argue that, while the human body may have evolved from animal predecessors, humans have a special place in God's eyes because they alone possess immortal souls. Pope Pius XII was one thinker who employed this strategy. But how can the physicalist respond? A more recent pope provides an example. Pope John Paul II, in an address to the Pontifical Academy of Sciences on the theory of evolution, spoke not of the special creation of the soul, as did Pius XII, but of "the moment of transition to the spiritual." Science cannot determine this point, he says, but it can determine at the experimental level a series of signs indicating what is specific to the human being. In addition, philosophical analysis can reflect on what is distinctively human. The Pope lists metaphysical

---

6. Imre Lakatos, "Falsification and the Methodology of Scientific Research Programmes," in *The Methodology of Scientific Research Programmes: Philosophical Papers,* vol. 1, ed. John Worrall and Gregory Currie (Cambridge: Cambridge University Press, 1978), pp. 8-101.

knowledge, self-awareness and self-reflection, moral conscience, free-dom, aesthetic experience, and religious experience. But only theology, he says, can bring out the ultimate meaning of these characteristics according to the Creator's plans.[7]

What, then, does it look like to reflect scientifically on the question of human distinctiveness? A number of scientists study the higher primates, and from these studies we could construct a list of things we can do and they cannot. As it turns out, most of the differences are matters of degree rather than the presence and total absence of certain characteristics. Small differences in basic capacities interact to produce huge differences in final outcome, however. For example, chimps can be taught rudimentary forms of language. There is debate over the question whether chimps also possess self-awareness (one of the distinctives listed by Pope John Paul II). Do chimps recognize themselves in a mirror? Perhaps it depends on what we mean: chimps do *recognize* themselves; but do they recognize them*selves*? Higher animals have emotions, but ours are more finely modulated. Animals can be angry, but cannot experience righteous indignation.

I want to emphasize two factors that seem most important to human distinctiveness: morality and religious experience. Morality has become a hot topic for debate among sociobiologists. Some claim that genetics can explain human morality. The arguments go something like this: Human morality has parallels in the animal world, in that the individual sacrifices itself for the good of the group. This can be explained in animal behavior because group survival is generally survival of kin, and kinship survival means survival of one's genes. Evolution favors whatever is good for the survival of one's genes. Hence, human morality can be seen, also, as a product of genetics.

On the surface it may appear that the sociobiologist has it just right: self-sacrifice is central to Christian morality. The sociobiologists' account, however, depends on similarity of genes in the group for which one sacrifices; that is, they must be family, kin. Christian morality is in some ways strangely anti-family. Jesus says, "I have come to set a man against his father, and a daughter against her mother . . . and one's foes will be members of one's own household" (Matt. 10:35-36). The em-

7. Pope John Paul II, Message to the Pontifical Academy of Science, *L'Osservatore Romano*, 44 (October 30, 1996).

phasis in Christianity is rather on loving the stranger. For Christians the one for whom one is to sacrifice is, most particularly, the enemy. Later New Testament teaching focused on reconciliation of Jews and Gentiles — whom no one at the time could have considered to be physically related. So Christian morality is different not only in motive but in content from kin-preserving altruism.

The ability to be in relationship with God, the ability to have religious experience, has often been thought of as dependent on the soul. Medieval mystics spoke of withdrawing from the world of the senses, entering into the soul, wherein they experienced God's presence. How could one conceive of experiencing God if there is no soul?

I recently came across an account of experiencing God, in fact an account of hearing God speak, in a book by Nicholas Wolterstorff, titled *Divine Discourse*. Wolterstorff says,

> Let me present part of the narration of some experiences which recently befell an acquaintance of mine who is a well-established member of the faculty of one of the other Eastern seaboard universities. . . . I shall call her "Virginia" . . . and call [her pastor] "Byron." Perhaps I should add, [says Wolterstorff,] that though Virginia is . . . a Christian, she neither is nor was what anyone would classify as an Evangelical. It's worth saying that because Evangelicals have the reputation of believing that God speaks to them rather more often, and rather more trivially, than most of us think God would bother with.

So here is Virginia's own account:

> On February 12, 1987, while folding laundry I suddenly knew with certain knowledge that Byron was supposed to leave St. Paul's Church. There was no external voice, but there was a brightening in the room at the moment of revelation. The experience was so overwhelming that I called my husband and invited him to come home for lunch. . . . I needed to reassure myself of reality. Later that afternoon . . . I found myself sobbing. I knew the knowledge I have been given was not me, and I knew it was correct. As the day progressed, it became clear to me that there were seven insistent statements that I needed to tell Byron. . . . I was awe-struck and terrified. . . .
>
> The next morning, when I went to see Byron . . . I told him the seven statements: "Your work is done here. You have accomplished

what you were sent to do. You are still young. There are great things in store for you. Do not be afraid. God will take care of you. I will help with the transition." This message was not a surprise to Byron. He had already come to that conclusion prior to our conversation.[8]

Virginia goes on to tell about the ways her message was confirmed in the days to come. There was a second message to be delivered to a meeting at church, which was well-received as just the thing that needed saying. Byron did get a call to another church. In addition, Virginia's own spirituality deepened.

Notice how ordinary this experience was — not ordinary in the sense that people regularly report getting messages from God, but in the sense that it used or depended on nothing but ordinary cognitive abilities that we all have. A set of *ideas* came into her mind. She had a variety of *feelings* — a feeling of certitude, a feeling of awe. I submit that for such an experience, nothing is needed beyond the ordinary neural equipment that we all possess.

What makes this a religious experience is that it was attributed to God. The question is, then, if it was so ordinary (in the sense I have specified), how could one *know* it was from God? Wolterstorff takes up this question, pointing out that the circumstances in which it happened, the consequences, and the confirmation by the community all pointed in that direction. I would add that this sort of judgment reflects quite well the regular criteria that Christians have used all along to distinguish between their own fancies and the voice of God.[9]

So I have mentioned a variety of features that are associated with our sense of what it means to be human, and animals share rudimentary forms of most of them. What matters is the way these enhanced capacities interact in human life. For example, put together our clear sense of self with finely tuned emotions and subtle linguistic abilities and we have immensely different capacities for interpersonal relationships. So nonreductive physicalism grants that we are biological organisms, but emphasizes that our neurological complexity and the history of cultural development have together resulted in the capacity for gen-

8. Nicholas Wolterstorff, *Divine Discourse: Philosophical Reflections on the Claim That God Speaks* (Cambridge: Cambridge University Press, 1995), pp. 274-75.

9. See Nancey Murphy, *Theology in the Age of Scientific Reasoning* (Ithaca, N.Y.: Cornell University Press, 1990), chap. 5.

uine moral reasoning, including the ability to recognize an objective obligation to obey the voice of the Creator.

Personal Identity

The term "identity" is used in reference to persons in several ways. In philosophical literature, numerical identity is distinguished from qualitative identity. It is the former that is at issue here: what are the criteria by which I am the same person now as I was forty years ago, even though qualitatively I am quite different?

This question is especially pressing when we consider resurrection. Christian dualists and physicalists have different ideas about what happens at death. Dualists generally believe that the soul survives the death of the body and is provided with a new or transformed body at the time of the general resurrection. Physicalists have two options. One is to say that at death each of us is immediately transformed in some other place or dimension — if we can make sense of this idea. The other possibility is that we are simply dead until the general resurrection, at which time God essentially re-creates us in a new, imperishable form.

Dualists raise the following objection: if humans are nothing more than their bodies, then the re-created person after the resurrection cannot be the same as the one who died; the physicalist cannot account for pre- and post-resurrection identity. Note that the "nothing more" in this objection should serve as a signal that we are facing another reductionist issue. I'll come back to this later.

There is a rich philosophical literature on personal identity. One longstanding argument is between those who stake personal identity on spatio-temporal continuity of the body and those who tie it to continuity of memories. That is, is it the fact that your body, despite its many changes, is a continuous physical object throughout your life that guarantees that the sixty-five-year-old you is the same as the ten-year-old? Or, given the fact that your body has changed so much, is your identity from year to year based on continuity of memories — you remember being that ten-year-old and a whole lot in between? To illustrate these two different criteria, consider this very clever thought experiment devised by Bernard Williams. This is a bit long and complicated, so bear with me.

The first half of Williams's essay reinforces the idea that it is the memory criterion, not the body, that is crucial. Two persons, A and B, enter a machine. When they emerge the A-body-person (that is, the one who has the physical features A had before) has all of B's memories and character traits, and vice versa. The experimenter announces beforehand that after the switch one person will receive $100,000 and the other will be tortured. It is entirely reasonable to expect that, given a choice, A will want the B-body-person to receive the money, rather than be tortured (and vice versa). Williams concludes: "This seems to show that to care about what happens to me in the future is not necessarily to care what happens to *this* body."[10]

This and further considerations introduced by Williams seem to confirm the description of the experiment as "changing bodies," and suggest that "the only rational thing to do when confronted with such an experiment would be to identify oneself with one's memories and not with one's body. The philosophical arguments designed to show that bodily identity was at least a necessary condition of personal identity would seem to be just mistaken."[11]

Now consider a different set of cases. You (we'll call you A) are told that you are going to be tortured tomorrow; you look forward to tomorrow with great apprehension. The person who holds this power over you says, in addition, that between now and then something will be done to you to make you forget everything you now remember. Will this relieve your fear? Absolutely not! Then you are told that your memories will be replaced prior to the torture by a complete set of memories from someone else's life. Does this relieve your fear? Williams says that this will not only *not* relieve your fear but will compound it with fear of mental derangement.

If you are told that your memories will be transferred simultaneously to the other person and that other will be paid $100,000 we have the same situation with which Williams began his essay, but now our intuitions are reversed: if given a choice, A would want the A-body-person to receive the money and escape the torture.

So which is correct? Is it your package of memories or your pack-

10. Bernard Williams, "The Self and the Future," in *Problems of the Self: Philosophical Papers 1956-73* (Cambridge: Cambridge University, 1973), pp. 46-63; quotation, p. 49.
11. Williams, "Self and the Future," p. 51.

age of cells and tissues that makes you you from one day to the next? We shall come back to this. For now I want to suggest that Williams's thought experiments push us to articulate the sense in which one's consciousness is *more* than a bundle of memories. Recognition of this "more" leads readily to belief in dualism, but I believe that it can be understood not as the mind's experience of its (nonmaterial) self, but rather as a product of the integration of various aspects of memory and awareness — a phenomenon that emerges sometime during early childhood. The ability to recognize my conscious self over time is so unproblematic most of the time (for example, when we wake up in the morning) that it may go unnoticed. An obvious case of failure is the phenomenon of split personality. Failure of the ability is also striking in certain sorts of the misidentification syndrome, in which patients believe they are being transformed into someone else's psychological identity. While we might speculate that this is the effect of reading too much philosophy of mind late at night, such patients show either localized or diffuse brain damage.[12]

Recognition of oneself as oneself over time and after interruptions of conscious experience may have been presumed to be part of what philosophers have been referring to all along as the memory criterion; I believe Williams has done us a favor by highlighting the distinction. I'll call this additional criterion the continuity-of-consciousness criterion.

I now want to argue that the combined memory-consciousness criterion is still too narrow, in that memory and continuity of consciousness together do not capture all of what we need in order to secure personal identity. Given the moral and social character of the kingdom of God, we need to add "same moral character" to our criterion.

Modern thought, following René Descartes, has presented an overly cognitivist account of human nature in general and of morality in particular.[13] Beginning in the 1970s and 1980s, however, both in Christian ethics and in philosophical ethics there has been a significant movement to return to an understanding of ethics in terms of character. Here the emphasis is not on the rules or principles one

---

12. Leslie Brothers, *Friday's Footprint: How Society Shapes the Human Mind* (New York: Oxford University Press, 1997), pp. 3-10.

13. David Hume's emphasis on sympathy and the motivating role of the passions is one notable exception.

ought to follow, but rather on the kind of person one ought to be. These approaches emphasize the development of *virtues*, the retraining of the *emotions*, and the development of new moral *perceptions*. For example, Alasdair MacIntyre argues that without the acquired capabilities we call virtues, we are not able to achieve the goods intrinsic to social practices.[14]

A book by G. Simon Harak, which offers a point of view complementary to MacIntyre's, bears the title *Virtuous Passions*. This phrase would sound like an oxymoron to those who hold a purely intellectualist account of morality. His goal is to work out a moral-theological account of the rightness or wrongness of passions and to consider ways to transform morally blameworthy passions and to foster morally praiseworthy passions.[15]

On the basis of the foregoing, I propose that identity of persons depends as much on *character* identity as it does on memory/consciousness and bodily continuity. That is, a replica or transformed version of my body with all my memories intact would not be I unless she possessed my virtues (or vices), affections, and moral perceptions.[16]

Another factor that needs to be taken into account in understanding personal identity is our relationships. It is clear that a great deal of what makes us to be the persons that we are is our relations with other people, and particularly with God.

Recall now the dualist's challenge: if humans are nothing but bodies and if resurrection in one way or another amounts to there being a new and radically different body, then there is no sense in which that post-resurrection body is a continuation of me. There is no sense in which *I* survive death.

I need now to introduce a helpful philosophical clarification. David Wiggins has shown that to say "x is the same as y" or "x is identical

14. Alasdair MacIntyre, *After Virtue*, second ed. (Notre Dame: University of Notre Dame Press, 1984).

15. G. Simon Harak, *Virtuous Passions: The Formation of Christian Character* (New York: Paulist, 1993).

16. Brian Garrett broadens the memory criterion to a "psychological" criterion that includes memory together with other features such as well-entrenched beliefs, character, and basic desires. He also argues that the bodily and psychological conditions need to be taken together. See "Personal Identity," in *The Routledge Encyclopedia of Philosophy*, ed. Edward Craig (London: Routledge, 1998), 7:305-14.

to y" requires the specification of what he calls a *covering concept;* that is, one needs to be able to answer the question, "the same *what* as y?" This solves many traditional philosophical puzzles such as whether or not one can step into the same river twice. The puzzle is due to failing to distinguish between "same body of water" and "same mass of water molecules." Criteria of identity need to be tailored to fit the relevant covering concept.[17] Consequently, in discussing personal identity it is necessary to ask specifically what are the identity criteria for the covering concept *person,* and to expect that these will be different from identity criteria for a material object or even for a human body.[18]

The identity criteria for an ordinary material object clearly involve spatio-temporal continuity. How do I know that this pencil is mine, even though it is now three inches shorter than when I bought it? The answer is that it has been in my possession all along. What about identity criteria for "same body"? Here spatio-temporal continuity still matters, and this makes up for the fact that the body changes qualitatively from birth to death, and even for the fact that most of the matter of which it is made is replaced after about seven years.

So what are the criteria for "same person"? And what is there about you that seems to be necessary so that on the day of resurrection you will happily recognize yourself to have survived? I have argued that the criteria include continuity of memories, continuity of consciousness itself, continuity of moral character, and continuity of relationships. I especially want to emphasize continuity of one's relations to others in the Body of Christ and to Christ himself. Thus, I concur with those who emphasize that God's remembering, recognizing, and relating to me are essential to my post-resurrection identity.

What about bodily continuity? It is a fact that on this side of resurrection all of these other criteria are tied to the same body in the sense of same material object. But what if, given our faith in the resurrection, we revise our concept of personal identity accordingly, and define "my body" as that which provides the substrate for all of these personal characteristics? It is that which allows me to be recognized by others;

17. David Wiggins's solution is to require covering concepts to be *sortal* concepts, which serve to pick out individuals. Thus, *mass of water molecules* is not an appropriate covering concept. See his *Identity and Spatio-Temporal Continuity* (Oxford: Clarendon, 1967).

18. Wiggins, *Identity and Spatio-Temporal Continuity,* pp. 1, 35-36, 50.

that which bears my memories; and whose capacities, emotional reactions, and perceptions have been shaped by my moral actions and experience. It is these characteristics that make me who I am. So any body that manifests all of these is in fact Nancey Murphy.

This recognition allows us to avoid tortuous attempts, as in the early church, to reconcile resurrection with material continuity.[19] Early theologians raised gruesome questions such as the problem of chain consumption: what if you die and a fish eats your body, then someone else eats the fish? Who gets the matter in the end? These attempts are based on failure to distinguish the covering concepts of *same person* and *same collection of particles*. The contemporary dualist who takes the concepts of *body* and *person* to be the same is importing a reductionist view of persons and is making the same conceptual mistake as these early writers.[20]

Mental Causation

The physicalist thesis is that mental events, such as seeing a peach or thinking of the number 7, are brain events. (The identity needs to be qualified — many theorists say that mental events supervene on brain events or are constituted by brain events rather than being strictly identical — but I need not pursue this here.) The advantage of physicalism is that if mental events are brain events then there is no problem in explaining how they can be causally effective. For example, if I think "I should take my umbrella," the brain event that constitutes this thought can have a straightforward connection to my motor cortex, which puts my arm to work reaching for the umbrella. So far so good.

One way of expressing the problem of mental causation is as follows. If mental/neural events are connected by neurobiological causes, what work is left for reason to do? For example, suppose that I look at the sky and think "it's really cloudy," and then think, "it looks like

19. See Carolyn Walker Bynum, *The Resurrection of the Body in Western Christianity, 200-1336* (New York: Columbia University, 1995).

20. An earlier form of this section appeared in Nancey Murphy, "The Resurrection Body and Personal Identity: Possibilities and Limits of Eschatological Knowledge," in *Resurrection: Theological and Scientific Assessments,* ed. Ted Peters, Robert John Russell, and Michael Welker (Grand Rapids: Eerdmans, 2002), pp. 202-18.

rain." We think such a series of thoughts to be connected by reason, not by blind physical causation.

I cannot pretend to solve this problem here, but the solution, I believe, lies in recognition of the plasticity of the brain, and the fact that experience actually reconfigures neural structure in such a way that ordinary neurobiological causes produce reasonable chains of ideas. I do not want to attempt to deal with language here, so suppose that our practical reasoner looks at the clouds and a mental image of rain occurs.[21] How can this happen? The account goes something like this. Information is stored in the brain in the form of cell assemblies or neural schemas — both terms refer to networks of neurons that have been conditioned by experience to fire together. Here is an account from neuroscientist Alwyn Scott of what is going on in the brain when you think of your grandmother:

> [L]et us consider what may appear to be a simple memory: that of your grandmother. Most of us are conscious of our grandmothers. But how? What series of neural links, of connections to connections, allow us to conjure up those dear old dames?
>
> Presumably an image of grandma may come to mind, and that would appear to involve the optic lobes. But other parts of the memory relating to voice would have originated, presumably, in the temporal lobes. These recollections are connected to others related to things she said and did, the way her house smelled on Thanksgiving Day, the colors of her kitchen, and so on. Because the memory of your grandmother is no doubt imbued with emotional overtones, those cells, whose locations are not known, would also need to be activated. And finally there is the not inconsequential linguistic task of matching the word "grandmother" to one elderly or even long-deceased human female who happened to be the mother of one of your parents.[22]

21. I expect to publish a chapter on the neurobiology of meaning in Nancey Murphy and Warren S. Brown, *Did My Neurons Make Me Do It?: Philosophical and Neurobiological Perspectives on Moral Responsibility* (forthcoming). Chapter 5 will address language, and chapter 6 will address the problem of mental causation.

22. Alwyn Scott, *Stairway to the Mind: The Controversial New Science of Consciousness* (New York: Springer-Verlag, 1995), p. 78.

Something of this sort happens when you see clouds, and the same network of cells fires together later when you think of clouds. A different assembly of cells fires when you experience rain. Past experiences of clouds and rain together have trained your brain in such a way that perception of clouds causes your rain assembly to fire. That is, when two assemblies are caused to fire together, the connections between them are strengthened in such a way that in the future, the firing of one is more likely to cause the firing of the other, especially if there is some reward involved (such as success in keeping dry). This happens by means of physical changes at the synapses connecting the neurons involved in the two cell assemblies. To put it very crudely, your brain has been rewired so that its causal pathways realize or instantiate the inference: If the clouds look like this, then it is likely to rain. The clouds do look like this; therefore, it is likely to rain.

There is a fairly large body of literature on the problem of mental causation, and one of the most influential authors in philosophy of mind, Jaegwon Kim, has judged that the problem is insoluble. Consequently, he believes that nonreductive physicalism is an unstable position — one has to be either a reductionist or a dualist.[23] The problem with most of the literature, though, is that it does not incorporate any information about how the brain actually operates. So I would argue that it is much too early to give up on the problem. We need to see how my crude account in terms of the training of cell assemblies can be extended to more complex forms of reasoning and made more realistic in terms of actual brain physiology.[24]

Free Will

Immanuel Kant argued that having free will is a matter of being capable of being moved by reason rather than by natural causes. If this is an adequate account, then the problem of free will and the problem of

23. See Jaegwon Kim, "The Myth of Nonreductive Materialism," in *The Mind-Body Problem,* ed. Richard Warren and Tadeusz Szubka (Oxford: Basil Blackwell, 1994), pp. 242-60.

24. For a start on this project, see my "How Physicalists Can Avoid Being Reductionists," in *Interdisciplinary Perspectives on Cosmology and Biological Evolution,* ed. Hilary D. Regan and Mark Worthing (Adelaide: Australian Theological Forum, 2002), pp. 69-90.

mental causation turn out to be one and the same. Kant's conception, however, is an unusually narrow analysis of the meaning of free will. In this section I intend to build from the foregoing work on causation to a broader conception of freedom. We shall have to ask in the end if the result is in fact an adequate account of free will.

One obvious problem with Kant's understanding is that so few of the decisions we make can be determined solely by reason; life would be much easier if it were possible, when facing a decision, to know in advance *the* optimal solution. As an extreme case, consider the medieval philosophical fiction of Buridan's ass, starving to death between two equidistant and equivalent piles of hay. This thought experiment was designed to raise the problem of choice in the absence of sufficient reason to choose. Nicholas Rescher states that there is almost no discussion in current philosophical literature of the logical issues involved in resolving this problem.[25]

Current neuroscience, though, may have solved the problem. Neuro-ethologists have shown that organisms as primitive as fruit flies and even bacteria exhibit "initiating activity." For instance, the bacterium *Eschericia coli* has a motor that produces "random" change in the direction it swims. It is able to move to more suitable environments by means of a *delay* in the next change of direction if the milieu improves. Fruit flies exhibit similar periodic "random" changes in direction, and it has been possible to control their environments sufficiently to show that these movements are internally generated rather than responsive to external stimuli.[26] These self-initiated "random"[27] changes in behav-

---

25. Nicholas Rescher, "Jean Buridan," in *The Encyclopedia of Philosophy,* ed. Paul Edwards (New York and London: Macmillan, 1967), vol. 1, p. 428. Rescher notes that Buridan's opponents were inspired by a similar problem conceived by Al Ghazali involving equally desirable dates (from date palms, not singles' clubs).

26. Martin Heisenberg, "Initiating Activity and the Ability to Act Arbitrarily in Animals," translation by Beatrix Schieffer of "Initiale Aktivität und Willkürverhalten bei Tieren," *Naturwissenschaften* 70 (1983): 70-78.

27. I enclose "random" in quotation marks because it is not clear whether this is an appropriate term for this sort of event. "Random" is usually defined as uncaused. These movements are *not* uncaused — the nervous system produces them. They *appear* to be random, however, in that they lack any discernible pattern and are not responsive to changes in the environment. Heisenberg attributes the neural basis of these behaviors to spontaneous activity in brain cells: nerve cells that without apparent causes give off rhythmic or nonrhythmic potentials have been found in all types of brains. Are these

ior provide an optimal solution to the problem of survival in an environment too complex to be met entirely with instinctive behaviors.[28] The organism's behavior thus explores all possibilities in its possibility space (*Verhaltensfreiraum* in Heisenberg's text), and feedback selects the responses that further the organism's goals. Neuropsychologist Warren Brown (in personal communication) concludes that all organisms with more than the most rudimentary nervous systems have a "chooser" — a program to produce a multiplicity of behavioral plans that may or may not be used. This being the case, Buridan's ass will not starve; nature has designed it to choose one pile of hay or the other despite the lack of any adequate *reason* to do so.

Notice that another capacity with which nature has endowed even simple organisms is the capacity to change or choose among salient goals. If this were not the case, animal behavior would not be flexible enough to shift from, say, pursuing a drink of water to escaping from a predator.

In one of Heisenberg's articles he speaks of "free will in the fly."[29] He notes that the spontaneous initiating activity he discusses is *not* an adequate model for human free will. Yet the capacity for such activity is an important prerequisite for the evolution of genuine free will.

The foregoing suggests that although we do not attribute free will to animals there is much to learn about our own capabilities by examining simpler forms of life. What we have seen so far is that organisms are goal-directed systems and that when there is no predetermined behavior appropriate to the situation they act spontaneously and "randomly," allowing feedback from the environment to shape their behavior and to alter the goals they pursue.

What conditions need to be added to this spontaneous but goal-directed activity in order for it to qualify as free will? A central contention of this essay is that "free" action is best understood as self-determined or self-caused action. Free will is always a matter of degree

---

events truly random (in the sense attributed to certain quantum events) or are there "hidden variables"?

28. See Daniel Dennett, *Elbow Room: The Varieties of Free Will Worth Wanting* (Cambridge, Mass.: MIT Press, 1984), pp. 66-73.

29. Martin Heisenberg, "Voluntariness (Willkürfährigkeit) and the General Organization of Behavior," in *Flexibility and Constraint Behavioral Systems* (New York: John Wiley and Sons, 1994).

— no agent ever acts entirely independently of pre-existing biological drives or environmental influence (and no one should *want* to be free in this sense, since biology and society have been shaped to foster our survival). The question, then, is how self-determination gradually *emerges* within the dynamic interplay between biologically driven activity and reactions to the environment. I hypothesize that the following cognitive capacities, found almost exclusively in humans, are the necessary prerequisites:

1. symbolic language,
2. self-awareness and self-transcendence,
3. the ability to imagine behavioral scenarios involving one's own future action, and,
4. the ability to predict the consequences of such actions.[30]

Terrence Deacon argues that language is essential for detaching behavior from immediate, biologically salient stimuli in order to enable the pursuit of higher-order goals. He describes an instructive series of experiments with chimpanzees. A chimp is given the opportunity to choose between two unequal piles of candy; it always chooses the bigger one. Then the situation is made more complicated: the chimp chooses, but the experimenter gives the chosen pile to a second chimp and the first ends up with the smaller one. Children over the age of two catch on quickly and choose the smaller pile. But chimps have a very hard time catching on; they watch in agitated dismay, over and over, as the larger pile of candy is given away.

Deacon says that the task poses a difficulty for the chimps because the presence of such a salient reward undermines their ability to stand back from the situation and subjugate their desire to the pragmatic context, which requires them to do the opposite of what they would normally do to achieve the same end.

Now the experiment is further complicated. The chimps are taught to associate numbers with the piles of candy. When given the chance to select numbers rather than the piles themselves, they quickly learn to choose the number associated with the smaller pile. Deacon argues

---

30. Here I am closely following Warren S. Brown, "A Neurocognitive Perspective on Free Will," *Center for Theology and the Natural Sciences Bulletin* 19, no. 1 (winter 1999): 22-29.

that the symbolic representation helps reduce the power of the stimulus to drive behavior. Thus, he argues that increasing ability to create symbols progressively frees responses from stimulus-driven immediacy. So language is one piece of the solution to the free-will problem. It helps to account for our ability to detach our behavior from biological drives.[31]

The experiments with the chimps illustrate a second piece to the free-will puzzle. What the chimps in the first phase of the experiment are unable to do is to make their own behavior, their own cognitive strategy, the object of their attention. This ability to represent to oneself aspects of one's own cognitive processes so as to be able to evaluate them is what I shall call self-transcendence. Daniel Dennett points out that the truly explosive advance in the escape from crude biological determinism comes when the capacity for pattern recognition is turned in upon itself. The creature who is sensitive not only to patterns in its environment but also to patterns in its own reactions to patterns in its environment has taken a major step.[32] Dennett's term for this ability is to "go meta" — one represents one's representations, reacts to one's reactions. "The power to iterate one's powers in this way, to apply whatever tricks one has to one's existing tricks, is a well-recognized breakthrough in many domains: a cascade of processes leading from stupid to sophisticated activity."[33]

The combination of sophisticated language and the capacity for self-transcendence contributes to another dimension of human self-determination, the ability to run mental scenarios involving one's possible future behavior and to predict their likely consequences. This frees one from the need to implement the behavior in order to receive environmental feedback. Warren Brown writes:

> Consideration of potential future behavioral scenarios allows for these scenarios to be evaluated with respect to the desirability of the imagined outcomes. The evaluation would be of the kind "good to enact" or "bad to enact." Having been evaluated, the behavioral sce-

31. Terrence W. Deacon, *The Symbolic Species: The Co-Evolution of Language and the Brain* (New York: Norton, 1997), pp. 413-15.

32. Dennett, *Elbow Room*, p. 29; referring to D. R. Hofstadter, "Can Creativity Be Mechanized?" *Scientific American* 247 (September 1982): 18-34.

33. Dennett, *Elbow Room*, p. 29.

nario creates a memory trace that affects the future probabilities of expressed behavior. . . .[34]

Can we put these four factors together now to formulate an account of a free and morally responsible decision? We come into the world as goal-directed and spontaneously active systems. Conflict between goals that cannot be pursued simultaneously often brings those goals to conscious awareness. Conflicting goals can become prioritized by running scenarios and imagining long-term consequences of various constellations. Language gives us the capacity, in addition, to describe our actual goals in abstract terms and to imagine ourselves pursuing different goals. Thus, the achievement of higher-order abstract goals, such as acting fairly or pleasing God, may become a criterion for ordering lower-level goals.

I suggest that a hierarchical ordering of goals of this sort is a prerequisite for responsibility. *When actions are determined in light of such a hierarchy I claim that the person is acting freely.*

Notice that I have described the processes leading up to the "free" action without invoking any agency — no "homunculus" within the person's mind making choices. To do so would set up a regress problem: were any of *those* choices free? Rather, I have described a process that could be deterministic all the way through. More likely it is a mixture of deterministic outcomes and of selection among "randomly" generated alternatives. For example, when faced with a decision there may have been a process of free association resulting in a "random" selection among all of the possible options that might have come to mind. The highest-level goal might be a product of innate temperament and the various concepts of morality available in the person's milieu.[35] For this reason I think that the question of free will should *not* be taken to hinge on the issue of determinism versus indeterminism.[36]

---

34. Brown, "A Neurocognitive Perspective on Free Will," p. 27.

35. It is important here to remember that further iterations of self-transcendence are always possible. As soon as I become suspicious that my moral principles are merely conventional I have made them subject to evaluation and may change them as a result.

36. Another related issue in the philosophical literature turns on the argument that free will entails that the agent could have done otherwise, or might do otherwise in exactly the same circumstances. Dennett has argued persuasively against this analysis of free will on the grounds that identical circumstances never present themselves and thus

There will always be a host of prior causal events leading up to an act. The important question, I suggest, is whether or not the act can be said to be (largely) determined by the person him- or herself, considered as a goal-directed and self-modifying system. I insert the qualification "largely" because a human action that is entirely independent of biological and social causal influences is highly improbable, and if such acts do occur, they are far from the kinds of actions — such as moral choices — that we care about in arguing for free will.

I have not set out to argue *that* humans have free will, but rather have assumed it to be the case as a condition for the meaningfulness of any scholarly work, this essay included. I have attempted instead to fill in a part of the *explanation* of why it is *not* (always) the case that the laws of neurobiology simply determine human thought and behavior. In the previous section I suggested that interaction with the environment creates patterns of causal pathways that instantiate or realize rational connections; in this section I proposed that influences from higher-order evaluative or supervisory systems within the agent's total cognitive system reshape the agent's goals and strategies for achieving them. This "downward" mental causation also results in the reshaping of the agent's neural pathways.[37]

Conclusion

It has been a pleasure to contribute to this volume, and especially to participate in the conference on which it is based. The topic of human nature is so important and, as I mentioned at the beginning of this essay, it has received too little attention in recent years.

I come to this issue not as a biblical scholar or theologian, but as a Christian philosopher, pressing for consideration of a physicalist account of human nature. Some readers may have been frustrated with my essay because it does not attend to issues that they see as primary: What does the Bible say? Or, what difference does physicalism make to

---

there is no way to know of any given action whether it was free or not. It is a criterion that can never be applied in practice, and it is exactly for practical reasons that we need to know what free will amounts to.

37. An earlier version of this section appeared in my "How Physicalists Can Avoid Being Reductionists," in *Interdisciplinary Perspectives on Cosmology and Biological Evolution*.

theology? Philosophers, too, may have found this piece dissatisfying, and I must say that I join them in that sentiment. I would like to have been able to provide well-considered solutions to all of the problems I have raised. But, as I mentioned above, all of this is still work in progress, for myself and for the philosophical community generally. While philosophers have worked on modern mind-body dualism for three hundred years, the attention to physicalism is relatively recent, and it is greatly dependent on scientific results that are only now appearing. What I do hope to have accomplished is to convey a little excitement for tackling the intriguing problems involved in explicating a physicalist account of the person that does justice to Christian anthropology.

Stanton L. Jones
and
Mark A. Yarhouse

Anthropology, Sexuality, and Sexual Ethics

The Challenge of Psychology

Sexuality is central to a comprehensive Christian theological anthropology. We live at a moment in history, however, when the church is consumed with strife over sexual morality and deeply divided over its views of sexuality. Evangelicals and other traditionalists appear to be losing ground in the culture wars surrounding homosexuality and sexual ethics more generally, both within the church[1] and in the church's engagement with culture. In the interest of the continuing development of a lucid and compelling presentation of the traditionalist view of sexuality, we explore here some reflections on key themes relating to sexuality that we believe should be included in a fully formed Christian anthropology, and then examine the implications of these views of sexuality for sexual ethics, particularly the vexing problem of homosexual conduct.

---

1. We are referring here to the erosion of influence of the traditional formulations of sexual ethics in the mainline Protestant denominations of the West.

We would like to thank William Hathaway, Regent University, and Stephen Spencer, Wheaton College, for their comments on an earlier draft of this essay. The final version benefited greatly from engagement with the response to it by Laura Miguelez, Wheaton College, when it was originally presented June 21, 2002.

Anthropology and Sexuality[2]

The "Place" of Sexuality

Sexuality is not the only thing, or the most important thing, about what it means to be a person. Nevertheless, sexuality seems a vitally important, an irreplaceable and irreducible, aspect of personhood that has often been underappreciated in Christian reflections on anthropology. Sexuality pervades and conditions the whole of human existence, and a deep understanding of human nature would be impossible and utterly incomplete without careful consideration of our sexual natures. The sexual dimension of human nature, however, cannot stand alone without being contextualized by other irreducible human characteristics, and these other characteristics are no more or less foundational to the person than the sexual. Human nature is thus basically and intrinsically sexual, and yet not reducible to, or explicable only in terms of, the various facets of our sexuality.

If classic Christian formulations of personhood have underappreciated the role of sexuality in human nature, the current general overemphasis upon sexuality (indeed upon an extraordinarily narrow

---

2. Many of the issues discussed in this section are adapted from the discussion of Stanton L. Jones and Heather R. Hostler, "The Role of Sexuality in Personhood: An Integrative Exploration," in *Human Nature, Motivation, and Change: Judeo-Christian Perspectives on Psychology,* ed. W. R. Miller and H. D. Delaney (Washington, D.C.: American Psychological Association, in press). These reflections on theological anthropology and sexuality have benefited from study of such works as, on anthropology generally, G. Berkouwer, *Man: The Image of God,* trans. D. Jellema (Grand Rapids: Eerdmans, 1962); Emil Brunner, *Man in Revolt,* trans. O. Wyon (Philadelphia: Westminster, 1939); John Calvin, *Institutes of the Christian Religion,* ed. John T. McNeill, trans. Ford Lewis Battles, 2 vols. (Philadelphia: Westminster, 1960); C. Stephen Evans, *Søren Kierkegaard's Christian Psychology* (Grand Rapids: Zondervan, 1990); and H. D. McDonald, *The Christian View of Man* (Wheaton: Crossway, 1982); on pastoral care, W. Clebsch and C. Jaekle, *Pastoral Care in Historical Perspective* (New York: Jason Aronson, 1975); and Thomas Oden, *Care of Souls in the Classic Tradition* (Philadelphia: Fortress, 1984); and on sexuality, Stanley Grenz, *Sexual Ethics: A Biblical Perspective* (Dallas: Word, 1990); *Issues in Human Sexuality: A Statement by the House of Bishops; General Synod of the Church of England* (Harrisburg, Pa.: Morehouse, 1991); Morton Kelsey and Barbara Kelsey, *The Sacrament of Sexuality: The Spirituality and Psychology of Sex* (Warwick, N.Y.: Amity House, 1996); Lewis Smedes, *Sex for Christians,* rev. ed. (Grand Rapids: Eerdmans, 1994); Helmut Thielicke, *The Ethics of Sex* (New York: Harper and Row, 1964).

understanding of sexuality) should be noted as we begin this exploration, and a powerful case study is at hand. We are referring to evolutionary psychology,[3] which we view as one of the most virulently secular and dangerous intellectual fads of the day. What is dangerous about
evolutionary psychology is not that it posits a drive to reproduce as a
fundamental human motivation, but that it does so utterly
reductively.[4] In this paradigm, the drive to reproduce is presumed *the*
fundamental human motivation. Evolutionary psychologists then in-
terpret all facets of human behavior (including as behavior all thought
and emotion and culture) in the context of this presumed motivational
state, as when the behavior pattern or trait of altruism is analyzed in
terms of its contribution to reproductive efficacy.

Despite the fact that Christians' often unreflective initial response
tends to be a denial of any "breeding motive," on the basis of its Dar-
winian roots, we would argue that a deep motive to reproduce is not
alien to a biblical view of human nature. The creation narrative, after
all, includes God's pronounced intention that the land produce vegeta-
tion and his dual blessings on all animal life to reproduce, followed by
his pronouncement of a high blessing on the original human pair that
they "Be fruitful and increase in number; fill the earth" (Gen. 1:28). Is
there any reason to think then, in Christian perspective, that humans
have no fundamental motivation to produce children? No. But what *is*
alien to the Christian perspective is a failure to condition such motives
by placing them alongside other less reductive sexual motives, such as
the desires for relatedness in marriage and family, for pleasure, and for
intimacy, and also to place them alongside different, nonsexual motivations such as to work productively, to pursue truth, or to be in relationship with God. In contrast to the aggressively reductionistic evolu-

3. See, for example, David Buss, *The Evolution of Desire* (New York: Basic, 1994).

4. We join Mary Stewart Van Leeuwen in reminding the reader that criticisms of genetic reductionism as evidenced in evolutionary psychology should not be confused
with research conducted in molecular genetics (which has led to important findings
such as genetic risk factors associated with sickle cell anemia) and behavior genetics (the
interdisciplinary study of the relative weight of genetics and environment on behavior).
Nor is our critique necessarily a criticism of specific, modest claims sometimes found in
micro-evolution. See Mary Stewart Van Leeuwen, "Of Hoggamus and Hogwash: Evolutionary Psychology and Gender Relations," *Journal of Psychology and Theology* 30, no. 2
(2001): 101-11.

tionary psychologist, however, too many Christian theologians through history have been unwilling to consider our sexual embodiment as a vital dimension of humanness. Hence we may have something to learn even from such deeply flawed intellectual programs as that of evolutionary psychology. Christians have theological reason to believe that reproduction could be *a* core motivation (that is to say, one among many core motivations), and hence an analysis of human behavior in terms of that motive could be fruitful (pun intended) both conceptually and empirically.

The lesson to be learned for this essay from our brief engagement with this paradigm of evolutionary psychology, however, is that sexuality can be construed as fundamental, but that in so doing we must not slip into an unconscious reductionism either in construing our sexuality overly narrowly or in failing to place our sexuality in its proper relationship to other key facets of personhood. We will risk appearing to commit the latter error here, in that the focus in this essay on sexuality will allow only passing engagement with those other nonsexual aspects of personhood.

Embodiment

To be human is to be embodied, to be a physical, biological creature. Christians view all of physical existence, from the grandeur of the cosmos to the particularity of the human body, as the good creation of a benevolent God. Physical existence is not divine, but it is good by creational intent, and human existence as embodied persons is an aspect of this good physicality. The goodness of embodiment is also supported by and grounded in two additional key theological themes of traditional Christianity, the doctrines of the incarnation and of the resurrection of the body. Clearly, bodily existence must not be intrinsically evil or incompatible with the perfect good if God can become fully human. Clearly, the teaching that the final state of redeemed humanity will be as persons of resurrected and perfected bodies, and that we will, in that state, enjoy God forever, must deepen our appreciation of embodiment. We are more than bodies — there is a trans-materialistic, a spiritual or soulish, aspect of our persons — but we are bodies.

Christians have thus, throughout most of history, accepted views of their own existences as fundamentally embodied. Caroline Bynum,[5] for example, documents that consideration of the physical body was central to reflections about identity and personhood, and about the very nature of the soul, for most of a millennium of church history. But at various points in history, Christian theology has leaned dangerously in the direction of an incipient dualism that bordered on a gnostic denial of or minimization of the physical. In ancient times this seemed often to result from the engagement of Christian theology with Platonic or Stoic philosophy, or to be in response to gnostic understandings of spirit-physical dualism. In the Enlightenment, the temptation may have been to exalt human reason and to distance human experience from its grounding in "lower" faculties. In recent times, reaction against aggressively reductionistic understandings of human nature may feed the same dynamic. The proper balance, it seems to us, is to affirm that to be fully human is necessarily to be embodied, but also to affirm that while we are irreducibly and necessarily physical, we are never merely physical.

"Sexualized" Embodiment

We are not merely physical beings; we are engendered and hence sexual physical beings. Unlike some other creation stories in the ancient world, the Genesis creation narrative declares God's creation of a gendered people to have been by divine intent, with both sexes declared to have been made in the "image of God" (Gen. 1:27), and humanity corporately, male and female, declared to be "very good" (Gen. 1:31). This was a radically egalitarian stance in the context of the ancient world. The "earthy" implications of this embodiment as sexual beings are not avoided in the biblical narrative: the prospect of bearing children is voiced as a blessing on the first couple (Gen. 1:28) and on other subsequent persons in Scripture; Scripture itself extols the physical pleasures of sexual union (Prov. 5) and links eroticism explicitly with romantic love and intimacy in the Song of Songs; and the apostle Paul even gives stern admonition to married couples that fulfillment of sexual need is a legitimate function

---

5. Caroline W. Bynum, *The Resurrection of the Body in Western Christianity, 200-1336* (New York: Columbia University Press, 1995).

that each spousal partner should provide for the other (and again, in a remarkably egalitarian fashion; 1 Cor. 7:1-6).

But caution must be exercised in celebrating our sexual natures. The concrete implications just mentioned — procreation, physical pleasure and eroticism, sexual need — are all tied to the physical union intended by God for married persons, and yet single persons are no less fully sexual than the married. We have in the example of our Lord Jesus himself a fully sexual existence as a Hebrew man but without sexual union in marriage. We are given little guidance in Scripture for how to understand his experiencing of his sexuality, but must assume from his full humanity and our instruction that "he had to be made like his brothers in every way," that he "suffered when he was tempted," and indeed that he was "tempted in every way" (Heb. 2:17, 18; 4:15), that he fully entered into his sexuality as a single man, and "yet was without sin" (4:15). We must conclude that our sexuality is expressed in but not composed of the sexual experiences of married union. Single persons, indeed all persons single or not, are fully sexual in being gendered beings, beings with particularized bodies (unique male or female bodies), beings with sensations, desires, and indeed gender-grounded emotional or cognitive capacities. We signal here our inability to precisely define sexuality. Gender is only one facet of sexuality, and gender itself is a multifaceted construct with biological dimensions that are usually (but not necessarily) concordant with gender, including genetics, gonads, secondary sex-characteristics, and circulating hormones, but also including the psychological/emotional/relational dimensions of gender identity, enacted gender role, and erotic preference and desire. Sexuality, the broader and more inclusive construct, is even more complex, and must include at some basic level relationality.

Relationality

We are given clear indications of the fundamental importance of a relational conceptualization of human nature in the creation narrative. The first man, living in a state of perfection himself in the perfect environment and in the context of a perfect relationship with the triune (and hence intrinsically relational) God, is judged incomplete by his creator. "It is not good for the man to be alone," God says (Gen. 2:18), and God then creates the perfect partner for the man. The man himself recognizes the profound complementarity of this new creation, and God declares that because of this reality, "a man will leave his father and mother and be united to his wife, and they will become one flesh" (Gen. 2:24). Our relationality is experienced as the longing for and realization of romantic love, but not only here.

This relationality is experienced also in friendships and relationships of all kinds; it is grounded in part in, but is certainly not reducible to, our sexuality. Our sexuality can be thought of as a grounding in incompleteness. To be a sexual being is to experience incompleteness. Perhaps we are to understand Adam and Eve to have had the chance for the experience of perfect completion in union with each other and together with God in Eden before the fall, but our common human experience is of fracture in all our relationships, with God and with each other. If the primal human sin is prideful assertion of self-sufficiency against God, our sexuality stands witness to the lie as our biology cries out that we are at core and inescapably complementary to "the other." Thus, single or married, we know that we are made for relationship. Relationships other than marriage offer profound opportunities for good, and opportunities to meet our needs for relatedness.

Conflicted and Broken

Humanity is broken and in rebellion against God. This reality has not eradicated the primal good of human nature, but it conditions all of human experience. Our sexual longings are grounded in our good capacities for union and love and pleasure, but are tainted with such tendencies as selfishness, sensuality (the disconnection of physical appetites from the transcendent purposes to which they are connected), and subjugation (flowing from inclinations toward domination of the other). Hence, we experience a deep conflictedness in our sexuality (as in all our experience) wherein we know the potential and realized good of our sexual natures, but never experience that good distilled and pure, disconnected from our sinfulness. It is because of the reality of our brokenness that, *contra* sexuality theorists who take what *is* for what should be, we can learn only so much about true human nature from the observed state of our sexuality.

Objective Meaning of Sexual Union

The Christian belief in an objective meaning of sexual intercourse is pivotal to our anthropology and to our ethical reflections. Philip Turner[6] correctly argues that if sexual intercourse has no objective and unique meaning, then we effectively have erased its moral significance; it has become only one among many other ways to achieve certain desired ends (each of which may be morally valuated) such as the expression of affection or the experience of pleasure. Turner, standing in the apostolic tradition, argues for an objective meaning of sexual intercourse, that being one-flesh union. In the creation account, and in such pivotal passages as Paul's teaching in 1 Corinthians 6 and 7, we are taught that sexual intercourse was made by God to create and sustain permanent union, one-fleshedness, in a male-female married couple.

That such physical union creates some sort of metaphysical entity that transcends the individuality of its participants would seem to have profound intellectual implications for theological anthropology, most obviously for whether we can understand humanity individualistically or must also engage some sort of complementary and complex collectivism to account for supra-individualistic aspects of personhood. It is commonly and correctly argued that the distinctive evangelical theology, particularly of America,[7] is profoundly and unbiblically individualistic. The creation of a union of persons that is "one flesh" through a physical union in intercourse confronts us with a profound challenge to individualism. This is not, though, the only such challenge, as we learn from Paul when he teaches us that the mystery of marriage union itself testifies to something bigger than itself (Eph. 5:32). The Old Testament pursuit by God of a covenant people, a tribe, a nation included a pursuit of individuals, but was surely more than that. The Pauline emphasis on our participation in a mystical body, the very body of Christ, in 1 Corinthians 12, and the eschatological depiction of the consummation of history not as the redemption of a gaggle of individuals but as a marriage (with its potential for union!) between the Bridegroom Lamb and his bride (collective singular), speak of a collective

6. Philip Turner, "Sex and the Single Life," *First Things* (May 1993): 15-21.
7. See, e.g., Mark Noll, *America's God* (New York: Oxford University Press, 2002).

identity that neither evangelical theologians nor psychologists have begun to properly comprehend.

But we cannot leave consideration of this objective union of persons without noting the puzzles it presents. This entity, this one-flesh union, does not achieve a permanence that transcends death; Jesus noted that marriage is only for this life and that there will be no marriage in heaven (Matt. 22:30). This presents perplexing problems: It is common to think of the eschaton as the re-creation of or return to the original state of perfection of Eden, but the Edenic state was not fully good without the institution of marriage. If people will not be married in the final state, and yet marriage was an integral part of human reality in the Edenic state, then we would seem to need to conclude that there will be some fundamental transformation of human character from its original given state. What could this fundamental difference between Eden and the New Eden be? Could the transformation be external; that the eternal incarnation of the Son now glorified will fill all human needs for relatedness in glory in a way not possible in a perfect first Eden? Is the difference a transformation of our resurrected bodies?

The Formation of the Soul

Fundamental to anthropology is the question of whether the true self is a given that is discovered or something that is progressively formed. The answer would appear to be that the true self is both discovered and formed. Our discipline, psychology, often errs dramatically in its clinical manifestations in the direction of discovery. Exploration of the ethical dimensions of our lived sexuality as developed by two Christian ethicists can help us better understand the ways in which we participate in the formation of our souls. Christian ethicist Gilbert Meilaender[8] rightly argues that we live all of our lives in a "distinct place in creation," "between the beasts and God." In our lives as sexual creatures we live within the limits of our creatureliness, and yet as beings created in the image of God — and hence as creatures who are not wholly defined by our bodily creatureliness — we are called to transcend partially our creatureliness to

8. Gilbert Meilaender, "Between Beasts and Gods," *First Things* (January 2002): 23-29; quote p. 24.

live in obedient response to God's revealed will. Yet that transcendence is always incomplete; we must accept the limits of creaturely life. In refusing to be creatures limited by our creatureliness, we seek the freedom properly accorded only to God, in short the freedom to be "godlike." Meilaender notes that many of the "advances" of the "sexual revolution" can be understood in part as attempts to transcend utterly our creatureliness and become godlike in our control of the definition of our existence: birth control that allows us to control procreation, the various "breeding control" technologies that allow us to determine the babies we want, and the severing of sex from marriage (and hence lifelong union). The proper formation of the soul requires submission to the given realities of our creatureliness, and yet also the strength and courage to respond in obedience to God's Word; such formation requires both the acceptance of what is and the formation of our souls through obedience, an obedience that creates that which is not yet.

Turner[9] offers a complementary analysis. Drawing on the work of Charles Taylor, Turner argues that in our society we are increasingly assuming that who we are as selves is defined only inwardly or subjectively in the context of our everyday lives. The most important dimension of our inwardness for many, if not most, is the attainment of happiness and fulfillment, this again in the context of everyday life. With this as the foundation, morality is transformed; the most basic moral principle becomes the obligation to act to enhance our growth and gratification. Add to this the commonplace that our sexuality "in some way defines the inner depths of the self" and that our sexuality is thus fundamental to the very "powers and abilities [of the self which] the self is to discover, develop, and exercise in the course of daily life," and it then follows that "Denial of one's 'sexuality' is akin to denial of 'oneself' and so also one's basic 'identity.'"[10]

The Christian vision of anthropology takes us in a profoundly different direction. According to Turner, the grounding for our understanding of our selves is first and primarily objective before it is secondarily subjective. A self, in the Christian view, is not defined solely or

9. Turner, "Sex and the Single Life." We are here summarizing and adapting our discussion of Turner in chapter 4 of Stanton L. Jones and Mark A. Yarhouse, *Homosexuality: The Use of Scientific Research in the Church's Moral Debate* (Downers Grove, Ill.: InterVarsity Press, 2000).

10. Turner, "Sex and the Single Life," p. 17.

primarily by subjectivity, but rather by meanings given by God by revelation and worked out in a community beyond the autonomous self. Further, our selves are grounded in visions of virtue and possibilities every bit as much as in how we live in everyday life. Turner applies this analysis to understanding the role of sexuality in the formation of the self. Our sexuality, particularly the act of sexual intercourse, has meanings and implications that exist independently of what we might think we mean by such acts, meanings and implications that are intrinsic to those acts; we referred to this earlier as the objective meaning of sexual union. We form our selves as we respond to these objective realities and pursue (or not) the virtues entailed; obedience or disobedience marks us and makes us. Again we see this dynamic of discovery and formation; we discover the reality of who we really are in response to God's revelation, and then we form the selves we are becoming by our responses. In the context of these objective meanings (narrowly, the meanings of our sexuality, and more broadly in the entire light of God's revelation to us of who we are before him), our subjective appropriation of and response to these meanings become most meaningful. This analysis should not be taken to mean that the subjective — such as the desire for pleasure or happiness, or the hunger for self-identity — is unimportant, but rather that it is the human condition to find the proper answers to these questions, the proper alignment of these subjective perspectives, only through engagement with the objective, the self-revealing God. This argument parallels that of C. S. Lewis in *Surprised by Joy* when he suggests that the hunger for joy is real and meaningful, but that true joy is ultimately found not through its direct pursuit but rather as a natural by-product of the proper alignment of the self with transcendent reality.

Our argument here may be summarized as follows:[11] There is a "given" nature to the self such that part of what it means to be a self is to "discover" who we are. But it is also fundamentally the case that human selves are formed by the choices we make in response to the objective realities we confront, and the teleology of self formation is that what is discovered about one's self is in turn submitted to God for transformation via obedience to his revealed standards and via living in

11. See Stanton L. Jones, "Response to 'A "Perfect Standard"?' Exploring Perceptions of Student Life and Culture at Wheaton College" by Cumings, Haworth, and O'Neill, *Religion & Education* 29, no. 1 (2002): 90-93.

an abiding relationship with an active Savior who indwells and molds his people. A self that is only discovered is an undeveloped, impoverished self; a self discovered and then *formed* in the painful, humbling, and intimate process of dying to one's sinful nature and living in costly obedience to God will be the truest and most real self.

Sexual Ethics

These are only some of the important aspects of sexuality that are relevant to theological anthropology, but we turn now to the practical implications of this theological anthropology. Anthropology gets lived out in ethics, and hence these discussions are not merely academic. They have implications for sexual ethics and even potentially in social policy, because who God intends us to be is tied to how we live together in the church and in the broader culture. In turning to this subject, we again acknowledge that we are not professional theologians but have been, if you will, activists or combatants in the sexual morality controversies of our day. We are convinced that part of the ineffectiveness of traditionalist or evangelical voices in the public sphere can be attributed to their (our) focus on making negative claims — once with pietistic denunciations of the licentiousness of the sexual revolution and lately the solitary claim that homosexual practice is immoral — instead of embedding rightly negative condemnations in a positive ethic.

In arguing this, we are acutely aware that God himself takes a negative strategy in the Scriptures in the provision of many "Thou shalt not's," but it is worth noting that eroticism and its linkage to romantic love and marital intimacy are celebrated in the Old Testament in passages such as Proverbs 5 and in the Song of Songs, and that such New Testament passages as Hebrews 13:4 and 1 Timothy 4:1-5, and even 1 Corinthians 6, declare the goodness of sexual union in marriage. Fundamentally, the Christian sexual ethic is a positive ethic. The anthropology sketched to this point establishes our sexuality as a profoundly positive gift. The Christian sexual ethic, then, far from a dour, Scroogish asceticism, is a constructive protection of a divine gift from misuse. It is a guide for proper use, even when sacrificial obedience leads to temporal pain.

In Deuteronomy 10:13 we learn that the "commands and decrees" of the Lord were given "for your own good"! And despite the interpretations of secularists, the social scientific empirical literature can help with sermon illustrations that depict the promised benefits. An immense literature attests to the quality-of-life benefits of traditional marriage and of two-parent family arrangements. Religious faith has rarely been measured in psychological studies of marriage but interesting results have emerged when it has, perhaps none more interesting than the Greeley report[12] on a Gallup study of marriage that found that the single most powerful predictor of a good marriage was whether couples pray together regularly, that joint prayer was highly correlated with sexual satisfaction, and that the couple able to pray together and enjoy good sex together was the least likely to divorce. Empirical studies of cohabitation consistently suggest, contrary to the received wisdom that cohabiting relationships facilitate better preparation for and judgments about marital compatibility, that cohabitation on average is associated with higher post-marriage divorce rates and rates of extramarital affairs, and with less sexual satisfaction in marriage. An immense literature attests to the quality-of-life benefits of traditional marriage and of two-parent family arrangements.[13] This literature does not "establish" the truthfulness of God's moral laws; such positive outcomes are probabilistic only, with many individual exceptions. But the *pattern* of outcomes is consistent with the outcomes to be expected if a loving, beneficent God truly gave his commands "for our own good"!

But we cannot merely proclaim a positive ethic in words. We must live out that positive ethic in the public sphere with conviction. People need to be "witnessed to" by the lives of the individual members that corporately comprise the holy, pure Bride of the Lamb of God. Yet at this moment in history (as throughout all history), our witness is compromised by our own hypocrisy in many areas (such as our lack of concern for racial reconciliation and social justice, and our lack of dedication to the poor) but perhaps nowhere more clearly than in the area of sexual morality. It is widely reported that divorce statistics for evangelical Christian families are as high or higher than for the general popula-

12. Andrew Greeley, *Faithful Attraction: Discovering Intimacy, Love and Fidelity in American Marriage* (New York: Tor, 1991).

13. For a recent review of the research, see Linda J. Waite and Maggie Gallagher, *The Case for Marriage* (New York: Broadway, 2000).

tion. Our young people have premarital sexual intercourse statistics that trail those of the nonreligious public by only a few percentage points. And many of those Christian young people who are technically preserving their virginity by not having sexual intercourse are anything but sexually inexperienced and chaste, as non-intercourse sexual gratification, particularly oral sex and mutual genital stimulation of other types, is becoming common among "virgins."

The persuasiveness of our stance on the immorality of certain contemporary practices is compromised by our lack of a living out of the positive sexual ethic. Our churches need to put a premium on a moral revitalization of our communities so that we truly become lights in the darkness, fragrant aromas. In addition to faithful obedience to God's call on our lives in areas of sexual morality, Christians gain credibility in public discourse when they actively demonstrate a positive ethic of compassion and hospitality toward those in bondage to sexual immorality — compassion and hospitality demonstrated in our homes, churches, and communities. This should include standing with the gay community against violence against self-identifying lesbian, gay, or bisexual persons, and also taking a proactive stance in meeting the needs of those in the gay community suffering and dying from HIV/AIDS.

The Ethics of Homosexual Conduct in Anthropological Context

In this final section we want to explore one of the most pressing moral issues of the day, homosexual conduct, in the light of the anthropology developed above. Paul's discourse in Romans 1 provides the theological key for understanding both homosexuality per se and the broadening acceptance of homosexuality by those not personally drawn to that particular sinful behavior: both are grounded in our rebellious human temptation to attempt to be gods unto ourselves. This tendency is in turn grounded in our proclivity to worship that which is created rather than the Creator (that is to say, in idolatry), and in our sinful suppression of available knowledge of God and of ourselves.[14]

---

14. Several recent exegetical/theological studies of Romans 1 converge on a persuasive understanding of Paul's message, but we are most directly indebted in the following

Romans 1 does not teach that homosexuality is in any simplistic sense a result of individual idolatry, as if a person engaged in idolatry and then immediately was "stuck" or "cursed" with the homosexual condition either as a natural consequence of or as divine punishment for the idolatry. Rather, argues Robert Gagnon,[15] Paul's logic follows a five-step process of decline for the entire human race: (1) "God's invisible transcendence and majesty is visibly manifested in creation"; (2) humans knowingly and deliberately exchange the truth of God (in the vertical God-human dimension) for an idolatrous lie; (3) God gives us over to our destructive and degrading passions; (4) humans exchange the natural for the unnatural (in the horizontal human-human dimension); (5) God gives rebellious humanity over to the ultimate consequence of our rebellion, death. In short, as a race we suppress knowledge of the divine and of the created order, we suppress the truth in unrighteousness, and from that rebellious denial of the truth flow remarkable distortions of "what is natural" (that is, what God created us for). Homosexuality is one case example; according to Gagnon,

> Same-sex eroticism functions as a particularly poignant example of human enslavement to passions and of God's just judgment precisely because it parallels in the horizontal-ethical dimension a denial of God's reality like that of idolatry in the vertical-divine dimension. In other words, idolatry is a deliberate suppression of the truth available to pagans in the world around them, but so too is same-sex intercourse.[16]

God's judgment of and wrath toward humanity is manifested in "God stepping back and allowing the sinful passions of the flesh to take control of those who have turned their back on the living and true God."[17]

As psychologists, we see no conflict between such a theological

---

to the thorough study of Robert A. J. Gagnon, *The Bible and Homosexual Practice: Texts and Hermeneutics* (Nashville: Abingdon, 2001). The most helpful other studies are those of Richard Hays, *The Moral Vision of the New Testament: A Contemporary Introduction to New Testament Ethics* (San Francisco: HarperCollins, 1996), and of Thomas Schmidt, *Straight and Narrow? Compassion and Clarity in the Homosexuality Debate* (Downers Grove, Ill.: InterVarsity, 1993).

15. Gagnon, *The Bible and Homosexual Practice,* pp. 252-53.

16. Gagnon, *The Bible and Homosexual Practice,* p. 254.

17. Gagnon, *The Bible and Homosexual Practice,* p. 251.

analysis of the genesis of homosexuality and the various psychological and even biological accounts of processes contributing to the formation of homosexual orientation. The "twistedness" of human existence is the product of the very theological forces described here, with the ensuing physical, emotional, relational, and spiritual brokenness of the human condition serving as proximal contributing causes of the homosexual condition.

We would apply this analysis to the growing acceptance of homosexuality in popular culture as well. The idolatry discussed in Romans 1 in turn seems grounded in our refusal to submit to God's rightful reign over our lives. It is part of the general human condition to long to be our own gods and to construct our own realities. This human tendency was captured in the most remarkable way by D. H. Lawrence:

> Liberty is all very well, but men cannot live without masters. There is always a master. And men live in glad obedience to the masters they believe in, or they live in a frictional opposition to the master they wish to undermine. In America this frictional opposition has been the vital factor. . . . [America is] a vast republic of escaped slaves[,] . . . [of] the masterless.[18]

It does not seem to us an understatement to regard the "normal" fallen state of humanity to be that of living in frictional opposition to the master we wish to undermine. Homosexuality represents a paradigm case for the aggressive assertion of human freedom, human will and choice, against not only cultural and moral constraints, but also, on the one hand, against even basic biological constraints of our physical, gendered bodily realities such as what our bodily organs are meant for, and, on the other hand, against the very definition of the self before God with the insertion of sexual preference into the essentialist definition of the core of the self. Hence, the acceptance of homosexuality as valid by the tolerant heterosexual constitutes an instance of the suppression of knowledge as grave in some ways as the behavioral choices of the homosexual person. The homosexual becomes, if you will, a heroic figure in the mind of the non-homosexual observer, a paradigm case of the existentially free human in the process of constructing his

18. D. H. Lawrence, quoted in Wilfred M. McClay, *The Masterless: Self and Society in America* (Chapel Hill, N.C.: University of North Carolina, 1994), p. 1.

Stanton L. Jones and Mark A. Yarhouse

or her own sexual and personal reality in autonomy from all constraints of morality, culture, biology, and (in the Pauline sense) reason. The happy, well-adjusted homosexual becomes the paradigm case, the Kuhnian exemplar, demonstrating that human will truly knows no boundaries.

To be clear, nothing in this analysis denies the operation of the various etiological variables under contemporary discussion in the causation of homosexual orientation; genetic influences, brain structures, hormonal factors, temperamental factors, family dynamics, experiential factors such as sexual abuse, and cultural factors may all be operative in various ways. Even so, the embrace of what is "discovered" of the developing self, a denial of one's fallenness, and a rebellion against (or frictional opposition to) the biological givens of gender, against the objective meanings of sexual intimacy as revealed in the Scriptures, and against the express command of God, are equally in play in the formation of the gay or lesbian person.

To the extent that there is any validity to this analysis, it suggests that there are powerful forces at work in the human heart in Western culture, among those not personally drawn to the homosexual preference, to accept and embrace it. The modern gay-affirming movement is in some ways symbolic of the human condition when people turn from the communion God offers with himself through his Son. The general acceptance of homosexuality in our culture represents a broader expression of idolatry as people turn away from their Creator to worship the created. The countervailing forces are the Holy Spirit's continuing work in the restraint of evil, and the background truth of Romans 1 that humans can be rescued from foolish rebellion and suppression of truth through honest engagement with the self-revelation of the Father in both general and special revelation.

After diagnosing our American condition as that of "the masterless," D. H. Lawrence accurately if vaguely diagnosed the cure for our disorder:

> But men are free when they are in a living homeland, not when they are straying and breaking away. Men are free when they are obeying some deep, inward voice of religious belief. Obeying from within. Men are free when they belong to a living, organic, *believing* community, active in fulfilling some unfulfilled, perhaps unrealized pur-

134

pose. . . . Liberty in America has meant so far the breaking away from all dominion. The true liberty will only begin when Americans discover . . . the deepest *whole* self of man.[19]

Lawrence was no Christian prophet, but he was dead-on right in this. Meilaender states a complementary formulation: "To be human, then, is to learn to live and love within limits — the limits of our embodied, mortal life, the limits of those whose being opens to God. It is to acknowledge, honor, and esteem the particular place — between the beasts and God — that we occupy in the creation."[20]

The Christian church has rightly taught throughout its existence the importance of sexuality to the understanding of personhood, and of sexual ethics to the formation of the person. It has rightly diagnosed homosexual practice as immoral and disordered, and must rightly preach the gospel as the ultimate cure. We face a daunting challenge in trying to effectively, strongly, and wisely carry our testimony to a skeptical and increasingly rejecting secular culture that is addicted to a self-conception of autonomous, godlike beings who can create themselves in their own image. We need to be clear that we are seeking to deliver faithfully to others that which has been delivered to us: the true revelation of the living God. It is ultimately only in this living Word that we understand the brokenness of our human condition and its cure. It is only through costly discipleship that we have any chance to model for a watching world the profound good of a people living by God's good standards.

Living out such a prophetic calling will be extraordinarily difficult, inside the church and without. The apostle Paul, in the words of Gagnon, enjoins believers to exercise "mutual toleration" as

> the proper approach for matters of indifference such as diet or calendar. . . . He [God] does not take the same approach of accommodation on all matters, however. In matters involving sexual ethics . . . , Paul does not countenance accommodation. . . . In short, homosexual practice whether among men or women was *not* a matter of indifference for Paul.[21]

19. D. H. Lawrence, quoted in McClay, *The Masterless*, p. 1.
20. Meilaender, "Between Beasts," p. 26.
21. Gagnon, *The Bible and Homosexual Practice*, pp. 243-44.

Neither can it become a matter of indifference for those who are Christ's followers.[22] We believe that the church must believe and proclaim that homosexual sexual intimacy is always wrong, and must do so with clarity and conviction. We must strive to see that faithful Christians adhere to and profess a biblical understanding of human sexuality that affirms our sexuality as a good of creation, that affirms our humanness and our inherent physicality with respect to what it means to be sexual beings, that affirms our sexuality as an important dimension to who we are as persons, and that affirms that what it means to be gendered as male and female in the image of God has pre-existing meanings and hence claims on our sexuality and our sexual behavior. In this, Christians continue to function as faithful stewards of the revelation we have regarding God's will for us in all areas of our lives, including our sexuality as seen in the broader context of our experience of redemption and sanctification.

22. Wolfhart Pannenberg has argued that, given the unambiguous condemnation in Scripture of homosexual practice, those who advocate for its moral acceptance are no longer part of the faithful, gospel-confessing church; in "Homosexual Experience," *Christianity Today* (November 11, 1996), pp. 35-36.

SECTION III | **Suggestive Proposals**

David H. Kelsey | **Personal Bodies**
A Theological
Anthropological Proposal

In this essay I reflect on the use in Christian theological anthropology of the term "person" and related terms from the point of view of a constructive proposal in theological anthropology. Because the proposal is not yet complete, what I suggest here will unavoidably have the tentativeness of a thought experiment. The essay will have four parts. In the first I shall focus the question lying behind the project, and in the second sketch the basic thesis and structure of the proposal. In the third I will offer reflections on the dominant ways in which "person" (and related terms) are used in modern Western secular cultures. In the fourth I propose in outline a theocentric concept of human person.

What Has Christian Faith to Add?

Behind my own theological reflection on human being has been the question, "What has Christian faith to add to general human wisdom about what it is to be human?" Some years ago when I was preparing the bibliography for a course I co-taught in pastoral theology, I came across *Pastoral Care in Historical Perspective,* a volume edited by William A. Clebsch, a historian of Christianity, and Charles R. Jaekle, a pastoral theologian.[1] Following a remarkable essay of theological and historical analysis of the intellectual history of practices of Christian

1. William A. Clebsch and Charles R. Jaekle, eds., *Pastoral Care in Historical Perspective* (New York: Harper and Row, 1967).

pastoral care, they offer a series of "exhibits," texts drawn from every period in Christian history, from the *Second Epistle of Clement* to William James, addressing a large range of human questions. Clebsch and Jaekel rightly construe pastoral care broadly so that it includes not only what we now call counseling but also instruction in the faith, spiritual direction, healing, reconciling, and moral guidance. The advantage of this broad construal of pastoral care is that it brings out the fact that what we now separate as pastoral theology, moral theology or theological ethics, apologetics, and dogmatics all have their roots in and are in the service of the communal practices that make up the common life of the Christian church.

Working my way through Clebsch and Jaekel's exhibits focused four points that had been right there in front of my theological nose all the time, so obvious they had gone unnoticed.

1. For the most part, the questions that form the core of the agenda of the subsection of dogmatics called "anthropology" have historically been rooted in, and thus pre-selected by, the core problems on which pastoral and moral theology have been focused. When we look for the theological anthropologies of pre-modern Christian thinkers we mostly have to look to their discussions of catechetical, moral, or Christian life ("spirituality"?) questions. Indeed, "anthropology" emerged as a locus in its own right only in the modern period, when the main task of theology came to be construed as address to Christianity's cultured despisers, on the supposition that a shared picture of human nature was the strongest point of intellectual contact with the skeptics.

2. Perhaps because of its roots in pastoral practices, theological anthropology's agenda has consisted, not of one, but of three different types of question. (a) Most obviously, it has addressed the question *what* is a human being? What is the nature of this creature to whom we are trying to provide pastoral care, broadly understood? It is, I think, a metaphysical question. Call it the "What?" question. But there are two more types of question that have been equally important. (b) *How* ought I to be set into my world? This is, I suggest, not in the first instance a moral question — What should I do? How should I act? — but an existential question — How should I be most fundamentally oriented to my neighbors, myself, my context? Call it the "How?" question. (c) *Who* am I, who are we? This is a question about one's unsubstitutable personal identity. It is not basically, I suggest, a psy-

chological question — What is my self-image? What is my personality type? — although it overlaps with such questions. Nor is it basically the ethnic- or group-identity question central to so much contemporary "identity politic," although it overlaps even more with it. Rather, it is a social-historical question about which narrative most aptly conveys "my" and "our" unsubstitutable personal and social identities.

These three types of question do not easily collapse into one another. It is controversial whether answers to any two of them can be deduced from the answer to the third. Not all Christian thinkers take up all three. Very often the *locus* "theological anthropology" is explained as theological address to the "What is a human being?" question. It cannot, however, be confined to that question. All three questions are centrally important to its agenda.

3. In attempting to address anthropological questions Christian thinkers have always borrowed what they took to be the best anthropological wisdom of their host non-Christian cultures. And in borrowing the wisdom, they borrowed conceptual schemes. To be sure, Christian thinkers were guided by a relatively small set of biblical tropes, chief among them that human beings are created "after the image of God." But the material content of Christian explanation of what those tropes mean has largely been borrowed from other sources. The point is a commonplace about the history of doctrine, beginning with the apostle Paul's borrowing of concepts and themes from the Cynics and continuing with contemporary borrowing from depth psychology and existential phenomenology. What Clebsch and Jaekel brought out was that such borrowing in theological anthropology has consistently had its roots in similar borrowing in Christian practices of pastoral care, spiritual direction, and ethical counsel.

4. What Christians borrowed from their host cultures by way of anthropological wisdom, they borrowed selectively, and then they *bent* it. Over and over, historical studies show that when Christian writers borrow anthropological (and other) concepts from their host cultures, they use them in ways different than their ordinary use in their original contexts. Hence, insofar as meaning lies in use, these concepts come to mean something slightly different in their new Christian theological contexts.

Now at last my central question came into focus. Given that the conceptual content of theological anthropology was largely (if selectively) borrowed from the general fund of human anthropological wisdom, does Christian faith bring with it any non-negotiable anthropological claims of its own? What has Christian faith to add to Christianly borrowed anthropological wisdom? Moreover, just what functions as the principle of selection of the wisdom borrowed, and just what commitments generate the gravitational force by which what is borrowed is bent?

I propose an answer whose apparent simplicity turns out to be very misleading: What Christians claim about humankind that nobody else does is that the triune God relates to humankind, and to all else, to create it, to draw it to eschatological consummation, and, when it is estranged, to reconcile it. That's what Christian faith has to add. Hence, a properly *theological* anthropology will be theocentric at every turn. It is under the conceptual pressure of claims about divine relating that borrowed anthropological conceptualities are theologically bent. I turn now to that.

God Relating

In reference to God it is less misleading, I think, to use as consistently as possible the participle "relating" and the verb "relates" rather than the nominative "relation" and the abstractions "relatedness" and "relationship." At least three considerations support this.

First, canonical Christian Scripture typically narrates God actively relating to reality other than God rather than abstractly describing a static "relationship" between God and creatures. I shall return to this theme in a moment. Note that throughout I use "narrative" very broadly in reference to a story with a distinct plot or pattern of movement that is made explicit in, or assumed by or implied by, a text, whatever its literary genre.

Second, the verbal forms bring out the distinction between God relating to humankind and humankind relating to God. Not only are these two not identical, the Christian claim is that humankind's relating to God is generally not congruent with, nor an appropriate response to, God's relating to humankind. That is, human relating to God is generally sinful. To declare abstractly that human creatures have the property of "God-relatedness" simply obscures the distinction between God relating to us and our relating to God. What makes Christian theological anthropology *theological* is that it is ruled by claims about God relating to us. More exactly, it is ruled by claims about the *triune* God relating to us. Such anthropology must be theocentric. Only in and from that context should we derive claims about our relating to God. Speaking of "God relating" rather than about "the God relation" brings that out.

Put the first and second considerations together and they yield a third, more controversial reason for preferring to speak of God actively relating to humankind rather than more abstractly of humankind's God-relatedness. It provides conceptual space for stressing that "God actively relating" is said in several senses, not in one.

To begin, it may be true that canonical Christian Scripture typically narrates God actively relating to reality other than God, but the canon seems to me to be a good bit more complicated than that. To call the Bible "canonical" Scripture implies that it is some sort of whole. But the canon is an internally very complex sort of whole. Since Irenaeus there has been a nearly unanimous tendency among theologians in the West to construe that wholeness as constituted by a single, extended, loosely organized narrative in three major moments: God creates, God reconciles a self-estranged creation, God draws creation to an eschatological consummation (end of story). I have become skeptical of that way of construing the unity of the canon.

If the unity of a narrative lies in the structure of its plot, then, I suggest, canonical Scripture embraces three classes of narratives distinguishable from one another because each has a distinct plot structure or narrative logic:

1. narratives of God relating creatively to all that is not God;
2. narratives of God relating to estranged creatures to reconcile them;
3. narratives of God relating to all that is not God to draw it to an eschatological consummation.

These three are braided together in a certain order in canonical Christian Scripture. They resonate with one another. They can each be told in ways that use episodes and tropes from the other two as metaphors for features of their own story. Hence they may not be separated. Indeed, the full significance of each can be told only when it is narra-

*tively braided with a telling of the other two. Nonetheless, they tell of three distinguishable ways in which God goes about relating to all that is not God. Hence in its telling no one of them may be conflated with the telling of the other two.

It is the differences between, and the quite definite order among, these three classes of biblical narratives that have made me skeptical of the time-honored practice of treating them as serial moments in a narrative that has a single plot structure or narrative logic.

It may help to examine two illustrations.

First, in canonical Scripture, stories of God relating *creatively* consistently tell of God's creating as an active relating into which God enters without there being another term for God to relate to except for the very act of relating creatively. This is theologically summarized, of course, in the formula that God creates *ex nihilo* all that which God affirms to be unqualifiedly good in its kind. The narrative is so plotted that that which God creates is radically dependent for its ongoing reality on God's creative relating. Hence at least part of what is meant by creation's "kind" ("It is good in its kind") is thoroughgoing finitude, limitedness by virtue of dependence, vulnerability, and fragility. Whatever the consequences may be across time of this finitude, they do not qualify God's creative affirmation of creation's goodness precisely as radically dependent, vulnerable, and fragile. This narrative logic entails that there can be absolutely no resistance by creation to its being created, no resistance to God's creative relating to it, simply because absent that relating there is nothing "there" to engage in resistance. Further, the narrative logic of this class of stories assumes or affirms that what is real in virtue of divine creative relating is good.

On the other hand, canonical Scripture also tells stories of God relating to creation to draw it to *eschatological* consummation, in which creatures will be transformed in unimaginable ways. What is "good" in its creaturely kind is promised that it will in some way participate in God's own "glory." This kind of story tends to be told in ways that suggest that God's relating in this way is as primordial as God's relating to create. God drawing to eschatological consummation does not follow God creating serially; it is coevally concurrent with it. Nonetheless, this kind of narrative is so plotted that, unlike stories of God creating, it *does* presuppose that the term of God's relating — that is, the totality of creatures — is logically already "there" and that what is being drawn to glory is already fully actual and good in its kind, independent of being glorified. Eschatological consummation does not actualize creation's goodness as though it had its goodness only as a future promise. It had eschatological glory only as a promise, but it is fully actualized as good by God's creative relating to it independent of consummation. At the same time, the narrative logic of this type of story entails that the possibility must be left open that at least some creatures may resist God's relating to draw them to eschatological consummation. Biblical narratives of this sort do not entail that creatures have resisted or will resist, only that there is the logical possibility that they may.

Now, it seems to me that if narratives with these two different narrative logics are conflated as successive moments of a single narrative with a single plot (as happens, it seems, in the theological proposals of Wolfhart Pannenberg, Karl Rahner, and John Zizioulas), either the narrative logic of stories of God creating or the narrative logic of stories of God drawing to eschatological consummation is distorted.

That is, either eschatological consummation is told as the final full actualization of what God only began to do in creating, or it is told as a restoration of the goodness of finite creation as created. In the former case, eschatological glory is flatly identified as creatures' "good," and what obtained by God's creative relating was at best only potentially good, awaiting eschatological consummation to be actually good. Here God relating creatively is merely the opening moment in an overarching narrative of God drawing to eschatological consummation. It is hard to see how creation stories read this way, narratively absorbed into stories of eschatological consummation, are anything more than thinly disguised stories of a relatively incompetent creating that stands in need of a second and more competent creative act to bring creatures to their full creaturely actuality and goodness. Read this way, the narrative logic of canonical stories of God creating appears to be systematically distorted.

In the latter sort of telling, when eschatological consummation is told as a restoration of the goodness of finite creation as created, stories of consummation are absorbed into stories of creation. They presuppose the narrative logic of stories of God relating to create that which God affirms to be good precisely in its finite creatureliness, but then smuggle in a second narrative element according to which creatures distort and deface their goodness and stand in need of having it restored. Read this way, the narrative logic of canonical stories of eschatological consummation is distorted in two ways: The glory associated with eschatological consummation is simply conflated with the goodness given with creation. And God's giving of glory is made to be contingent on creatures' distortion and defacement of their creaturely goodness, rather than being independent of that contingency and as primordial as God's relating to them creatively. It won't do, I submit, to read these two types of canonical scriptural stories as successive moments in an overarching narrative made a narrative by its single plot line. Better to tell them distinctly, albeit interrelatedly.

A second example: In canonical Scripture, stories of God relating to draw creation to eschatological consummation and stories of God relating to reconcile estranged creatures are tightly interwoven because they both center on the incarnation.

On one side, canonical stories of God's enacting across history an intention to draw the good creation to an *eschatological* glory are plotted in such a way that their narrative climax is quite particularly and concretely the resurrection of the Incarnate One, the event when the long-promised future eschatological consummation proleptically invades the here and now.

On the other side, the canonical stories of God enacting across time an intention to *reconcile* estranged creatures are plotted in such a way that their narrative climax is quite particularly and concretely the resurrection of the crucified Incarnate One.

It is clear that both classes of stories presuppose a third type of story about God relating *creatively;* absent that, there is nothing "there" either to be consummated or to be reconciled.

Furthermore, it is clear that if creatures are, as a matter of contingent fact, estranged, stories about their eschatological consummation presuppose stories about their (logically) first being reconciled, for estranged creatures are incapable of participating in God's promised eschatological consummation. Conversely, it is clear that New Testament stories of God reconciling estranged creatures in Jesus Christ presuppose that the larger narrative context of God's doing so is told in stories of God drawing them to eschatological consummation through their oneness with Jesus Christ.

For all of these reasons it is clear that these two classes of canonical scriptural stories of God actively relating to humankind cannot be told in separation from one another.

Nonetheless, I suggest, the differences between biblical narratives of God drawing creatures to eschatological consummation and God reconciling estranged creatures mean that the two sorts of stories cannot be conflated into a single narrative without distortion of the narrative logic of one or both of them. If, on one hand, stories about God reconciling creatures are told as the opening episode of longer stories about God drawing those creatures to a glorious eschatological consummation, then the estrangement that is the necessary condition of stories of divine reconciliation (if there is no estrangement, no reconciliation is needed) also becomes the necessary condition of the larger story of consummation. But not only does the narrative logic of canonical scriptural stories of eschatological consummation not presuppose that creatures are estranged, but, as stories about how what is good by God's creativity is further blessed with eschatological glory, their narrative logic positively presupposes that creatures are *not* estranged. To read them otherwise is to distort their narrative logic by making creaturely estrangement narratively necessary to them.

If, on the other hand, canonical scriptural stories of God drawing creatures to eschatological consummation are told as the happy-ever-after consequence of stories of God reconciling estranged creatures, told chiefly as an affirmation of the permanence of the restoration of right relationship with God effected by reconciliation, then the narrative logic of either or both types of story is distorted. To tell the story of eschatological consummation as nothing more than the restoration of creatures' pre-estrangement relationship with God is inadequate because it is inherent to the narrative logic of such stories that the outcome of the story is a glorification of the creature that far transcends its creaturely relationship with God. On the other hand, if the story of reconciliation is told as though it moves creatures directly into a relationship with God that transcends their creaturely relationship without any change in them, that too is inadequate, because it is inherent to the narrative logic of canonical stories of reconciliation that they tell of a freeing of creatures from their self-distortion in estrangement and a restoration of their undistorted creaturely relationship with God, precisely as the pre-condition making it possible for them then, once reconciled, *also* to be drawn into eschatological consummation. To read scriptural stories of reconciliation otherwise is to distort their narrative logic.

These illustrations are intended to show the inner complexity of the set of narratives that constitute canonical Christian Scripture as a "whole." They demonstrate why it is wise not to oversimplify that complexity by treating these three types of scriptural narratives as successive moments in a serial narrative, and why it would be wiser to treat them theologically as distinguishable narratives told in ways that weave them inseparably together while honoring their different and distinct narrative logics.

The differences among the three classes of canonical stories about God actively relating to all that is not God may be signaled by the different prepositions that are appropriate to each way of relating: In relating to create, God the Father, through the Son in the power of the Spirit, is creatively present *to* creatures, but is not one among them nor circumambiently between them. In relating to draw to eschatological consummation, God the Spirit, sent by the Father with the Son, is circumambiently *between* creatures, not one among them or merely present to them. In relating to reconcile alienated creatures, God the Son, sent by the Father in the power of the Spirit, is one *among* them, sharing their common creaturely field, not just relating to them nor circumambiently with them. It is, I suggest, the differences among these three classes of biblical narratives that are a major reason for canonical Scripture's internal complexity.

If that is the case, then the concept "God relating to humankind" must be used analogically and not univocally. The expressions "the triune God relating to create," "the triune God relating to draw to eschatological consummation," and "the triune God relating to reconcile" are not interchangeable alternative variations on some one more precise and logically basic concept such as "God-relatedness." Rather, they are different ways in which God actively relates, each a "relating" in an importantly different sense of "relating."

In my view this has two major implications for theological anthropology: First, the conceptual pressures under which borrowed anthropological wisdom is selected and bent come from implications of these three ways in which God relates to humankind, not from some single, abstract "God-relatedness." Second, Christian theological anthropology's answers to the "what," "how," and "who" questions are suggested by the implications of these three ways in which the triune God relates to humankind.

Teasing out those answers is the anthropological project I'm trying to work out. The claim that the triune God relates to us creatively chiefly implies some answers to the question "What are we?" but also implies some answers to the "How?" and "Who?" questions. The claim that the triune God relates to us to draw us to eschatological consummation chiefly implies some answers to the question "How ought we to be?" but also implies answers to the "What?" and "Who?" questions. The claim that the triune God relates to us to reconcile us in our estrangement chiefly implies some answers to the question "Who are we?" but also implies some answers to the "What?" and "How?" questions. Each of the ways in which God is said to relate to humankind also implies a distinct account of human flourishing or blessedness. Conversely, each implies a distinct sense in which human beings fail to respond appropriately to the concrete way in which God relates to them and thereby bind themselves in a distinct sense of "sin." Exploring these anthropological implications of each of the ways in which the triune God relates to us thus constitutes a separate part of the project as a whole.

"Personhood"

Now let us use the foregoing as a framework within which to consider one major cluster of related concepts borrowed by contemporary theological anthropology from its host culture. Arguably the most important family of concepts borrowed by contemporary theologians from modern secular culture's anthropological wisdom includes concepts of "person," "personality," "personal," "personhood," and the like. There is no way to avoid borrowing them. I want, however, to urge extreme caution about how we use what we borrow, and to identify ways in which they need to be deeply bent when used theologically.

"Person" and related terms are used in contemporary culture in three broad interrelated ways: classificatory, descriptively metaphysical, and evaluative.

David H. Kelsey

1. "Person," "personal," and the like are used descriptively to *classify* certain living beings, distinguishing them from the class of "impersonal" or "nonperson" beings. There are two major criteria for inclusion in this class: "Personal beings" or "persons" are free such that they can be held morally accountable for their actions; and they are subjects in contradistinction to objects, centers of consciousness. "Consciousness" is usually discussed as though it were some one thing. In secular intellectual culture consciousness tends to be analyzed either in psychological, especially psychoanalytic, terms or in existential-phenomenological terms. "Consciousness" is complexly dynamic.

   It is, perhaps, a hallmark of distinctly "modern" thought to select "consciousness" as definitive of human personhood. Philosophical anthropology in the pre-modern period by and large settled on "mind," "intellect," or "rationality" as definitive of properly human being. Picking "consciousness" rather than "rationality" as a key criterion for inclusion in the class "human persons" does not, however, necessarily devalue reason. Rather, it may allow for including reason holistically along with sense experience, emotions, passions, and feelings in their complex interrelations within consciousness.

   A particular pattern or organization of sensibilities, emotions, passions, feelings, and types of intelligence is called a "personality."

2. In a classic essay philosopher P. F. Strawson[2] argued that in ordinary discourse we informally use "person" in a *descriptively metaphysical* way to designate that to which it is appropriate to attribute two quite different classes of properties — "M-predicates" (five feet, ten inches; weighs 190 pounds; brown eyes; and so on) and "P-predicates" (anxious; polite; thinks slowly; and so on) — but which is not itself predicated of anything. Strawson's analysis of this use of "person" formally parallels Aristotle's definition of substance as that of which things are predicated but which is not itself predicated of anything else. Strawson, however, was not interested in developing a theory of substance; he simply observed that used in this way "person" is a "primitive" concept, that is, a concept that cannot be explained by analysis into more basic concepts. We

---

2. P. F. Strawson, "Persons," chap. 3 in his *Individuals: An Essay in Descriptive Metaphysics* (London: Methuen, 1959).

might add that concepts of self, ego, and agent are sometimes used informally as primitive concepts filling the same role as "person."

3. "Person," "personal," and the like are also used *evaluatively* to assess a living being as deserving to be treated always, in Kant's phrase, as an end and never as a means. Here our family of concepts is used to assign a living being to a certain moral *status,* a certain moral dignity.

It is my contention that three theologically worrisome tensions, if not incoherences, among these commonplace uses of "person" and related terms in modern culture caution extreme care in any theological appropriation of them.

First, the classificatory use of "person" and related terms trades on a bifurcation of "personhood" from material bodiliness. If what constitutes something a "person" is having subjectivity or being a subject, and if "subject" is defined in contradistinction to "objectivity," and if what makes something "objective" is its material bodiliness, then a human being's bodiliness is excluded from what makes her or him belong to the class of persons. But, theologically speaking, *what* God creates and declares to be good in creating human persons is living organic bodies that *are* objects. This theological claim appears to exclude the type of anthropological "bifurcation" that is inherent in classificatory uses of "person" that are commonplace in characteristically modern discourse. The anthropological dualism such bifurcation generates is conceptually quite different from many of the body-soul distinctions that have traditionally been employed in Christian anthropology. There may still be strong speculative philosophical arguments in support of the latter type of distinction, although developments in neurophysiology and artificial intelligence may make such arguments much more difficult to mount. Even so, the distinction such arguments defend is not at all the distinction between mutually exclusive modes of reality implied by modern culture's classificatory uses of such terms as "person."

Second, the descriptively metaphysical use of "person" seems to be in considerable tension with its classificatory use.[3] Roughly speaking,

---

3. A particularly careful and nuanced discussion of this problem from a philosophical, but theologically sensitive, perspective is provided by R. S. Downie and Elizabeth Telfer in their *Respect for Persons* (New York: Schocken, 1970).

in the *descriptively metaphysical* use of "person" a human person is identifiable with neither its objective bodily properties nor its subjective mental properties. A person is *tertium quid*. On the other hand, a person is *classified* as person precisely in virtue of certain P-predicates only. Certain P-predicates, namely, freedom and consciousness, make something count as a person. On the other hand, used as a primitive concept, "person" designates something conceptually distinct not only from its M-predicates but also from those very same P-predicates of consciousness and freedom. This is theologically troubling because, once again, use of the term "person" consistently marginalizes human beings' bodiliness. The family of concepts related to "person" in modern culture seems to be inherently dualistic.

Third, it is critically important that the classificatory and the evaluative uses of "person" and related terms be held together, but it is just as critical that the evaluative force not be a function of the classificatory use. Having the properties of freedom and consciousness cannot be the *reasons* for being respected as an end and not a means. Otherwise, for example, massively deformed newborns and elderly victims of advanced Alzheimer's disease do not classify as persons, and, presumably, may then be treated as mere means. Our culture's concept of person does not provide grounds for holding these two uses together.

These problems are not solved theologically simply by borrowing modern culture's concept of person, stressing its descriptively metaphysical use, and adding that the beings designated by this primitive concept are created, reconciled, and eschatologically consummated by God. This will not work because the added theological claims are inconsistent with fundamental features of modern culture's concept of person.

As conceptualized in modern culture, a person's defining freedom and consciousness (or subjectivity) is understood in such a way that Christian claims about God relating to persons to create them, to draw them to eschatological consummation, and to reconcile them can be understood only as claims about interruptions and invasions, *violations* of their freedom and subjectivity, that is, as negations of precisely the properties that classify them as persons. If persons' moral status is a function of their being classified as persons, then such violation is also the negation of their status as ends and not mere means. As conceptualized in modern culture, "person" is a primitive concept that cannot be analyzed into more basic concepts, such as "created by God's relating to it." To claim that the triune God relates to it in the ways in which canonical Christian Scripture narrates is to declare it violated, not grounded, by God's relating. Hence, this concept of person can be borrowed by Christian theological anthropology only with great caution, and only if it is bent in some important ways.

A Proposal in Outline

My own proposal goes roughly like this:

1.0. We cannot help but borrow our culture's concept of "person"; however, we should use it within the context of the theological claim that the triune God relates creatively to humankind. Using the family of concepts related to "person" in that context will require some bending of their conventional uses, some change of meaning.

This proposal, therefore, limits Christian anthropological use of "person" to the context of reflection on the anthropological implications of the claim that the triune God relates *creatively* to all that is not God. That is, the proposal addresses the family of concepts centered on "person" only in the context of theological address to the question, "*What* is a human being?" and not in the context of the other two questions that make up theological anthropology's agenda, "*Who* am I? Who are we?" and "*How* ought I, how ought we, to be?" In other words, the topic of "personhood" is addressed in the context of anthropological implications of the doctrine of creation rather than in the context of anthropological implications of eschatology and soteriology.

This restriction to the doctrine of creation as it applies to human beings is appropriate given the order that obtains among the three classes of canonical narratives about God's active relating. Stories about God drawing persons to eschatological consummation and stories about God reconciling estranged persons both presuppose God relating creatively to persons. So the latter is the context in which Christian theological appropriation of modern culture's concept of person ought to be located.

2.0. I urge that "person," "personal," "personhood," and the like cannot be usefully used in a collective or generic way to embrace such ontologically different realities as the triune God, the "persons" of the

Trinity, angels, human beings, and, perhaps, enormously complex computers and robots. The concept "person" and related concepts that are commonly used in our contemporary, largely secular host culture in reference to human beings have very little overlap with the traditional Christian technical concept of person used in Trinitarian discourse, John Zizioulas's historical contentions to the contrary notwithstanding.[4] In *Concepts of Person and Christian Ethics*, Stanley Rudman[5] briefly touches on reasons for doubting Zizioulas's historical claims. More detailed studies of Gregory of Nyssa by Lewis Ayres, Michel Barnes, and Lucian Turescu in a special issue of *Modern Theology*[6] do the same. There is not space to summarize them here, except to stress that even if there were a genetic historical link with the fourth-century Father's borrowing-and-bending of technical Greek metaphysical categories in service of elucidating the doctrine of the Trinity, the disanalogies between the uncreated triune Persons and created human persons are so great as to render equivocal the use of the term "person."

Furthermore, the technical sense in which Father, Son, and Holy Spirit are "persons" cannot be the sense in which the triune God might be said to be "a person." And even if one could show some analogy between the sense in which the Three are "persons" and the sense in which the One as such is "a person," the ontological distinction between the uncreated triune God and creatures subverts significant overlap between the sense in which the triune God is "a person" and the sense in which human beings are "persons." I have been urging that when "person," "personal," and related terms are used in reference to human beings in theological anthropology, that use must be ruled in theocentric ways in order to be properly *theological*-anthropological. For the reasons given above, however, I follow a different strategy from those who seek to develop a theological anthropology on analogy with analysis of inner-Trinitarian relations.

3.0. *What* the triune God creates in relating creatively to humankind is human living bodies which, for reasons to be given below, may properly be characterized as "personal." God does not create "human

4. John D. Zizioulas, *Being as Communion* (Crestwood, N.Y.: St. Vladimir's Seminary Press, 1985), chap. 1.

5. Stanley Rudman, *Concepts of Person and Christian Ethics* (Cambridge: Cambridge University Press, 1997).

6. *Modern Theology* 18, no. 4 (October, 2002).

persons" but "personal bodies" (the phrase is Paul Ricoeur's), or, more exactly, "personal human living bodies." Personal living bodies is *what* God creates in creating us.

Favoring the qualifier "personal" over the nominatives "person" and "personhood" signals that when used in the context of Christian anthropology the concept of person loses its status as a "primitive concept" (Strawson). Some expression such as "human creature" assumes that conceptual status. Thus the problematic tension, noted above, between conventional descriptively metaphysical use of "person" and its classificatory use is neutralized.

To forestall misunderstandings, some comments on "human living bodies" may be added:

3.1. The phrase "human living bodies" expresses the integral psycho-somatic unity of human beings. This move is not necessarily ontologically reductive of human being to some sort of metaphysical naturalism or materialism. Since the root of the idea of "soul" is "principle of life in a living being," the word "living" points to what theories of soul speculate about, without commitment to any particular metaphysical view.

3.2. For theological anthropology, the class of living bodies that are characterized as "personal" is the class of *human* living bodies, where the criteria for inclusion in the class are genetic (human DNA).

3.3. "Living" must be construed broadly in several interrelated but distinguishable senses. Certainly it includes the systems of biological energy that constitute organic life. In human beings, however, it also includes systems of emotional, intellectual, social, and cultural energies. The "livingness" of "human living bodies" is multidimensional because the range and plasticity of capacities of such bodies are so extraordinarily broad and rich. Some of these include capacities for certain sorts of self-management. They include a range of capacities that are conventionally lumped together as *the* capacity for "consciousness." Just as human beings have capacities for different sorts of human intelligence, however, such that it is unhelpful simply to think of intelligence as a single power, so too they have capacities for different sorts or modes of consciousness, such that it is unhelpful to think of consciousness as a single phenomenon. These two ranges of human capacities are important. Use of "personal" in this conceptual context, however, bends the notion of person borrowed from our host culture in that it no longer inherently separates and privileges "consciousness" and "freedom" from other types of capacities as that which constitutes the "personal."

3.4. Somewhere in this discussion of what God creates in creating us one would traditionally have expected to find a discussion of the "image of God" (Gen. 1:26). It is missing here by design. I see no exegetical basis for linking the reference to the *imago dei* in Genesis with the concept of a person, which is the topic here. Furthermore, there seems to be an exegetical consensus that the idea of "image of God" plays very little role in the Old Testament. Interpretations of what it does mean in Genesis 1:26 vary enormously, and it is difficult to see any exegetical move, as opposed to some *a priori* hermeneutical framework for exegesis, that could decisively settle interpretive disagreements. It is dangerous to rest much theological weight on so slim a basis.

Perhaps most important for my decision not to invoke *imago dei* in this context is the fact that the notion does play an important role in New Testament accounts of Jesus. Accordingly, I prefer to reserve use of "image of God" for exploration of anthropological implications of Christian claims that in Jesus Christ the triune God relates to humankind to draw it to eschatological consummation and relates to reconcile estranged humankind, rather than to use it in the context of exploration of anthropological implications of the claim that the triune God relates to humankind creatively. Nevertheless, all the features of human creatureliness associated with the *imago dei* by the full array of theological interpretations of Genesis 1:26 can be affirmed here as features of what God creates in creating us, features of created human nature, but without suggesting that selection of those features is somehow specially warranted by Genesis 1:26.

Back to the theological concept of the personal!

4.0. The criterion that marks human living bodies as "personal" should be specified in a theocentric way, not by reference to freedom and subjectivity. "Personal" names a status before God given to human living bodies by God in creating them. Human living bodies are "personal" because the particular *way* in which the triune God relates to them creatively places them in a certain status.

God's creative relating is most aptly likened to a self-involving performative utterance by God by which God is self-committed to the flourishing of the society of creaturely beings, and is in particular self-committed to human creatures as ends in themselves and not as mere means to any further end. God's relating creates a society of creaturely beings, a society to whose well-being God is committed but of which, strictly speaking, God is not a member. It is a society consisting of mutual interdependencies characterized by networks of giving and receiving. Some members of the society of creatures are living bodies. In the case of human creatures, because of their peculiarly broad and rich array of capacities, the principal medium of the giving and receiving that characterizes the interdependencies among them is language. Human living bodies constitute a community of discourse in which God is an interlocutor. In and through that community of discourse human creatures are called by God in their practices to act wisely for the well-being of their fellows in the society of creaturely beings, and through that community of discourse they are not only able to respond to God with their whole being, but also able to give an account of how they respond to God.

In this context, the *evaluative* use of "personal" is grounded theocentrically in God's creative address to human living bodies, and is not grounded in any subset of their creaturely capacities (such as capacities for freedom and subjectivity). That is, theologically speaking, human living bodies are "personal" in the sense that they are to be treated always as ends in themselves and not as means to further ends precisely because they have been given that dignity by God's own self-involving creative address to them wherein God commits to them and to their well-being — commits to them as creaturely ends in themselves and not as means to further divine ends.

Moreover, since, by God's creative address, human living bodies are created for just this status as members of this community of discursive giving and receiving with God, the *classificatory* force of "personal" in a Christian theological context follows from its theocentrically grounded evaluative force, rather than the other way round, as in conventional uses of "personal." Human living bodies are to be classified as personal just in case they are evaluated as personal by God's creative address to them, rather then being evaluated as persons because they have been discovered to have the subset of properties that classify them as persons. This bending of conventional uses of "personal" avoids the danger of making the evaluative force depend on attributes that some human living bodies may in fact lack.

With the terminology used in these ways, subject to conceptual bending under the gravitational pull of the Christian theological claim that the triune God relates creatively to humankind, we may say that God's human creatures are not so much persons as personal in a properly theocentric use of the term "personal," a use that would also help avoid theologically problematic features of ways in which "person," "personal," "personhood," and the like are used in our host cultures.

Mark R. Talbot

Learning from the Ruined Image
Moral Anthropology
after the Fall

Millie, having married Adam, now hopes to humanize him.[1] Consequently, she embarks on an ambitious although somewhat covert project. It includes trying to get Adam to stop and think before he speaks or acts. And so, for example, when they are out for an evening with the kind of people who tend to loosen Adam up too much, Millie starts to posture herself to him in a specific way.

What is that posture and how does Millie convey it? The posture involves her stepping back from the fun, evaluating it, and then trying to moderate it appropriately. Her standards of appropriateness may range from the trivial to the momentous — from helping Adam to avoid committing minor social faux pas, through encouraging him to moderate what he eats and drinks and smokes so that he can remain a healthy human being, on to laying down the law concerning what she takes to be beyond the pale morally or religiously. In public settings, since Millie is wise, she first tries to convey her sense of these standards to Adam nonverbally. She may just touch his hand if he is laughing too loudly. She may signal her sense that he has eaten enough by simply declining, in her own case, to order dessert. Moral or religious transgressions are of a different order, so if Adam commits one, then Millie may abandon all discretion and just tell him outright to quit acting in such wicked ways.

---

1. Lest I offend someone, I should say that I don't think that such humanization between spouses goes just one way. It is merely for ease of exposition that I take Millie to be humanizing Adam rather than vice-versa.

Now exactly what is Millie trying to do by taking this posture; and what would it mean for her to succeed? What would it be like for Adam to become fully humanized? In other words, what does Millie strive and pray for each and every day?

She wants Adam to internalize her standards, to live his life in their light, and thus become properly "socialized." In other words, she wants him to become a real *person* — that is, a properly self-regulating human being.

I

Calvin opens his *Institutes* by declaring, "Nearly all the wisdom we possess, that is to say, true and sound wisdom, consists of two parts: the knowledge of God and of ourselves. But, while joined by many bonds, which one precedes and brings forth the other is not easy to discern."[2] The remainder of the first section of the first chapter of the *Institutes'* final edition is devoted to stating how our knowledge of ourselves — and especially our knowledge of that "miserable ruin, into which the rebellion of the first man cast us" — "compels us to look upward." Each of us, Calvin claims, "must be so stung by the consciousness of his own unhappiness as to attain at least some knowledge of God." And thus, he concludes,

> from the feeling of our own ignorance, vanity, poverty, infirmity, and — what is more — depravity and corruption, we recognize that the true light of wisdom, sound virtue, full abundance of every good, and purity of righteousness rest in the Lord alone.

Indeed, he claims, "we cannot seriously aspire to [God] before we begin to become displeased with ourselves." And so "the knowledge of ourselves not only arouses us to seek God, but also, as it were, leads us by the hand to find him."

Calvin adds, in the first chapter's next section, that we shall not achieve this sort of accurate knowledge of ourselves unless we first look

2. John Calvin, *Institutes of the Christian Religion,* ed. John T. McNeill, trans. Ford Lewis Battles (Philadelphia: Westminster, 1960), p. 35. Hereafter cited intratextually by book, chapter, and section (e.g., in this case, 1.1.1).

at God and then descend from contemplating his perfections to scrutinize ourselves. Realizing that we really are miserable, foolish, and corrupt requires us to look beyond earthly things to God and ponder "his nature, and how completely perfect are his righteousness, wisdom, and power" as the standard or norm or "straightedge," as Calvin puts it, "to which we must be shaped" (1.1.2).

Thus, for Calvin, the knowledge of God and the knowledge of ourselves are inextricably intertwined. Yet, in finally choosing how he will proceed, Calvin says, at the very end of his first chapter, that "the order of right teaching" requires us first to consider the knowledge of God and only then to proceed to treat the knowledge of ourselves (1.1.3).

In my final section, I will reflect a bit on this final claim. Yet for now I want us to proceed from the opposite direction, for I believe theological anthropology can avoid much confusion and wasted intellectual motion if it keeps certain platitudes about human nature in mind. Moreover, I shall, for the most part, state these platitudes in a way that deliberately avoids a lot of the language that Christian theologians have used to discuss anthropology — and especially to discuss the doctrine of the *imago dei* — because this may keep us from hackneyed thinking and thus allow us to see Christian truth afresh.

II

We can get a first glimpse of what human beings are meant to be simply by noting what all societies want done with their younger human beings.

Consider Rachel, who has just had the birthday that allows her parents now honestly to say, "She's going through the terrible twos." Rachel is the third — and last! — of Kim and John's children. She takes after her mother, which means that she is usually a very pleasant, fun child, but one with a short fuse. Very early, she discovered she had a will, and she immediately knew how to use it. Making eyes at Daddy is fun, as is getting the goat of her older brother Matthew.

Right now, while she is with her mom at the grocery, Rachel has decided to occupy herself with her mother's lipstick, which she removed from her mother's opened purse as Kim began to check out. She has smeared it all over her lips and her face. The clerk tells Kim, who is busy writing a check, that Rachel is now eating what's left of it. Kim, with the calculated indifference of practiced motherhood, decides to let her finish it so that she can continue checking out without risking the kind of petulant explosion that might mark the beginning of World War III.

Most of us know what "the terrible twos" are like and so we don't blame Kim for handling Rachel this way. In fact, watching Rachel's busy little toddler hands, noticing her mother's harried look, and remembering what those child-rearing days were like probably make our hearts go out to Kim.

Now flash forward three years and imagine the same scene but with Rachel five instead of two. If Rachel were to all appearances a normal five-year-old, then our reaction to the same behavior on her and her mother's parts would probably be quite different. Rachel would probably strike us as "spoiled" and Kim as inappropriately indulgent. Rather than our hearts going out to her, we would probably blame Kim for not having done what we think she should have done with Rachel in the intervening years.

In other words, if we were to see Rachel behaving like this at five, then our perception of her and her mother would change as our awareness of their violation of some societal norms or standards kicked in. To be inclined to consider Rachel "spoiled" is, of course, to take something to have gone wrong with her — in fact, to take others to have damaged her in specific ways. That is why a standard dictionary definition of "spoil" reads "to impair the disposition or character of [someone] by overindulgence or excessive praise."[3] In the situation we are imagining, we would most likely assume that Kim or John had indulged Rachel in ways that had impaired her normal development because we would see this lipstick-smearing-and-eating behavior as age-inappropriate. Rachel would not be what we, in our society, think a five-year-old ought to be.

So, as Augustine noted centuries ago, we overlook specific attitudes and behaviors in infants that "when grown, we root out and cast away."[4] Augustine thought that all of these attitudes and behaviors involve sin, but perhaps we can be a little less quick in at least some cases

---

3. *Webster's Seventh New Collegiate Dictionary* (Springfield, Mass.: G. & C. Merriam, 1971), *s.v.* "spoil."

4. Augustine, *Confessions,* bk. 1, chap. 7, Pusey translation. The remaining quotations from Augustine in this paragraph are from the same place. Hereafter I will cite the *Confessions* intratextually by book and chapter (e.g., "1.7").

to condemn. In spite of what Augustine suggests, tears from an inarticulate newborn may be an appropriate way to signal hunger or thirst, although in a child articulate enough to identify and state her needs verbally they are an undesirable and perhaps naughty thing. Yet Augustine is right that while we "bear gently" with much that infants do because we know that it "will disappear as years increase," attitudes and behaviors that are tolerated in infancy can become "utterly intolerable when found in riper years."

What makes them intolerable as an infant grows? It is that we consider these attitudes and behaviors to be socially disruptive or personally harmful or aesthetically displeasing (think of nose-picking) or otherwise objectionable; and we know that developmentally normal human beings can and to a large degree will, with the proper rearing, learn to avoid acting or attitudinizing in these ways. In other words, these acts and attitudes are "intolerable" at least in the sense that we — specifically, the surrounding society — won't tolerate them. If they crop up in human beings whom we deem old enough to avoid them, then our intolerance will manifest itself in some sort of bad reaction either toward the perpetrators themselves or toward those who we think have botched rearing them.

More generally, what we as a society want is for parents to rear their children in ways that will raise[5] or elevate what at first appears to be only a little more than a peculiarly helpless kind of animal to a distinctively higher level of creaturely being. What is this distinctively higher level of creaturely being? It is the level that Millie is trying to produce in Adam, the level where she could relax because she would know that he would no longer be likely to do socially intolerable things. It is the level where he would tend to stop and think before he said what he shouldn't or otherwise misbehaved. In fact, it is the level where he would actually *want* to behave in the appropriate ways, where he would perceive such behavior as a desirable thing. Then Millie would no longer have to monitor Adam by being the one who, in his stead, steps back from an evening's fun, evaluates it, and then tries to moderate it appropriately. Instead, Adam would have come to own the appropriate standards and he would freely conform his life to them.

---

5. Our English word "rear" derives from the Middle English *reren,* which is related to the Old Norse *reisa,* which means to raise.

If this were to happen, then it would be exactly right to say that Adam had finally been properly "socialized," for producing this kind of properly self-regulating being is the goal of every human society. In a particular human society, a set of human beings share a specific outlook. Of course, sharing such an outlook depends on more than merely occupying adjacent physical spaces. A particular human society is more or less united in its social orientation, which requires its members to interact in specifically *social* ways. The social dimension of human life includes but cannot be reduced to a set of people perceiving things to have specific social meanings or significance,[6] where objects and events not only *have* specific meanings or significance (like this being the fifth day in a row that it has been under 80 degrees) but where at least some of those objects and events *get* their specific meanings or significance from *being intended and taken to have* those meanings or significance (such as my intending and your taking my not greeting you as you entered the room this evening as a sign of disrespect).[7] But having a more or less united social orientation involves more than that. The members of a particular human society must not only share a common lexicon of social meanings; they must also be inclined to accept at least most of the same norms and standards.[8] If our society considers public nose-picking to be aesthetically displeasing and consequently labels it as "rude," then we see it to be part of Kim's and John's job to teach Ra-

6. In other words, having a perceived social meaning or significance is a necessary but not a sufficient condition for something counting as a human society, because some animal acts are perceived by other animals as having a particular meaning or significance. For example, a male dog perceives another male dog's rolling over on its back and exposing its soft underbelly to it as a sign of submission.

7. The issue is a bit more complex than I have just represented it to be because, for example, Adam's committing a social faux pas involves his making a kind of social misstep that others perceive but that he does not intend. Yet we cannot repair my representation by simply removing the reference to the agent's intention, because if someone has taken an act of mine to have a specific social meaning or significance and I convince him that I didn't intend it to have that meaning or significance, then (social faux pas aside) he will probably no longer take it to have that meaning or significance. (For example, if you become aware that I didn't greet you when you entered the room because something legitimately distracted me, then you will probably no longer consider my not greeting you to be a sign of disrespect.) All of this emphasizes that social meaning or significance is a kind of *shared* meaning or significance.

8. My "more or less" and "at least most of" qualifiers in this paragraph are meant to acknowledge that, for example, contemporary American society is rather pluralistic.

chel, when she reaches the developmental stage where this teaching can "take,"[9] not to do it. In other words, a society's having a more or less united social orientation involves most of its members subscribing to roughly the same set of moral and nonmoral values, interpreted and expressed in approximately the same ways.

I have descended to an unpleasant example of one of the kinds of behavior that a society may label "intolerable" because our very reaction to the mention of it corroborates how pervasive societal pressure is for us to shape ourselves into our society's image of what a proper human life should be. Many of us cannot even conceive of circumstances where we would be willing to pick our nose in public, no matter how much we might recognize our nostrils to be in need of it. Indeed, to the degree that you are feeling right now that I shouldn't be using this example, you show yourself to have been socialized to avoid even the mention of such unpleasantness.

Yet if nothing other than social inconceivability stops us from doing or mentioning such things, then here we have a paradigm case of personal self-regulation, of someone's voluntarily doing or avoiding some act (or feeding or starving some attitude) because he or she accepts the norm or standard requiring or encouraging or discouraging or prohibiting it. We come to accept such norms and standards because our society, through proxies such as spouses, parents, and peers, conveys them to us.[10] In this way, if Rachel grows up to become someone who regulates herself according to our society's norms and standards, then this will signal the success of a specific kind of project, enjoined by our society and pursued primarily by her parents. And if what it means to be a human person is to be this sort of self-regulating being, then if Adam were to become a proper person, that would be an achievement — Millie's astounding achievement![11] As I explore in my next section, human

9. If you have been to children's Christmas pageants, then you probably know that this seems to be around age six. In this sort of case, peer reaction probably also figures in. Children may stop picking their noses at around age six as much because their schoolmates react negatively to it as because their parents tell them not to do it.

10. Christians will probably maintain that there is more to it than this, for some Scriptures seem to imply that God himself directly urges such norms and standards on human beings.

11. I hasten to add that if we adopt this technical conception of human personhood and thus recognize that becoming a person really is an achievement, then we must make

beings, as we arrive in this world, are probably less what we can and indeed must become than any other creaturely being.[12] Yet what all societies want done with their young makes clear what kind of creatures we should be. In this sense, we can say that human societies view their members as "meant" to function in particular self-regulating ways.

Of course, the particular norm I have just highlighted is neither here nor there to this more general point. Who knows if public nose-picking is considered intolerable everywhere? And even if it *is*, that would not establish that it *ought* to be. We can acknowledge the relativity of large numbers of societal standards without relinquishing the claim I am now making. My point is simply this: human beings flourish only in societies, and a set of people constitutes a specific human society only if it succeeds to some degree in encouraging its members to regulate themselves in particular ways. Such self-regulation is, then, clearly part of what human beings need to achieve. Consequently, self-regulation according to some set of norms or standards is the general *telos* that societies invariably aim at with human beings. And so it is not inappropriate to say that if Millie were to succeed in getting Adam to act and attitudinize more appropriately, then she would have succeeded, in a real sense, in humanizing him — in making him more like what creatures of our genetic makeup are meant to be.

III

Here is another way to put the main point made so far: proper child-rearing involves taking the wantonness out of little human beings. A

---

merely being human — (roughly) in the sense of being made of human genetic stuff — the basis for respect and human rights, because otherwise having not (yet) achieved or not maintaining personhood could be taken to justify, for example, abortion, infanticide, and euthanasia. (As, indeed, Princeton University philosopher Peter Singer claims. See both the first and the second editions of his *Practical Ethics* [Cambridge: Cambridge University Press, 1979 and 1993], where he makes slightly different claims about babies, personhood, and the right of neonates to life.) Yet, as I shall attempt to show in my final section, adopting this technical conception of human personhood is crucial to correctly understanding ourselves and our place before God.

12. "Must become" in the sense that we will not even survive if we don't develop in specific ways.

wanton is an impulsive, unruly, and unreflective creature, a creature dominated by whichever of its impulses is strongest.[13] Becoming a person consists in becoming such that you are no longer prone simply to give way to your impulses, for you now reflect on them and at least try to rule them accordingly. When we become persons, in this sense of becoming reflectively self-regulating beings, then and only then do we begin to live as human beings should — that is, in a way that corresponds to our using all of our natural human capacities. Bishop Butler still said this best. In the second of his now unjustly neglected three sermons on human nature, he acknowledges that a human being may act wantonly — that is, he may "act according to that . . . inclination which for the present happens to be strongest [in him], and yet," as he says, "act in a way disproportionate to, and [in violation of] his real proper nature." To illustrate this, he frames out the following case:

> Suppose a brute creature by any bait to be allured into a snare, by which he is destroyed. He plainly followed the bent of his nature, leading him to gratify his appetite: there is an entire correspondence between his whole nature and such an action: such action therefore is natural [to him]. But suppose a man, foreseeing the same danger of certain ruin, should rush into it for the sake of a present gratification: he in this instance would follow his strongest desire, as did the brute creature: but there would be as manifest a disproportion, between the nature of a man and such an action, as between the meanest work of art and the skill of the greatest master in that art: which disproportion arises, not from considering the action singly in *itself* or in its *consequences;* but from *comparison* of it with the nature of the agent.[14]

13. I take the claim that becoming a person involves overcoming wantonness from Harry Frankfurt's seminal piece, "Freedom of the Will and the Concept of a Person" (in Harry G. Frankfurt, *The Importance of What We Care About: Philosophical Essays* [Cambridge: Cambridge University Press, 1988]), although his characterization of a wanton is a bit different than mine. C. S. Lewis makes very similar points in the first book of *Mere Christianity* (San Francisco: HarperCollins, 2001; first published in 1952), bk. 1, "Right and Wrong as a Clue to the Meaning of the Universe," especially chap. 2.

14. Joseph Butler, *Fifteen Sermons Preached at the Rolls Chapel,* with introduction, analyses, and notes by the Very Rev. W. R. Matthews (London: G. Bell & Sons, 1958), pp. 54, 55 (sermon II, paragraph 10). The emphasis upon "unnatural" in the next sentence is mine.

"And since," Butler concludes, "such an action is utterly disproportionate to the nature of man," as a creature who can assess the relation between the bait and the snare and thus foresee that taking the bait will result in his death, "it is in the strictest and most proper sense *unnatural*" for a human being to take the bait, because taking the bait under these circumstances does not correspond with our using all of our natural capacities. This is what saying that this kind of action is "disproportionate" to this kind of nature means. Wantonness, whether in five-year-old Rachel or in grown-ups like Adam, is unnatural or disproportionate to what human beings can and should be.

Put more generally, wantonness is unnatural to human beings because we, unlike Butler's "brute creature," possess the capacity for a kind of stratification of our consciousness, where we can step back or away from whatever we are thinking or desiring or feeling right now (such as strongly desiring to reach for the cake that makes up the snare's bait) to ask ourselves if we ought to be thinking or desiring or feeling this way. In this situation, is it prudent — or moral, or Christian — for me to be thinking or desiring or feeling like this? To pose this sort of question is, in effect, to stratify my consciousness, because I am then *elevating* some rule or norm to be a proper arbiter over my thoughts and desires and feelings.[15] Complete wantonness is unnatural to any but the youngest of human beings because normal human be-

15. It seems there can be several levels. For example, I may at first judge my wild desire to surprise Cindy with a trip to Paris at Christmas just prudentially (If I arrange that sort of expensive trip, then am I going to end up in Cindy's doghouse?) and then morally (Given the need to contribute to African relief funds that save starving children, am I morally obliged not to spend my money on such an unnecessary trip?) and finally as a Christian (Is it appropriate for Christians to indulge themselves like that?). Both Butler and Frankfurt assume there is a hierarchy of levels of reflective evaluation. For Butler, the levels are as I have suggested: there is the prudential level of reasonable self-love, which is trumped by the level of moral conscience; and conscience seems for him to be in some sense subordinate to Christian commitment. Frankfurt simply acknowledges that just as we can have second-order desires and volitions, so we can have third-level desires and volitions, and so forth.

But while this picture of a hierarchy of "levels" of reflective evaluation is initially illuminating and consequently seems plausible (think of Lawrence Kohlberg's stages of moral reasoning), it isn't clear that it is ultimately accurate to the way that we bring the various kinds of rules or norms or standards we possess to bear on our raw thoughts and desires and feelings. See, for example, Susan Wolf's criticism of Frankfurt's hierarchical theory in her *Freedom within Reason* (New York: Oxford University Press, 1990).

ings who have gotten through the "twos" — which are terrible precisely for their wantonness — are now developmentally capable of asking some of these questions and thereby eschewing impulsiveness and unruliness by becoming properly reflective about whatever is passing through their heads.[16] So when a child — or even an adult — is overcome by some attitude (think of the bromide "If Momma ain't happy, then nobody's happy!") or given always to acting self-indulgently (think of impulsively ordering whatever book sounds interesting), we sometimes hear exasperated onlookers say, "Grow up!" or "Don't be such a baby!" Infantile behavior befits only infants.

As "Grow up!" suggests, we try to work the wantonness out of human beings by *addressing* them. Millie's touching Adam's hand shows that we can address each other nonverbally; with children, as with adults, a lot can be conveyed by just giving a properly prepared potential offender nothing but a particular look. But usually a look doesn't convey much if it isn't framed by words. Millie's touching Adam's hand if he is laughing too raucously will have a more certain effect if she has previously spoken to him in private about the need to watch his laugh.

In that previous conversation, Millie will have enunciated a norm to Adam, probably in the context of a larger story about how his laughing too loudly can offend others and make him appear socially inadept. Her nonverbal prompts (just like someone else's "Grow up!") then serve to remind him to think twice and gauge how he is acting in terms of the norm she previously expressed.

Thus language is central to the humanizing process. In fact, our linguistic capacities are probably the most crucial factor in our distinctively human kind of being. The *differentia* between humans and the higher animals at least includes our ability to communicate in relatively sophisticated ways, and this is probably key to the growth of our other distinctions.

So Augustine was probably right to draw the line between infancy

16. Developmentally, young children seem first to gain a capacity for being prudent; for example, a mother's tone of voice as she says, "Rebekah, that's Caleb's!" can prompt a child to reconsider some course of action because it is clear that to act like that would mean catching heck. But Scripture may, again, suggest that more is going on here than purely human interaction. For a theological interpretation of the way that God figures into even the earliest childhood experience, see John Baillie, *Invitation to Pilgrimage* (New York: Charles Scribner's Sons, 1942), chap. 6.

and childhood at the acquisition of speech.[17] Indeed, language is crucial to our development in far more pervasive ways than any we have noticed yet. This follows from the peculiar helplessness and cluelessness that accompany human infancy. As I have argued, every human society assumes that human infants are a very far cry from what mature humans are meant to be; in fact, the distance the little human critter must travel to become a normally functioning adult is probably much further than the distance that confronts any other creaturely being. At the start, we can't do all sorts of things. And yet these initial incapacities are seedbeds for the specific abilities that flower later on.

For instance, infant immobility probably spawns a baby's first attempts at communication. By about nine or ten months, a baby's relative immobility prompts it to engage in a kind of pre-linguistic communication. It will use gaze alternation[18] or pointing to show that it wants something brought to it. Its initial immobility "forces the young infant into finding other, *interactional* means of reaching certain goals." Gazing strategies or pointing gestures "therefore start out as instrumental requests."[19]

As Augustine represents language acquisition in the *Confessions,* this sort of "proto-imperative" behavior is emblematic of all human communication. For Augustine, an infant's only motive for learning to communicate is that it wants to express its will so that it can get others to do its bidding (see 1.6, 8). Gazing and pointing are pretty crude ways to accomplish this; words are much better for making our wills clear; and so infants are sinfully motivated to acquire them. Learning to talk just launches human beings "deeper into the stormy intercourse of human life" (1.8).

Some of Augustine's observations about his parents and teachers bear out how sinful talk can be (see especially 1.9-18); but, once again, as with his remarks about infant tears, he is too quick to condemn. An in-

---

17. See *Confessions* 1.8: "I was no longer a speechless infant, but a speaking boy."

18. Gaze alternation refers to looking at someone's eyes, then at some desired object, then back and forth again.

19. Annette Karmiloff-Smith and James Russell in *A Companion to the Philosophy of Mind,* ed. Samuel Guttenplan (Oxford: Basil Blackwell, 1994, 1995), *s.v.* "developmental psychology." The unidentified quotations in the next three paragraphs and the next footnote are from the same place.

fant's coos are not mere practice for its making verbal demands. And, as developmental psychologists note, an infant's proto-imperatives "rapidly become proto-declaratives" — that is, "a point becomes the infant's means of making a non-verbal comment about the state of the world (the equivalent of, say, 'look, that's a nice dog')." Of course, proto-declarative behavior involves a desire to share and not merely to boss; and so the human infant's drive toward language seems to be not nearly as self-centered as Augustine suggests.

Interestingly, autistic children don't progress to the proto-declaratives, which seems linked with their failure to engage much in other forms of what is called "social referencing," such as when an infant or a child "gauges how she should respond to a novel event (is this danger or is it OK?) from [watching her] mother's [face]."

Such social referencing is vital to proper human development; it is among the earliest ways in which an infant's society (by means of its parents) starts to transmit to it its social outlook. This takes direct human-to-human contact because (to resort to some computer terminology) a human being, compared to (say) a cat, has relatively little "hardwiring" that is dedicated to producing particular results.[20] So it is only by learning lots from more mature human beings that we start to get a fix on things. The "architecture" of distinctively human being is, in other words, much more dependent on the deliberate installation of some specific "software" — some particular social outlook on things — than it seems to be with other living beings. In fact, there is a sense in which it is not too strong to say that, for human beings, the "software" is *everything*. For example, a human baby will simply perish if those surrounding her have not learned what kinds of and how much care she needs.

Perhaps the best way to sum up this point is to observe that, with human beings, our "psychologies" are not nailed down to our "physiologies." We are capable of being — and, indeed, we *must* be, if we

---

20. In developmental psychology, such dedicated "hard-wiring" is often referred to in terms of "input systems" or "'domain-specific' modules" that "operate swiftly, mandatorily and independently from [each other]" as well as being "relatively unaffected by higher-level, knowledge-based [or 'central'] systems and by current states of consciousness." In other words, dedicated "hard-wiring" carries out very specific tasks. In that sense, to talk about such "hard-wiring" is pretty much equivalent to talking about what is determined by instinct.

are to flourish or even to survive — much more than just the sum of our physiological drives. We can be — and as we mature, we inevitably are — occupied with much more than our immediate physical wants and needs. In this sense, thanks to our lack of dedicated hardwiring — thanks, in other words, to our initial cluelessness — we are unavoidably "spiritual" creatures in the sense that we need what our culture has come to call "a spirituality" — that is, a whole way of looking at and evaluating things — if we are to function in anything like a distinctively human way.[21]

Any adequate global "operating system" or "spirituality" must be content-rich in a way that only the subtleties of natural human languages can convey. Of course, such languages convey a lot more than bare information; not only do they inform us about what there is and how to evaluate it, but when mature persons use them they address and affect us in numberless ways. Neonates, we now know, are innately social — they are, in other words, "hardwired" to pay attention to, imitate, and make emotional sense of the gross features of the primate face.[22] But probably even more crucially, they are "hardwired" to attend to the human voice. At birth they can already distinguish human speech from other sounds, and at four days a baby begins to attend preferentially to its parents' native tongue. No wonder, then, that it is by other persons using words to address us that we come to grasp our own significance; words — and not visible objects — supply us with the horizons between which we actually live. Stop and think, just for a moment, how often you have hungered for some word from some human being. In that and other senses, you and I really are "verbivores" — word-eaters. If we don't get enough words, then we not only fail to achieve a distinctively human orientation on life, but we also lose our very taste for living.

---

21. I develop and defend the claims made in this and the next paragraph in my "Starting from Scripture," in *Limning the Psyche: Explorations in Christian Psychology,* ed. Robert C. Roberts and Mark R. Talbot (Grand Rapids: Eerdmans, 1997), and in "Growing in the Grace and Knowledge of Our Lord and Savior Jesus Christ," in *For All the Saints: Evangelical Theology and Christian Spirituality,* ed. Timothy George and Alister McGrath (Louisville: Westminster John Knox, 2003).

22. See the Karmiloff-Smith and Russell article again. I am paraphrasing some of their claims in this and the next two sentences.

IV

If you were to walk into Kim's kitchen and find her rubbing Rachel's nose in a puddle of her own piddle and then applying a newspaper to Rachel's rear-end while saying in a stern voice, "Bad girl!" or if you were to hear her trying to engage Annie, their black Labrador retriever, in a conversation, then you would be reacting charitably if all you con-cluded was that Kim had gone off the deep end. Even for humans who have only poked through what we Christians know to be merely this world's ruins of human nature, there are clear hints of what sets hu-man beings apart from other creatures, hints that suggest what human beings perhaps once were and are clearly still meant to be.[23] It is also pretty clear how they need to be formed as well as how they are and are not to be treated and addressed. In other words, by examining what ev-ery society tries to do with its human beings and how it tries to do it — and then recognizing that it inevitably fails to pull off that task — we can and should begin to see through the ruined image to what the true image should be.

Of course, this does not mean that I intend the kind of platitudes that I have emphasized here to function as a kind of indispensable em-pirical warrant for Christian anthropology. Like Calvin, I think that while our knowledge of God and ourselves is inextricably intertwined, the correct order of Christian teaching requires us first to consider the knowledge of God, as revealed in the Scriptures, and then to proceed from that to the knowledge of ourselves. The Protestant post-Reformation scholastics, as Richard Muller shows, cut a number of close but helpful distinctions here, including distinguishing between

---

23. For instance, in attempting to explain "why human beings have to live by rules which can frustrate their desires," Mary Midgley observes that people "tend to look backwards, asking whether there was once an 'unfallen' conflict-free state before the rules were imposed, a state where rules were not needed, perhaps because nobody ever wanted to do anything bad" ("The Origin of Ethics," in *A Companion to Ethics,* ed. Peter Singer [Oxford: Basil Blackwell, 1991, 1993]). She thinks this backward glance is natural for human beings who are seriously asking why they should be moral now and who real-ize that we need some supreme principle for adjudicating between clashing duties. She thinks we tend to answer these questions in terms of some sort of "origin-myth," which describes "not only how human life began, but also why it is so hard, so painful, so con-fusing, so conflict-ridden." One kind of myth postulates a state of original innocence and then asks both how we lost that innocence and how we might get back to it.

two kinds of natural theology, the one proceeding independently of Scripture and that is consequently "pagan and false" *(theologia naturalis irregenitorum),* and the other "redeemed and belonging to the category of *theologia vera"* because it is read out from the supernatural or revealed theology found in our Scriptures *(theologia naturalis regenitorum).*[24] Although *theologia naturalis irregenitorum* proceeds independently of Scripture, Scripture represents it as producing a kind of rough and confused awareness of God and our duties (see, for example, Acts 14:8-18; 17:16-33; Rom. 1:18–2:16). As such, it may discover some theological truths and thus be one more way in which sinners are rendered "without excuse" (see Rom. 1:20). But its freedom from Scripture inevitably results in a mix of truth and falsity that makes its deliverances unreliable. *Theologia naturalis regenitorum,* however, by starting from Scripture, can identify what is true in unregenerate thinking as well as what even the unregenerate should know (see, for example, Rom. 2:1-16) and then deploy those truths in articulating and defending Christian belief.

From the standpoint of the latter sort of project, it is not difficult to show that Scripture endorses virtually all of the platitudes I have stressed. For instance, it accentuates our verbivorousness (see, for example, Amos 8:11, 12; Matt. 4:4; 1 Thess. 4:18; 1 Tim. 4:6; 6:3; 2 Tim. 1:13) and the various differences I have specified between human beings and beasts (see Ps. 73:22; 32:8, 9; 2 Peter 2:12). Its declaration that we are "fearfully and wonderfully made" (see Ps. 139:12-15) may even hint of some of the fascinating complexity that we are only now discovering about how our special capacities get booted up from the hardwired modularity of some of our earliest and most instinctive responses.

Scripture also draws attention to the way in which some human claims and judgments are self-implicating,[25] suggesting a strategy that

---

24. Richard A. Muller, *Post-Reformation Reformed Dogmatics,* vol. 1: *Prolegomena to Theology* (Grand Rapids: Baker Academic, 2003 [second ed.]), p. 296. The whole chapter, entitled "Natural and Supernatural Theology," is immensely helpful in formulating a genuinely Protestant view of natural theology and natural revelation. The claims I make following this sentence in the text represent my own use of this Protestant scholastic distinction between two kinds of natural theology.

25. For instance, at Romans 2:1-5 Paul argues that whenever we judge others we condemn ourselves because we invariably practice the very things that we condemn. Alvin Plantinga seems to have pioneered this strategy in contemporary analytical philosophy

Christian academics should pursue in order to give the claims of an explicitly scriptural and theological Christian anthropology some scholarly space. For instance, Christians and non-Christians alike can see that, because of human infancy's peculiar helplessness and cluelessness, a human being's survival depends on his or her being formed to some image. Each human being must be reared in some particular way. Even Richard Rorty acknowledges this when he says that each of us needs some "final vocabulary," some set of core convictions to which we can adhere unflinchingly. A "final vocabulary," he tells us, consists in some "set of words which [we] employ to justify [our] actions, [our] beliefs, and [our] lives"; these are the words "in which we formulate praise of our friends and contempt for our enemies, our long-term projects, our deepest self-doubts, our highest hopes"; these are the words "in which we tell, sometimes prospectively and sometimes retrospectively, the story of our lives."[26] The fact that Christians, then, are committed to a particular "word" on life does not distinguish them from anyone else; the need to be committed to some such word is a feature of distinctively human being that we share with everyone.[27]

It is equally incontestable that human beings must become *persons* if we are to survive and thrive. Because so little of human nature is hardwired we enjoy degrees of cognitive and volitional freedom that are almost surely unparalleled by any other earthly beings. But this freedom rings as a death-knell if we do not internalize some particular (and more or less consistent) set of norms and rules and standards that then shape and discipline us. We must encourage each other to become and remain genuinely self-regulating beings. This happens primarily through our addressing each other in terms of our "final vocabulary," which includes conveying to each other our image of what a human person is meant to be.

Finally, it is obvious that human persons never succeed in regulat-

---

with his claim that some philosophical positions are "self-referentially incoherent." See, for example, his *Warranted Christian Belief* (New York: Oxford University Press, 2000), pp. 94-97 and especially pp. 442-47 on the "abstemious pluralist" who charges that there is something arbitrary about accepting Christian belief.

26. Richard Rorty, *Contingency, Irony, and Solidarity* (Cambridge: Cambridge University Press, 1989), p. 73.

27. I say a lot more about everybody's need for such a "word" in my "Starting from Scripture."

ing themselves as they should. We often don't know what we ought to do. But even when we do, we often lack the motivation to do as we know we should. This, as Mary Midgley observes, prompts human beings to try to find some account of the origin of life's rules that explains why we have to follow them and why following them can be so frustrating.[28]

Christians believe that God has revealed the correct "final vocabulary" in his holy Scriptures. Those Scriptures speak of humanity as the *imago dei*. And so, as Calvin said, we will not achieve an accurate knowledge of ourselves, of what has gone wrong with us, and of what we are meant to be, unless we lift our eyes from ourselves to ponder God's "nature, and how completely perfect are his righteousness, wisdom, and power — the straightedge to which we must be shaped." We also know that, even when we have begun to shape our lives according to this straightedge, we never "internalize" God's word and its norms and standards as well and as accurately as we should; and we know that, even if we were to internalize it perfectly, we would never, in this life, regulate our lives by it as perfectly as we should. Here the great gospel truths recovered at the Reformation resound for our comfort and encouragement. In Christ Jesus, we have been justified, and we are being sanctified, because we have been "created in [him] for good works" (Eph. 2:10). Yet until glory we shall never become the perfectly self-regulating persons that we should.

Perfect creaturely personhood would involve unfailing, glad, and prompt obedience to the God who has created us. On this side of glory, it would involve believing and obeying every jot and tittle of God's Word. For it is through his Word that God now addresses us. And, as Montaigne declared, "It is the proper office of a rational creature to obey."[29] In this way, Adam's harkening to Millie's counsel and Kim's and John's attempts to socialize Rachel just faintly echo (and indeed sometimes disfigure) the commands that the almighty, sovereign Lord of All is continually revealing to all human beings.[30]

28. See note 23.

29. This is my paraphrase of his comment that "to obey is the principal function of a reasonable soul," as Donald M. Frame has translated him in his *Essays,* bk. 2, "Apology for Raymond Sebond" (New York: Alfred A. Knopf, 2003), pp. 436f.

30. To my mind, one of the very best accounts of how God is constantly requiring our obedience is found in John Baillie's *Invitation to Pilgrimage,* chapter 6. In analyzing

So, by looking closely at the ruined image, we should, by God's grace, begin to be displeased with ourselves and the way that we never become the persons that we, in some vague and confused way, know we are meant to be. Even in human beings so faint, so spiritless, so dull, and so dead, God's image and his glory are not completely effaced.

---

his tendency to rebel against his parents' authority, even though he often knew that what they asked was right and that they as well as he were called upon to obey a "Greater Will" that he knew was God's, he speaks of his rebellion as "naughtiness," which etymologically means not to be a true wight — that is, not to be a true man.

Michael S. Horton | **Image and Office**
Human Personhood
and the Covenant

As is well known, modernity after Descartes was dominated by a notion of the self that was constrained by substance metaphysics. And yet, a line is often (and not entirely without warrant) drawn from Augustine to Descartes in this respect. Among others, Charles Taylor provides a reliable summary of this complex relationship.[1] If I were to attempt such an ambitious argument here, it would go something like this: Somewhat overdetermined by questions more germane to neoplatonic speculation, traditional Christian anthropologies have too often sought to ground human selfhood on the *imago dei,* the latter understood in quite essentialist terms. So whether one was an intellectualist or a voluntarist, the self was usually understood as the soul or mind. Returning more directly to classical rather than biblical categories, modernity radicalized and secularized this essentialist enterprise, especially with the addition of a sharp emphasis on autonomy. Personhood thus became reduced to knowing, duty, feeling, striving, overcoming, authenticity, and so on.

1. Charles Taylor, *Sources of the Self: The Making of the Modern Identity* (Cambridge, Mass.: Harvard University Press, 1989). This trajectory undoubtedly provided a basis for grounding selfhood in an inward quest, although for Augustine this was meant to lead through the noumenal self to God, while for Descartes it was meant to underwrite what has come to be known as modern autonomy (albeit, in his case, with an apologetic for God's existence added on). See also Phillip Cary, *Augustine's Invention of the Inner Self: The Legacy of a Christian Platonist* (New York: Oxford University Press, 2000).

This essay was adapted from the author's *Lord and Servant: A Covenant Christology* (Louisville: Westminster John Knox, 2005), chapter 4.

In all of its modern forms, it includes the crucial element of *disengagement,* to borrow Taylor's term, despite attempts to resituate the self in "lived experience," through language, culture, and history. What we often fail to see is a corresponding biblical-theological effort to resituate selfhood in the "lived experience" of the covenant and eschatology.[2] Wilhelm Dilthey correctly discerned that in the empiricism and idealism of the Enlightenment period, "No real blood runs in the veins of the knowing subject that Locke, Hume and Kant constructed."[3] Regardless of the classical and modern roots of this approach to our question, it is hoped that this proposal will provide an alternative paradigm for anthropology over against the more neoplatonic rivals and their secularized successors, without running into the arms of a reactionary reductionism (namely, seflhood reduced to relations or language). Post-structuralist anthropologies, for very different reasons, bear some ironic similarities with a number of recent theological proposals. Space does not permit us here to raise the question as to just how far John Zizioulas and, in his own way, Karl Barth approximate Michel Foucault's prediction that "man" is about to be "erased like a face drawn in the sand at the edge of the sea."[4]

I will approach our topic in terms of two concentric circles: humanness more generally and the *imago* specifically. In this way, I hope to steer a course between the more traditional essentialist approaches and the denial of a genuine human subject. I will aim at identifying the character of the *imago dei* in its context of covenant and eschatology

---

2. While we realize that the so-called "hermeneutical turn" belongs to the same line of history as modernity, identified as "this present evil age," God's common grace may be discerned in the availability of certain conceptual schemes that emphasize the emergence of meaning in concrete contexts. Notions such as "language games" (Wittgenstein), *Wirkungsgeschicte* and horizons of expectation (Gadamer), "paradigms" (Kuhn), "plausibility structures" (Berger), and "conventions" (Searle) provide tools for articulating a renewed covenant theology.

3. Cited by Anthony Thiselton, *Interpreting God and the Postmodern Self: On Meaning, Manipulation and Promise* (Edinburgh: T&T Clark, 1995), p. 47.

4. Michel Foucault, *The Order of Things: An Archaeology of the Human Sciences* (New York: Random House, 1970), p. 387. Let's not forget that modernity was never wholly individualistic. Remember Spinoza? Hegel? Fichte? Marx? Freud? Not to mention the philosophy of history from Dilthey to the present. Furthermore, postmodernity celebrates atomistic individualism as often as communitarianism. In both modernity and postmodernity are many mansions.

and then suggest some ways in which this perspective might interact fruitfully with some recent approaches to the problematic status of the "postmodern self." Covenant and eschatology do not exhaust the meaning of the human but do significantly contextualize and orient it.

Covenant

The mature federal theology typically advanced three covenants: an eternal, intratrinitarian covenant of redemption, with the Son as mediator, and two covenants made between God and human beings, executed in time. The covenant of works (also designated covenant of "creation," "nature," or "law") was the natural state in which Adam and Eve were created and under which humanity "in Adam" stands condemned under the original covenant curses.

The *protoeuangelion,* however, announces a gracious covenant. Without setting aside the original covenant, God promulgates a covenant of grace in anticipation of the second Adam whom he will send. As the tree of life was the sacrament of the covenant of works, Adam and Eve are clothed sacramentally in animal skins by God to prefigure "the Lamb of God who takes away the sin of the world" (John 1:29). Through Abraham, God gives greater clarity to this gracious covenant by swearing unconditional loyalty to Abraham for the sake of his seed, identified by the apostle Paul as Jesus Christ (Gal. 3:16), and ordains circumcision as the sign and seal of the old covenant administration, with baptism as the new covenant sacrament of incorporation (Matt. 28:18-20; Mark 16:15-16; Col. 2:11-12).[5]

Thus, even after the fall, human existence remains intrinsically covenantal, even though it is divided between Cain's proud city (Gen. 4:17-24) and the City of God represented by Seth, whose descendants are distinguished by their invocation of the Great King for their salvation: "At that time people began to invoke the name of the LORD" (v. 26). Those who do not acknowledge God or embrace his covenant of grace are nevertheless included "in Adam" under the *original* covenant. Intrinsic to humanness, particularly the *imago,* is a covenantal office or

---

5. Of course, Passover and the Lord's Supper are added to the old and new covenant administrations, respectively, but here we are indicating the sacrament of incorporation.

commission into which every person is born; it is, therefore, as an equally universal phenomenon, the basis for God's righteous judgment of humankind even apart from special revelation (Rom. 1 and 2). This is to say that "law" — in particular, the divine covenant-law — is natural, a *verbum internum* identified with the conscience. Hardwired for obedience, human beings fell from this state of rectitude through no ontological weakness (such as finitude or concupiscence) but through an inexplicable rejection of the reign of God. The gospel, by contrast, is entirely foreign to the human person in this natural state. It comes as a free decision on God's part in view of the fall and can be known only by a *verbum externum.*

We will therefore look for an answer to the question, "What is it to be human?" not in ontological definitions of inner states or essences, much less in terms of contrasts with the nonhuman creation, but in terms of the unique *commission* given to human beings in the biblical narrative. For the biblical writers at least, "What is it to be human?" is ultimately a narrative-ethical rather than a metaphysical-ontological question. It cannot be named apart from the drama of creation, fall, redemption, and consummation. As covenant theology argues, then, the satisfactory answer to that question of human identity is to point to Jesus Christ — not because anthropology is subsumed under christology (*pace* Barth, Jüngel, and others), but because it was he alone who fulfilled the covenant of works and did so not merely for himself but representatively (that is, federally) for his new humanity: "For their sakes I sanctify myself, that they may be truly sanctified" (John 17:19).[6]

Eschatology

The notions of covenant and eschatology are closely intertwined in biblical theology. Both are oriented toward promise and fulfillment. Furthermore, both eschew any ontological dualism. As the covenant idea in Scripture excludes a nature-grace antithesis by emphasizing the ethical dimension (sin-and-grace), biblical eschatology similarly concentrates its antithesis between "flesh" and "Spirit" in terms of "this pres-

---

6. It is typical to read in the federal theologians such expressions as, "And he did this not just for himself but as a public person," that is, as a representative figure.

ent aeon" and "the aeon to come," respectively. It is this world *in its ethical rebellion* that is under divine judgment, and it is this same world — "far as the curse is found" — that will be finally liberated when the work of the second Adam has resulted in the Spirit's consummation of all things in him. Thus, both body and soul are included in this image-bearing task and only in a psychosomatic unity enjoy the consummation in Jesus Christ.

According to this eschatological perspective I am proposing, which builds on the older Reformed theologians, creation was not the goal, but the beginning, of God's purpose for humankind specifically and the natural world generally. As Geerhardus Vos reminds us, the particular covenantal and eschatological orientation found in Scripture is thoroughly concerned with the ethical and personal sphere, not with abstract metaphysics and ontology. "The universe, as created, was only a beginning, the meaning of which was not perpetuation, but attainment." Thus, eschatology is prior to soteriology: creation began with a greater destiny lying before it.[7] (Affinities with Irenaeus, particularly with the doctrine of recapitulation, may be recognized here as elsewhere.)

This has obvious implications for the concept of human immortality. While death should not, without qualification, be regarded as "a characteristic of frail, temporal creation,"[8] Jürgen Moltmann is nevertheless right to point out, on the basis of God's command to be fruitful and multiply, "that human beings were mortal from the beginning."[9] Miroslav Volf correctly sees in Moltmann's construction a classic debate between Eastern and Western approaches, the former indwelling categories of corruption and completion, while the latter inhabits the paradigm of sin and redemption.[10] By recognizing that creation even before the fall was awaiting its completion under Adamic dominion, however, and that this consummation included the confer-

---

7. Geerhardus Vos, *The Eschatology of the Old Testament,* ed. James T. Dennison Jr. (Phillipsburg, N.J.: P&R Publishing, 2001), pp. 73-74, where Vos goes on to write that " Eschatology aims at consummation rather than restoration. . . . It does not aim at the original state, but at a transcendental state of man."

8. Jürgen Moltmann, *The Coming of God: Christian Eschatology,* trans. Margaret Kohl (Minneapolis: Fortress, 1996), p. 78.

9. Moltmann, *Coming of God,* p. 91.

10. Miroslav Volf, "After Moltmann: Reflections on the Future of Eschatology," in *God Will Be All in All,* ed. Richard Bauckham (Edinburgh: T&T Clark, 1999), pp. 249-50.

ral of immortality as well as indefectibility, covenant theology is able to integrate both of these strands — the eschatological and the soteriological, immorality and redemption. Thus conceived, death did not come as a consequence of mere human finitude (*pace* Barth, Moltmann, and others), nor was immortality a human possession from the beginning (especially not in virtue of an immortal soul). Immortality was a goal, not an origin; the Tree of Life was a prospect, not a presupposition, of human existence. Prior to the fall, Adam and Eve lived between the two trees: "You shall be confirmed in righteousness and immortality" and "You shall surely die."

As human beings are by nature covenantal, they are also constitutionally prospective — even utopian, despite the distorted ways in which fallen humanity seeks to win its glorification apart from and even against God. The fact that Adam and Eve were representatively created in God's image and yet were to attain the perfection and consummation of that image in the future gives to human personhood both a retrospective and an anticipatory eschatological identity. This fact becomes crucial to the account of personhood that I will elaborate below in terms of *dramatic narrative emplotment.*

Person and Image

As we gesture our way through a covenantal-eschatological approach to the vexing question of human personhood by specifying within that larger question the character of the *imago dei,* we might begin by distinguishing between what we may call prerequisites for image-bearing and the *imago* proper. The prerequisites are the broader concentric circle encompassing the narrower circle of the image proper.

Prerequisite Characteristics for Human Image-Bearing

The Platonic rooting of the *imago* in reason has had disastrous effects, as recent criticisms have highlighted.[11] Furthermore, there is not a hint

11. The mind-body dualism leads us "into the problems of individualism and ecology," as Colin E. Gunton warns in *The One, the Three and the Many: God, Creation and the*

in Scripture of the oft-repeated theological axiom that human likeness to God has to do with a shared "spirituality," since the concept of *ex nihilo* creation blocks any emanationist scheme with its chain of being. The human soul is no more to be identified with God than the human body.

While my proposal rejects any identification of the image of God with any faculty or substance, mental or physical, can there be any doubt that human beings are uniquely suited among the creation to be covenant partners with God? And can we not point out fairly obvious prerequisites such as certain natural capacities for deliberative reason, intentional relationality, moral agency, and linguisticality? Without identifying the image of God with any or all of these distinguishing traits, we can nevertheless affirm that they are endowments that render humankind uniquely suited to the commission that will constitute the image proper. Due to space, we cannot pursue a treatment of each of these prerequisite characteristics. Suffice it to say that human personhood requires these characteristics if it is to be construed as covenantal personhood, and yet the *imago*, properly considered, cannot be identified with these. Rather, the image is to be understood in this account as an office or embassy, a covenantal commission with an eschatological orientation.

Further, this approach necessarily directs our attention away from the inner quest, out toward a conception of the self that is inseparable from though not reduced to its external relations in a specific "form of life" defined by mutual obligations. Although Calvin himself did not sufficiently develop this aspect of his thought, covenant theology is unthinkable apart from a basic commitment to relational categories. In fact, Stanley Grenz cites a number of representative sources for his claim that the Reformation in general and Calvin's theology in particular led to "the birth of the relational self."[12] A. N. Whitehead's famous quip, "Religion is what the individual does with his own solitariness,"[13]

Culture of Modernity (Cambridge: Cambridge University Press, 1993). The contrast between the biblical creation narrative and modernity's antithesis of the human and non-human spheres could not be greater. In the former, humans are clearly represented as belonging to the natural world, serving it as stewards of fellow-creatures.

12. Stanley Grenz, *The Social God and the Relational Self: A Trinitarian Theology of the Imago Dei* (Louisville: Westminster John Knox, 2001), pp. 162-70.

13. A. N. Whitehead, *Religion in the Making* (New York: Meridian, 1960), p. 16.

may fit well with rationalism, idealism, and romanticism, but it is at far remove from any view of the self that is oriented covenantally.

Although he does not use the concept of covenant to identify this theological understanding of social personhood, Francis Watson has judiciously analyzed the socio-linguistic conditioning of human personhood while avoiding the common tendency to eliminate individual subjectivity.[14] He reminds us that this corporate aspect of self-identity isn't always felicitous: "The intersubjective matrix which forms individual, related persons also simultaneously *de*forms them."[15] This is where Christian theology will want to raise the subject of human fallenness — sin.

The Image of God (Properly Considered)

So far I have outlined essential features of a covenantal anthropology as touching the subject of human personhood generally. We now turn to what I regard as "the image proper." I will argue that the image, properly speaking, is constituted by the following four characteristics: sonship/royal dominion, representation, glory, and prophetic witness.

Sonship/Royal Dominion Concurring with Calvin's exegesis, accepted by a consensus of contemporary Hebrew scholars, I regard *ṣelem* ("image") and *demut* ("likeness") as synonyms. And at least part of the significance of the *imago dei* is that it is the royal investiture of a servant-son. In his person and work, Jesus Christ receives in the place of fallen Adam his royal investiture in the Seventh Day as the image-son of God. Despite superficial similarities, the royal sonship motif in Genesis 1:26-28 differs significantly from ancient Egyptian and Mesopotamian myths. For instance, while the king in these myths is represented as the royal son of the chief deity — an incarnation, in fact, of the deity — the

14. Francis Watson, *Text, Church and World: Biblical Interpretation in Theological Perspective* (Edinburgh: T&T Clark, 1994), chap. 8. See also Paul Ricoeur, *Figuring the Sacred*, trans. David Pellauer, ed. Mark Wallace (Minneapolis: Fortress, 1995), esp. chap. 20; Paul Ricoeur, *Oneself as Another*, trans. Kathleen Blamey (Chicago: University of Chicago Press, 1992).

15. Watson, *Text, Church and World*, p. 110.

creation of Adam and Eve was never regarded by the Jews as a divine incarnation. Furthermore, this royal investiture in Genesis included all human beings, "male and female," and not just a single ruler.[16]

As Meredith Kline notes, the three principal elements of likeness that appear in all their redolence when the royal son appears are the following: *temple* (dominion, kingship); *the ethical dimension* (the foundations of the temple are justice, equity, truth, righteousness, holiness, goodness); and *glory* — physical beauty.[17] "To be the image of God is to be the son of God."[18] Similarly, Phyllis Bird observes that while *ṣelem* by itself tells us nothing, "The *selem elohim* in Genesis 1 is, accordingly, a royal designation, the precondition or prerequisite for rule."[19] This interpretation, Bird argues, fits well with the parallel passage in Psalm 8, where coronation language and dominion language once more converge.

This sonship-likeness is seen most clearly, of course, in Jesus Christ, of whom Adam was himself a proleptic reflection. It is essential to recognize that in this sense the incarnate Lord of the Covenant is its servant, and that as the new Adam his royal sonship-likeness is not the same as his eternal sonship. In his humiliation, he must attain this sonship-likeness — this royal image — on behalf of his brothers and sisters. This is

---

16. Phyllis A. Bird, "'Male and Female He Created Them': Gen. 1:27b in the Context of the Priestly Account of Creation," *Harvard Theological Review* 74:2 (1981): "The genius of the formulation of Genesis 1:26 may be seen in its use of a common expression and image of Mesopotamian (-Canaanite) royal theology to counter a common image of Mesopotamian (-Canaanite) anthropology, viz., the image of humanity as the servant of the gods, the dominant image of Mesopotamian creation myths. The language that describes the king as the one who stands in a special relationship to the divine world is chosen by the author of Genesis 1 (perhaps under the influence of Egyptian wisdom tradition) to describe humanity as a whole, *adam qua adam*, in its essential nature" (pp. 140, 155-58).

17. Meredith G. Kline, *Images of the Spirit* (self-published, 1986), p. 35.

18. Kline, *Images of the Spirit*, p. 36.

19. Bird, "'Male and Female He Created Them,'" p. 140. Further, Bird appeals to parallels in Egypt, where the notion of the pharaoh as the divine "image-son" or representative on earth is common, yet she reminds us that the further implication that the pharaoh was an incarnation of the chief deity would have been "an idea foreign to Israelite thought." If there is any direct connection on the writer's part, it is the "language of analogy rather than representation. . . ." Whatever parallels there may be with Akkadian and Egyptian literature, however, the origin of these analogies in the biblical text must be located in "a still unknown 'Canaanite' tradition," and the most direct parallels for the biblical comparisons and contrasts are with Mesopotamian religion (p. 140).

how we might understand a reference such as that in Psalms 2:7 and 89:26, repeated in Hebrews 1:5: "To which of the angels did God say, 'You are my Son. Today I have begotten you'?" In John's Gospel especially, Jesus' fulfillment of this destiny of royal sonship is repeatedly underscored (cf. John 5:17-21). Without separating the two natures of Christ, we must nevertheless distinguish between the everlasting sonship of Christ as a possession and his fulfillment of this human, Adamic sonship *as a commission*. Jesus is not only the Son of God but is also the Son of Adam, Seed of Abraham, Son of David, and Son of Mary who fulfills the *human* destiny of becoming the royal son of God.

Representation To speak of the image of God as representation is to place it in the realm of judicial commission rather than, as in the more traditional understanding, considering it a mirror of the divine essence. It refers not so much to a correspondence in attributes (even the so-called communicable ones), but to an official embassy. In the ascension, the royal repatriation and acceptance of reward are accomplished by Jesus acting not as a private person but as a federal representative of his covenant people. Thus, just as was the case in connection with the royal sonship theme, a robust emphasis on the humanity of Christ is essential.

While there has been a widespread tendency throughout church history to treat the victory of Christ almost exclusively as the victory of God, covenant theology — particularly in its insistence on the necessity of the original covenant being perfectly fulfilled — has underscored its significance as the victory of a human person. To be sure, this person is the God-Man, but as the second Adam he is entrusted with a thoroughly human task. This emphasis of covenant theology has been challenged from time to time by what Alan Spence has identified as "Apollinarian" tendencies that fail "to conceive of the incarnate Christ as 'normative man,'" despite formal adherence to the humanity of Christ.[20] In fact, Spence offers an insightful analysis of John Owen's anti-Apollinarian christology, sharply contrasting it especially with Barth's.[21] But we can discern similar tendencies in Zwingli's ascription

20. Alan Spence, "Christ's Humanity and Ours: John Owen," in *Persons Divine and Human*, ed. Colin Gunton and Christoph Schwobel (Edinburgh: T&T Clark, 1991), p. 77.

21. Spence, "Christ's Humanity and Ours," pp. 93ff. See also Karl Barth, *Christ and Adam: Man and Humanity in Romans 5* (New York: Harper and Brothers, 1957), p. 36: "The guilt and punishment we incur in Adam have no independent reality of their own but

of the saving efficacy of Christ exclusively to his divinity.[22] At least in Barth's case, we may wonder if the weaknesses in his understanding of Jesus' saving humanity have some connection with his tendency to treat Christ as a universal form and Adam as a mere appearance, with the correlative reduction of the covenant of creation to the covenant of grace and anthropology to christology.[23]

Jesus is, therefore, according to Calvin and the confessions and consensus of Reformed scholasticism, not merely the Son of God as to

---

are only the dark shadows of the grace and life we find in Christ." If one does not take Adam (that is, the human *as human*) seriously, it is difficult to see how a due appreciation of Jesus Christ as the historical fulfillment of Adam's original task will be conceived. For Barth, it appears that "Adam" represents a mere copy, appearance, or shadow of the eternal Form (Christ), the latter swallowing the former.

22. While Zwingli was in many respects a Reformed forebear, his neoplatonism is evident in his tendency to sharply contrast the divine and the human, spirit and matter, the internal working of the Spirit and the external means of grace. All of this is inimical to later Reformed theology (especially that of Calvin and his successors). Zwingli even displays some of these "Apollinarian" inclinations when he says under discussion of the sacraments, "We must note in passing that Christ is our salvation by virtue of that part of his nature by which he came down from heaven, not of that by which he was born of an immaculate Virgin, though he had to suffer and die by this part . . . " (*Commentary on True and False Religion,* ed. Samuel Macauley Jackson and Clarence Nevin Heller [Durham: Labyrinth, 1981], p. 204). W. P. Stephens concludes, "As the stress in Zwingli's theology as a whole is on God rather than on man, so the stress in his Christology is on Christ as God rather than on Christ as man" (*The Theology of Huldrych Zwingli* [Oxford: Clarendon, 1986], p. 111). By contrast, the more mature Reformed emphasis on the union of the two natures in salvation is evidenced by Calvin's remark that, "In short, from the time when he took on the form of a servant, [Christ] began to pay the price of liberation in order to redeem us" (2.16.5). Under his discussion of the sacraments, Calvin writes that not only did Christ become flesh, "But he also quickens our very flesh in which he abides, that by partaking of him we may be fed unto immortality. . . . By these words ['I am the bread of life come down from heaven'] he teaches not only that he is life since he is the eternal Word of God who came down from heaven to us [*pace* Zwingli], but also that by coming down he poured that power upon the flesh which he took in order that from it participation in life might flow unto us" (4.17.8). It is no wonder that the christology and sacramentology of the Reformed confessions operate with significantly different categories than those employed by Zwingli. The extent to which Karl Barth is influenced more by Zwingli than by the subsequent Reformed tradition on this point is worth pondering.

23. Even P. T. Forsyth remarked, "we must think of the *divine* element as constituting the historic personality" of Christ (emphasis added); cited by Spence, "Christ's Humanity and Ours," p. 80.

his divinity, but the true and faithful Son of Man who always obeys his Father's will in the power of the Holy Spirit.

This meritorious human life lived in full dependence on the Spirit (recapitulation) is not extrinsic but intrinsic to redemption; it is not merely a necessary prerequisite of a sacrificial offering, but part and parcel of that offering. Thus the Son of Man claims victory for himself by right and not merely by gift, nor indeed by virtue of his deity:

> Very truly, I tell you, the Son can do nothing on his own, but only what he sees the Father doing; for whatever the Father does, the Son does likewise. . . . For just as the Father has life in himself, so he has granted the Son also to have life in himself; and he has given him authority to execute judgment, because he is the Son of Man. . . . I can do nothing on my own. As I hear, I judge; and my judgment is just, because I seek to do not my own will but the will of him who sent me. . . . The works that the Father has given me to complete, the very works that I am doing, testify on my behalf that the Father has sent me. (John 5:19, 26-27, 30, 36)

And later in John Christ says, "I glorified you on earth by finishing the work that you gave me to do. So now, Father, glorify me in your own presence with the glory that I had in your presence before the world existed" (John 17:4-5). So from the cross, it is not only his suffering on behalf of sinners but his completion of the Father's commission that he has in mind when he cries out, "It is finished" (John 19:30).

Because of this human achievement, Paul can say concerning Jesus, "being found in *human* form, he humbled himself and became obedient to the point of death — even death on a cross. *Therefore* God also highly exalted him and gave him the name that is above every name . . ." (Phil. 2:7-9). Taking his cue from Daniel's vision of the four empires, Moltmann duly notes, "In the kingdom of the Son of Man, man's likeness to God is fulfilled. *Through this human man* God finally asserts his rights over his creation."[24]

Essential, then, to the representation that marks Jesus Christ's office is its reciprocity. The Father's approval of the Son is not a question of grace but of being rewarded for a commission fulfilled. This under-

---

24. Jürgen Moltmann, *Man: Christian Anthropology in the Conflicts of the Present,* trans. John Sturdy (Philadelphia: Fortress, 1974), p. 112, emphasis added.

scores the notion of mutuality, which is involved in all covenants of the suzerainty-type. The creation covenant is not set aside or subsumed under grace, but is fulfilled representatively on our behalf, and the Covenant Servant dispenses the fruit of his victory under the terms of a covenant of grace.

This approach emphasizes for Oliver O'Donovan that Christ's resurrection is representative not in a symbolic way of independent and prior truths, but inasmuch as it effects its concrete results representatively for a people.[25] It is "Not that the created order has changed, or was ever anything other than what God made it," O'Donovan writes, "but that in Christ man was able for the first time to assume his proper place within it, the place of dominion which God assigned to Adam."[26] To be sure, there is an already–not yet character to this, as Hebrews reminds us, after quoting Psalm 8:

> Now in subjecting all things to them [humans], God left nothing outside their control. As it is, we do not yet see everything in subjection to them, but we do see Jesus, who for a little while was made lower than the angels, now crowned with glory and honor because of the suffering of death, so that by the grace of God he might taste death for everyone. (Heb. 2:8-9).

Glory While royal sonship and representation find ample support in Scripture, perhaps the theme most closely attached to the relevant passages is that of "glory" *(kavod)*.[27] It is this notion that best ties together both testaments and indicates the closest connection between covenant and eschatology. Furthermore, once we recognize its central importance to the concept of the *imago dei,* the latter's significance in even the Old Testament is capable of being recognized as well.

---

25. Oliver O'Donovan, *Resurrection and Moral Order: An Outline of Evangelical Ethics* (Grand Rapids: Eerdmans, 1986), p. 15.

26. O'Donovan, *Resurrection and Moral Order,* p. 24.

27. Ricoeur observes that Paul's development of the *imago dei* theme (for instance, in 2 Cor. 3:18) anchors itself not in the Old Testament notion of creation in the image of God (Gen. 1:26) but in the Old Testament motif of glory (*Figuring the Sacred,* pp. 267-78). There is a lot of exegetical support for such a view, and this underscores how the importance of the *imago dei* concept in Scripture will be determined by corollaries or constituent aspects of the image rather than direct statements concerning the image as such.

Pillaging the ancient cosmogenic myths, the creation narrative recounts the Great King's completion of his cosmic house, then his filling of it with his Glory-Spirit as his own holy dwelling. One of the gains in this account is a greater integration of christology and pneumatology, as the Glory of God is identified directly with both the Spirit and the Son, and indirectly/reflectively with those whom the Spirit "fathers" by breathing into them the breath of life, rendering human beings prophetic witnesses to the Glory they reflect. Adam and Eve were created as temples of the same Glory-Spirit identified in Genesis 1:2. As Adam is represented as having been created by a "divine inbreathing" of the Spirit, Mary was told, "The Holy Spirit will come upon you and the Power of the Highest will overshadow you; therefore also that holy thing which shall be born of you shall be called the Son of God" (Luke 1:35). And in inaugurating his new creation, Jesus breathed on the disciples, saying, "Receive the Holy Spirit" (John 20:22). Individual believers and the corporate church are therefore re-creations in the image of Christ, the true temple filled with the Glory-Spirit.

All of this serves, retrospectively, of course, to illuminate the Genesis narrative. "As Genesis 2:7 pictures it," writes Ricoeur, "the Spirit-Archetype actively fathered his human ectype," showing that "image of God and son of God are thus twin concepts," as the birth of Seth in Adam's image seems to confirm (Gen. 5:1-3).[28] It is "a making of man in the likeness of the Glory-Spirit."[29] It is no wonder, then, that the Son sends the Spirit to inaugurate a new creation on the pattern of his own glory both as God and as the glorified new Adam.

The eschatological and the protological are thus coordinated with each other, as when Paul states, "Thus it is written, 'The first man, Adam, became a living being'; the last Adam became a life-giving Spirit. . . . Just as we have borne the image of the man of dust, we will also bear the image of the man of heaven" (1 Cor. 15:45, 49). In 1 Corinthians 11:7, as Stanley Grenz notes, "the apostle connects the *imago dei* with the concept of the divine glory *(doxa)*. The way was paved by the Old Testament, most directly by the declaration in Psalm 8:5 that God has crowned humankind with 'glory and honor.'"[30] This eschato-

28. Ricoeur, *Figuring the Sacred,* p. 23.
29. Ricoeur, *Figuring the Sacred,* pp. 23-24.
30. Grenz, *Social God and the Relational Self,* p. 205.

logical image, though effaced and marred by human sin, will be fulfilled in the new creation: the one who created us in his image by his Spirit in the beginning will re-create us in the same image by the same Spirit in the end. Thus, Christ identifies himself as no less than the Creator and Consummator, "the Alpha and Omega, the beginning and ending, the first and the last" (Rev. 1:8), "the faithful witness" to God's covenant (Rev. 1:5). The church is then the temple built according to the likeness of the heavenly city. The church therefore witnesses to Christ: that is its glory-image, and in its glorified state this witness is vindicated.

All of this serves to show the inextricable link between covenant, eschatology, and the judicial-official character of the divine image. Again, this glory is ethical-official, rather than corresponding to a particular essence in the human constitution. "As image of God," Kline writes, "man is a royal son with the judicial function appertaining to kingly office. The renewal of the divine image in men is an impartation to them of the likeness of the archetypal glory of Christ."[31]

In drawing together these various strands, we can say that the creation of humankind represents the appearance of the image-bearing son, although the investiture of that son in the royal office is in a sense already eschatologically oriented at creation. In other words, *'Adam* has not yet assumed the throne under God in the Sabbath glory. (See 2 Cor. 3:7-18; 4:4-6, with "the investiture figure" of "putting on Christ" in Eph. 4:24; Rom. 13:14; 1 Cor. 15:53; 2 Cor. 5:2ff.; Gal. 3:27; Col. 3:10.) Now those who even after the fall still bear an official glory are re-created to reflect the ethical glory of the Son in the power of the Spirit. Ricoeur therefore is justified in seeing union with Christ and not the imitation of Christ as the New Testament successor to the Old Testament prophetic idea: the summoned subject of the prophetic narratives is "the christomorphic self."[32]

Related also to this covenant-bearing glory-image is the concept of "name." Adam and Eve are both named by God (a clear indication of their equality in creation and as image-bearing officers), while Adam is given the prior task of naming the animals. Similarly, notes Ricoeur, believers are "named 'sons of God,' just as people customarily are surnamed after

---

31. Kline, *Images of the Spirit,* p. 28.
32. Ricoeur, *Figuring the Sacred,* p. 268.

the name of their forebears."[33] This "naming" practice is also a treaty-making practice. "The name 'Christian' is a covenantal identification for the servant-son people of the new covenant."[34] That we are not only created but created-in-covenant — and that we are named, both in creation (Adam) and then in redemption (Christ) — undermines all notions of autonomous self-creation. The federal or covenantal nature of this redemption undermines all anthropological individualism. Anthony Thiselton also indicates the significance of this naming in determining the biblical concept of selfhood: "In a distinctively theological sense the biblical text ... may be said to address the selfhood of the reader with transforming effects. It thereby gives the self an identity and significance as the recipient of loving and transforming address. In this sense, it 'names' the self."[35] In baptism, Christ claims believers and their children, writing his name on their foreheads, setting them apart for himself as images of his glory. To bear the name of God is to bear the glory of God.

The creature thus named is a prophetic witness, authorized to declare God's word of command and promise. It is important to recognize that in Adam, humankind, like Moses with his disobedient fellow-travelers on the verge of the Jordan, never entered the Sabbath consummation and therefore does not yet possess the glorification that royal investiture indicates. "As originally created, man was not yet endowed with this [physical] form of Glory-likeness. Physical glorification might only be contemplated in eschatological hope."[36] Adoption is finally and fully realized for us only in our bodily resurrection and glorification (Rom. 8:23).

Prophetic Witness Although something of the witnessing character of the image has been mentioned, we should add a bit more to this important aspect. As Kline observes,

33. Ricoeur, *Figuring the Sacred,* p. 54. Kline adds here, "The equivalence of the bearing of God's name and the bearing of God's image appears strikingly in Revelation 22:4. Here, in the midst of the description of the glorified covenant community, renewed after the image of the Lord, it is said: 'They will see his face and his name will be in their foreheads.' . . . To say that the overcomers in the New Jerusalem bear the name of Christ on their forehead is to say that they reflect the glory of Christ, which is to say that they bear the image of the glorified Christ" (*Images of the Spirit,* pp. 28-29).

34. Ricoeur, *Figuring the Sacred,* p. 55.

35. Thiselton, *Interpreting God and the Postmodern Self,* p. 63.

36. Kline, *Images of the Spirit,* p. 61.

The lives of the prophets caught up in the Spirit were prophecies of the eschatological destiny of mankind re-created in God's image. . . . In the beginning man was created in the image of God by the power of creative fiat after the paradigm of the theophanic Glory-Spirit. In redemptive history the reproduction of the image of God in the new mankind takes place through the mediatorial agency of Jesus Christ, in whom the divine Glory became incarnate. He is the paradigm of the Glory-image and he is the mediator of the Spirit in the process of replicating the divine likeness.[37]

Pentecost then, as a new creation, is nothing less than "a redemptive recapitulation of Genesis 1:2 and 27."[38] "In the command of the voice from heaven, 'Hear him,' Peter perceived [Acts 3:22ff.] the ultimate application of the Deuteronomic requirement that Israel obey God's prophet (Deut. 18:18). That was God's own identification of Jesus as *the* prophet like unto Moses."[39] The preincarnate Son, as "Angel of the Covenant" (Mal. 3:1; Zech. 3), "was that archetypal prophet behind the human prophet paradigm."[40] Through the descent of the Glory-Spirit at Easter and Pentecost, the "new creation" has dawned, equipping those once "dead in trespasses and sins" (Eph. 2:1) to be witnesses to the ends of the earth. The Son witnesses to the Father, and both the Father and the Spirit witness to the Son, as the Spirit sent by the Son makes of fallen office-bearers a resurrected prophetic priesthood. Kline observes, "In 2 Corinthians 3 and 4, Paul describes the Christian's transformation into the image of the glory of the Lord in terms of Moses' transfiguration. . . . According to 2 Corinthians 3 and 4, for Christ to re-create the church in his divine likeness is to create a prophet-church."[41] "Christ is the original light; the church which he creates in his likeness is a reflective light," a "prophetic witness."[42] The Son has witnessed to what he has seen and heard in the heavenly council, and now his disciples are to witness to what they have seen and heard as they have stood for these three years in that same council with the incarnate Lord himself among them.

37. Kline, *Images of the Spirit,* pp. 63-64.
38. Kline, *Images of the Spirit,* p. 70.
39. Kline, *Images of the Spirit,* pp. 81-82.
40. Kline, *Images of the Spirit,* p. 83.
41. Kline, *Images of the Spirit,* p. 84.
42. Kline, *Images of the Spirit,* p. 85.

In Revelation 11, "The figures in whom the likeness of Christ is re-produced are expressly denoted as witnesses (v. 3) and prophets (vv. 10, 18) and their mission is described as one of prophesying (v. 3), prophecy (v. 6), and testimony (v. 7)."[43] Now all believers enter the holy of holies (as priests) and are prophets in the Spirit, wearing the garments of the Spirit as a bride adorned for her husband. And yet, the church is the bride of Christ, not yet the spouse. The confirmation in righteousness and the consummation of the glory-image that constitute royal investi-ture await believers in hope.

That the image necessarily involves — even centrally — the ethical dimension is evident in the close connection it bears with the repeti-tion of God's work and rest in the seven-day pattern. Yet this is true only in the liminal state of the already–not yet, as believers — together with the whole creation — await their own resurrection from the dead and royal entrance into confirmed righteousness. The Glorification, al-ready semi-realized in the possession of the Holy Spirit as a down pay-ment, will be the full psychosomatic investiture of each believer as a royal son. This may be why Paul (Rom. 8:18-25) puts an eschatological spin on adoption, deferring its full accomplishment until the whole creation is able to participate with redeemed humanity in the Sabbath enthronement of God. Although the whole earth will be full of the glory of God, human beings are central in this construction for theo-logical reasons. As Watson notes, "The earth is at the centre of the uni-verse and humans are the pinnacle of creation not because the priestly writers had the misfortune to live before Copernicus or Darwin but be-cause such a presentation is indispensable within a non-alienated, theological account of human existence in the world and before God."[44]

I hope to have shown also in the preceding section how christology informs our understanding of these themes without collapsing protology into soteriology. Having allowed a space for the essential constitution of human beings as prerequisite conditions for a covenantal relationship, our conclusion is that the image of God in hu-mankind is itself official rather than essential; ethical rather than on-tological; eschatological rather than metaphysical.

43. Kline, *Images of the Spirit*, p. 91.
44. Watson, *Text, Church and World*, p. 148.

Conclusion

Arguing for a "praxis-oriented self, defined by its communicative practices, oriented toward an understanding of itself in its discourse, its action, its being with others, and its experience of transcendence," Calvin O. Schrag draws together insights from narrative approaches that are, as I have already indicated, quite congenial to my proposal.[45] In step with similar approaches by Charles Taylor, Alasdair MacIntyre, Paul Ricoeur, and others — all of whom share important affinities with Martin Heidegger's analysis at certain points — Schrag seeks to disentangle personhood from the "what" question initiated by Descartes to the "who" question, "putting us in quest not of an abstract universal nature but rather of a concrete and historically specific questioner. The question about the who thus becomes a question about the questioner."[46] Instead of the question, "What is man?" the question becomes, "Who am I?"[47] Although Schrag tends to see self-identity chiefly in terms of "constituting itself" and "self-formation," he provides an account of how discourse and action conspire to form a dynamic narrative of selfhood. An exclusively narrative approach leads to "narrative without a narrator."[48] It is in the terrain of "lived experience" that the event of discourse and narrative become united. "Narratives need to be told by someone to someone," and it is at the crossroads of discourse and narration that the self appears as "a who of discourse in the guise of a narrating self, a *homo narrans,* a storyteller who both finds herself in stories already told and strives for a self-constitution by emplotting herself in stories in the making."[49]

This narrative construction is easily contrasted with the "self-identical monad," a self that is "mute and self-enclosed, changeless and

---

45. Calvin O. Schrag, *The Self after Postmodernity* (New Haven: Yale University Press, 1997).

46. Schrag, *The Self after Postmodernity,* p. 22. See also Martin Heidegger, *Being and Time,* trans. Joan Stambaugh (Albany: State University of New York Press, 1996), pp. 108ff.

47. Heidegger, *Being and Time,* p. 13. It is worth noting that Psalm 8 does not ask, "What is man?" — an abstract metaphysical question — but, "What is man *that you are mindful of him?*" It is a rhetorical question about the psalmist's own existential sense of smallness (probably not only in ontological but also in ethical terms).

48. Schrag, *The Self after Postmodernity,* p. 22.

49. Schrag, *The Self after Postmodernity,* p. 26.

secured prior to the events of speaking," a "zero-point center of consciousness." Instead, "The who of discourse is an achievement, an accomplishment, a performance, whose presence to itself is admittedly fragile, subject to forgetfulness and semantic ambiguities."[50] At this point, Schrag appeals to Ricoeur's well-known distinction between *idem*-identity and *ipse*-identity, the former referring to a permanent and immutable self-sameness *(soi-même),* while the latter indicates "the sense of identity applicable to a person's character, which for Ricoeur finds its direct analogue in 'character' as a protagonist in a story."[51] Thus, the question "Who is speaking?" is about *ipse*-identity, while the atomic weight of silicon is an *idem*-identity question.[52] The subject of *ipse*-identity is a temporalized self of a given narrative. "The self that has nothing to remember and nothing for which to hope is a self whose identity stands in peril," says Schrag.[53]

This would seem to lend support to my view that being eschatologically oriented to the future — indeed, to a better world — is intrinsic to humanness.

The story of the self is a developing story, a story subject to a creative advance, wherein the past is never simply a series of nows that have lapsed into nonbeing, but a text, an inscription of events and experiences, that stands open to new interpretations and new perspectives of meaning. Correspondingly, the future is not a series of nows that has not yet come into being. The future of narrative time is the self

---

50. Schrag, *The Self after Postmodernity,* p. 33. We would add, of course, *sin,* as Watson's remarks above clearly mark. Schrag does not include theological reflections, and his account is clearly weighted toward human autonomy. At the same time, he does indicate the significance of self-identity as achievement, something to be won or lost. While it is certainly true that justification of the ungodly is a gift and in no way "an achievement, an accomplishment, a performance," Eberhard Jüngel (like Barth) seems to reduce human identity to soteriology without remainder. This is where, once again, a covenantal model seems to provide more conceptual space for a wider body of exegesis on this topic.

51. Schrag, *The Self after Postmodernity,* p. 35, based on Ricoeur's *Oneself as Another.* See also Paul Ricoeur, "The Image of God and the Epic of Man," in his *History and Truth,* trans. Charles A. Kelbley (Evanston: Northwestern University Press, 1965); Ricoeur, *Figuring the Sacred,* esp. pp. 262-75.

52. Schrag, *The Self after Postmodernity,* p. 36.

53. Schrag, *The Self after Postmodernity,* p. 36.

as possibility, as the power to be able to provide new readings of the script that has already been inscribed and to mark out new inscriptions of a script in the making.[54]

In this narrative construction, the self is neither wholly self-determined (either rationally or volitionally) nor wholly determined by the past or by the present but is relatively open to the future.[55] Further, "The communalized self is *in* history but not *of* history. It has the resources for transcending the historically specific without arrogating to itself the unconditioned and decontextualized vision of the world."[56] Schrag draws on Julia Kristeva's suggestive expression for the self as "a subject on trial" *(sujet en procès)*.[57] "As Kristeva reminds us, the subject constitutes itself at the same time as speaking and agentive subject against the backdrop of an ethos and a body politic of common goals and institutional involvements."[58] Once more we may be led back through such suggestive reflections to the theological concept of covenant for at least one of the language games in which selfhood is implicated, the one that matters in our topic under consideration.

Although Schrag's account is not explicitly theological, it bears closer affinities with the biblical orientation than the traditional, more neoplatonic (that is, ontological) approach. Nowhere in Scripture is the question of human identity asked or answered in the abstract, but only in terms of the covenantal — which is to say, ethical — commission that takes an explicitly narrative construction. Echoing the structure of ancient Near Eastern treaties, biblical covenant-making begins with a historical prologue that contextualizes the subsequent stipulations and sanctions. Thus, it is never a question of bare ethics — timeless, eternal moral truths — but of a particular form of

54. Schrag, *The Self after Postmodernity*, p. 37.

55. "The failure to distinguish between 'context-conditioned' and 'context-determined' has ushered in a profound confusion on matters of the degree and quality of transcendence required for making moral judgment and submitting critiques of culture" (Schrag, *The Self after Postmodernity*, p. 107).

56. Schrag, *The Self after Postmodernity*, p. 109.

57. Schrag, *The Self after Postmodernity*, p. 40. See also Julia Kristeva, "The System and the Speaking Subject," in *The Kristeva Reader*, ed. Toril Moi (New York: Columbia University Press, 1986), pp. 24-33.

58. Schrag, *The Self after Postmodernity*, p. 41.

existence that arises from a concrete narrative emplotment: "I am the Lord who brought you up out of Egypt." Walther Eichrodt's judgment that "the covenant-union between Yahweh and Israel is an original element in all sources," even the earliest, is shared more widely across the landscape of biblical scholarship than ever before.[59] In fact, it is the promissory character of this covenant that "provides life with a goal and history with a meaning."[60]

Modern anthropology is at even further remove from this biblical mentality in its addition of autonomy to inwardness. Grenz observes,

> Whereas the psalmist [in Psalm 8] sought to understand personal identity by appeal to the place of humans within a universe viewed as "creation," the modern era witnessed the birth of the individual, who, having been pried loose from creation, attempts to gain a sense of identity as a self and through the construction of the self. As a result, modern anthropology centers on the means for this self-construction.[61]

It is in the context of being a covenantal creature ("a little lower than the angels," endowed with "glory and honor") that the psalmist, lost in the immensity of the cosmos, rediscovers his bearings, his "Here I am" that gives him a place of narrative significance that would otherwise elude him. Eberhard Jüngel comments,

> Biblical texts certainly do not address people about themselves without at the same time addressing them about something else. This is a decisive clue for the proper understanding of the true humanity of human persons. It is only as the human 'I' is addressed not only about itself, but rather addressed in such a way that it is simultaneously claimed by something outside itself, that one is really speaking about the human 'I' as such.[62]

---

59. Walther Eichrodt, *Theology of the Old Testament*, trans. J. A. Baker (Philadelphia: Westminster, 1951), 1:36.

60. Eichrodt, *Theology of the Old Testament*, vol. 1, p. 37.

61. Grenz, *Social God and the Relational Self*, p. 98.

62. Eberhard Jüngel, "On Becoming Truly Human," in *Theological Essays II*, ed. J. B. Webster, trans. Arnold Neufeldt-Fast and J. B. Webster (Edinburgh: T&T Clark, 1995), p. 220. Despite appreciation for key points of Jüngel's theological anthropology, my account obviously differs in its understanding of "true humanness."

What I appreciate about Schrag's particular construction of a more nuanced narrative approach is that he, like Ricoeur, refuses to surrender personhood to either relations or the cogito. "The we-experience and the I-experience are more intricately entwined," he rightly urges, "than has been acknowledged by proponents of either the social doctrine of the self or the individualist doctrine. . . . The point is that both these doctrines trade on a common mistake of sundering the undivided portion of world-experience and then reifying the abstracted components."[63] For a host of reasons that we do not have the space to explore here, Christian theology cannot do without either side of such lived experience.

I have conveniently left out aspects of Schrag's account that I find inconsistent with my own proposal. His account does, however, help to indicate the direction in which a covenantal account of human personhood might be construed. In such an account, the modern notions of selfhood that pivot on autonomy are resolutely challenged even more vigorously than Schrag would allow. We have happily witnessed the deconstruction of the Cartesian subject, but equally reductionistic reactions have filled the void. I would suggest that the "we-experience" that is essential to self-identity, at least in connection with the topic before us, is constituted at least theologically by the covenant: first, there is the covenant of creation, which renders us responsible to the divine other and therefore to all human others and indeed to the entire creation whose care has been entrusted to us; and, second, *rightly ordered* selfhood is constituted by the covenant of grace, administered by the Covenant Lord through Word and sacrament in the power of the Spirit. Any account that takes sufficient note of the wide range of biblical teaching will have to appreciate both aspects of this "we-experience" without reducing one to the other.

The covenant of creation provides the basis for the unity of the human race, and even after the fall the features of this original human creatureliness are not in any way altered but are employed in ways that are ethically subversive of their original intention. The covenant of grace similarly determines human existence, but this time does relate entirely to the sphere of redemption, christology, and ecclesiology. It is at *this* point that we recognize the shape not of true humanness (onto-

63. Schrag, *The Self after Postmodernity,* pp. 79-80.

logically considered), not humanness as it is seen by Barth, Jüngel, Zizioulas, and others, but properly oriented and experienced true humanness (covenantally considered).[64] It is *here* that synergism is excluded: we are fallen image-bearers who need to be rescued, no longer innocent covenant partners who can cooperate in the mission of leading creation into its consummation. Only by being reconciled to God in Jesus Christ by the power of the Spirit working through the means of grace in the church can covenant-breakers be constituted covenant-keepers and be kept in that covenant until one day the image of God is finally not only perfectly restored but confirmed in everlasting righteousness.

In the Pauline eschatology, both "I-experience" *(ordo salutis)* and "we-experience" *(historia salutis)* are fully integrated, without surrendering to an exclusively social or individual understanding of self-identity. The covenantal self emerges in what Alasdair MacIntyre calls "the narrative unity of a life" and, we might add, the narrative unity of all the lives lived in the history of God's covenant people. And that life is told by God back to us as we find ourselves in the drama of creation, fall, redemption, and consummation. In fact, Ricoeur singles out Israel "because 'no other people has been so overwhelmingly impassioned by the narratives it has told about itself.'"[65] As this drama evolves and incorporates us, we find ourselves not merely imitating characters in the story, but finding our character in its unfolding plot. And while we are not masters or self-constituting and self-constructing authors of our own identities, we are nevertheless partners in the covenant and therefore contribute meaningfully to its development. This represents a dialectical development of self-identity

64. Among the chief dangers of a dualistic ontologizing of creation-fall-redemption is the tendency seen, for example, in Athanasius, Augustine, and Barth to exchange a natural rectitude–human depravity problematic for a neoplatonic being-nothingness one. For Athanasius, the fall made the human race "turn back again according to their nature; and as they had at the beginning come into being out of non-existence, so were they on the way to returning, through corruption, to non-existence again" (*On the Incarnation,* trans. Sister Penelope Lawson [New York: Macmillan, 1946], p. 8). For much of the patristic and medieval tradition, "nothingness," "corruption," and "natural state" become virtually synonymous, leaving the state of nature ambiguous at best.

65. Cited by Dan R. Stiver, *Theology after Ricoeur: New Directions in Hermeneutical Theology* (Louisville: Westminster John Knox, 2001), p. 172.

in which the reply "Here I am" reflects the acceptance of the terms of that covenantal selfhood.[66]

Although space does not allow an exegetical treatment of this theme, a lot could be said at this point about the recurring feature of this response. "Here I am" (Hebrew: *hinēh*, behold, plus *nî*, me), and its New Testament equivalent (Gk. *idou*, behold), is the typical marker of covenantal response on the part of God's servants. In fact, the flight of Adam and Eve from the divine call, "Adam, where are you?" (Gen. 3:9), is contrasted with the "Here I am" of Abraham, Moses, Samuel, Isaiah, Mary, and Jesus. After the angel's auspicious announcement, Mary declares, "Here I am, the servant of the Lord; let it be with me according to your word" (Luke 1:38). It is noteworthy that Jesus announces his triumphant arrival in heaven with the words, "Here am I [*idou ego*] and the children God has given me" (Heb. 2:13).

All of this underscores the point made above, that the self is a situated, narrated subject, an agent who, like God, is known from one's acts and not from one's essence. But the human self is not merely situated in a hermeneutically sealed cultural-linguistic bubble; it is able to be drawn out of a purely mundane, chronological, and immanent context of self-identity to be written into a script that cuts across all times and places through the vertical "intrusions" of the Spirit. The biblical narrative seems to support Schrag's suggestion that the question "What is man?" should be replaced with the query "Who am I?" It is in the context of the covenant that this question can even be properly asked, much less answered from a theological perspective. "The self's commitment to something," writes Dan Stiver, "provides a kind of self-constancy that also provides an answer to the question of identity."[67] In this way, narrative (resting on the indicative of God's mighty acts) and ethics (the imperatives that delineate the "reasonable service" of-

---

66. It may be worth noting that this "Here I am" formula brings nothing to the table that might be considered worthy of God's favor. In other words, it is nothing less than faith itself. The Westminster Larger Catechism expresses this well: "Faith justifies a sinner in the sight of God, not because of those other graces which do always accompany it, or of good works that are the fruits of it; nor as if the grace of faith, or any act thereof, were imputed to him for justification; but only as it is an instrument, by which he receiveth and applieth Christ and his righteousness" (Q. 73, *The Book of Confessions* [PCUSA, 1991], 7.183).

67. Stiver, *Theology after Ricoeur*, pp. 175-76; cf. Ricoeur, *Figuring the Sacred*, p. 170.

fered "in view of the mercies of God," Rom. 12:1-2) become integrated without reducing one to the other.

Thus, the covenantal self is, to borrow Ricoeur's phrase, "the summoned subject in the school of the narratives of the prophetic vocation."[68] These "narratives of vocation" constitute the self-identity of the prophet, and we should bear in mind that this vocation may be understood in the narrower sense (biblical prophets) and the broader sense (the general office of all human beings in creation and of all believers in redemption).

Against essentialism I have argued that the image of God is chiefly an office, but that it is an office for which human beings are suited by specific capacities as agents directed toward ends. Without surrendering the inalienable status of all human persons as divine image-bearers, I have nevertheless indicated the eschatological, soteriological, and therefore christological character of this image-bearing in its proper operation. Neither creation nor redemption is assimilated into the other; each retains its distinctive character and space.

68. Paul Ricoeur, *Figuring the Sacred,* p. 262. According to Ricoeur, the narratives of prophetic vocation include three phases: confrontation with God, an introductory speech of divine self-identification ("I am the God of your father Abraham"; "I am who I am"; and so on), and then finally the time when the "decisive word can be pronounced: 'I send you,' 'go and say to them . . .'" (pp. 265-66).

Richard Lints | **Imaging and Idolatry**
The Sociality of Personhood
in the Canon

*It is within society, and as a result of social processes, that the individual be-
comes a person, that he attains and holds onto an identity, and that he carries out the various projects that constitute his life. The person cannot exist
apart from society.*[1]

Introduction: What Is Personhood?

The increasingly obvious insight that human persons are essentially
"social" has done much to rehabilitate discussion of human identity
against the backdrop of the Trinity in recent decades.[2] Whatever else
may be said for the modernist notion of the "individual," clearly the
pendulum has swung in theological anthropology toward communi-
tarian notions of personhood and away from Cartesian "solitary
minds,"[3] from notions of the self as constituted by a listing of essential

1. Peter Berger, *The Sacred Canopy: Elements of a Sociological Theory of Religion* (New
York: Doubleday, 1967), p. 3.
2. Karl Barth's discussion in *Church Dogmatics,* vol. 1: *The Doctrine of the Word of God,*
second ed., trans. G. W. Bromiley, ed. G. W. Bromiley and T. F. Torrance (Edinburgh:
T&T Clark, 1975), part 1, is often cited as the locus for this renaissance of Trinitarian discussions of personhood. Stanley Grenz, *The Social God and the Relational Self: A Trinitarian
Theology of the* Imago Dei (Louisville: Westminster John Knox, 2001), offers a nice summary of the renaissance and its impact upon theological questions of personhood.
3. The phrase is borrowed from William Barrett, *Death of the Soul: From Descartes to
the Computer* (New York: Anchor, 1986).

attributes toward notions of the self as constituted by its relations. This has prepared the way to think of the Trinity, being the foundational set of "relations," as creating human persons in its relational image.[4] And the older substantial self has given way to the relational self — with much benefit. Most especially there has been a renewed interest in the church as the identifying community of the Christian life and the distinctive manner in which "belonging together" lies at the heart of the Christian life. In this essay, I want to extend the revisioning of the classic *imago dei* discussion, but also to raise a set of cautionary questions about the present affirmation of the "social self" against the backdrop of the canonical discussion of idolatry.

It is not uncommon to characterize the classic Christian treatments of human nature as two alternative explanations of what separates humans from the animal kingdom. The structuralist explanations suppose there is some structure inherent in the human make-up by which they are different from the beasts. At this point, concepts such as rationality, spirituality, morality, and so on enter into the discussion. These are the "faculties" which humans possess and which animals do not and which therefore define the essential attributes of a human person *qua* human person. Let me suggest (I hope without prejudicing the discussion) that these Christian anthropologies share a certain orientation "from below." They begin with the created order and argue from differences within that order that there is a definable essence to human nature, which therefore must be a gift from God. It is not less Christian by virtue of starting "from below," since these accounts still accord a fundamental role to God as the creator of all that is, and as the being whose final imprint of purpose and design is the effective cause of all that is.

These approaches ("from below") are distinguished from those that orient themselves "from above" — namely, those anthropologies which see in the language of "image" the essential reflection of the Cre-

---

4. So the recent and helpful work by Grenz, *The Social God and the Relational Self,* the first by a major evangelical thinker to appropriate relational notions of personhood. Influential theological works preceding Grenz's and offering "social" accounts of personhood include David F. Ford, *Self and Salvation: Being Transformed* (Cambridge: Cambridge University Press, 1999), Alan J. Torrance, *Persons in Communion* (Edinburgh: T&T Clark, 1996), and John D. Zizioulas, *Being as Communion: Studies in Personhood and the Church* (Crestwood, N.Y.: St. Vladimir's Seminary Press, 1985).

ator in the human person. In these accounts, the essential character traits of the human person lie in their degree of similarity to or difference from God. The central concern inevitably is to lay out the similarities between human persons and their Creator as that which constitutes the "image of God." This image consists variously of humanity's moral or spiritual nature, possibly even humans' rational faculties. They may coincide with a set of essential attributes that are grounded in the so-called communicable attributes of God.

What both of these approaches share in common is a search to define the *imago dei* in light of a list of essential attributes or characteristics — either as different from the animals, or as similar to God.[5] Let me suggest we call both kinds of accounts "essentialist" in this regard. They are concerned to locate a set of attributes or character traits which distinctively define the "essence" of the human person.

These kinds of "essentialist" accounts are to be distinguished from those theories which suppose rather that the *imago dei* consists in a unique set of tasks or functions which set the human person apart from the rest of the created order and from the Creator.[6] There is not necessarily a unique list of attributes distinctive to humanity as such, but rather distinctive kinds of activities to which all humans are called by the God who created them "in God's image." These accounts tend to think in terms of humankind's responsibility either to exercise dominion over the created order or to exercise those spiritual responsibilities of moral rectitude owing to the Creator.

The Trinity and Relational Notions of Personhood

I take the recent revisioning of theological anthropology after a Trinitarian model to successfully suggest that neither essentialist nor functionalist accounts adequately capture the larger context of personhood

5. Two of the standard contemporary evangelical treatments of the *imago dei* move in this general direction — Philip E. Hughes, *The True Image: The Origin and Destiny of Man in Christ* (Grand Rapids: Eerdmans, 1989), and Anthony Hoekema, *Created in God's Image* (Grand Rapids: Eerdmans, 1986).

6. I suppose the same sort of "from below"/"from above" distinction could be made regarding these functionalist accounts, but the theoretical move made in either direction appears less significant on these accounts.

as centrally defined by its relations-in-community. The very relational identity of the triune God is reflected in the created order most especially in the creation of persons-in-relation. To be more precise, humanness is a function of "being-in-relation," rather than of an individual who is in possession of certain qualities or functions and who derivatively enters into relations with other individuals. The relationality of personhood means that persons are not actually persons outside of relations. This is a move away from an ontology of human personhood as objects (substances) and toward a relational ontology of human personhood. Persons are constituted by their sociality, by being in the nexus of relations. In this regard human consciousness is not a sort of a "thing" which a list of attributes could accurately locate on the ontological map.[7] Human consciousness is a way to talk about our being in relation to the created order.

One obvious experiential reality which points in this "relational" direction is the very ambiguity of ordinary language when speaking of ourselves. We may sometimes use the first-person voice ("I") and other times the third-person ("he/she"). We experience ourselves in the middle of this ambiguity — as a person conscious of himself or herself. But this reminds us of the difficulty of dealing with ourselves as if we were merely "things." If we are "aware of ourselves," it may be asked, "who is aware of what?" Or reflecting on an older bit of wisdom, "it is important to talk to yourself and not simply listen to yourself," we may fairly ask, who is talking, who is listening, and are they the same? We can speak as if there is a little person "inside" us to which we speak and sometimes listen. But no one would suggest that there are in fact two ontological "things" which together may be called one person.[8] Rather, it is the mysterious character of human consciousness that resists an

7. See especially John D. Zizioulas, "Human Capacity and Human Incapacity: A Theological Exploration of Personhood," *Scottish Journal of Theology* 28 (Oct. 1975): 401-8.

8. In the eighteenth century, David Hume went so far as to suggest that there is no such "thing" as a person and further that the notion of personhood is reducible to the concept of "perceptions." The so-called "bundle theory of human identity" left its lasting mark on those philosophical movements of the twentieth century most closely associated with logical positivism. See Amelie Oksenberg Rorty, ed., *The Identities of Persons* (Berkeley: University of California Press, 1976) for a helpful discussion of this philosophical trajectory. The Humean tradition (as in positivism) remains resolutely individualistic in orientation.

easy description as a sort of "thing," and instead induces us to think in terms of a "subject."

All of this underscores the insight about the nature of persons as constituted by their relations. And what is distinctive about a Christian anthropology is precisely the affirmation that it is a peculiar relation which in the end most clearly and adequately explains human personhood — namely, the relation to the God who is, in some ontologically prior sense, personal. It is this distinctive and particular relationship which most nearly captures the identity of human personhood. It is also appropriate to say, Christianly speaking, that relationship to God is not only that which gives identity to us as humans, but also that which constitutes our humanity. Our existing as persons is rooted in our relation to God. It is also true to say, asymmetrically, that God's existence is not rooted in a relation to humanity. It is rooted in the triune relationships that exist prior to and apart from creation.[9] Further, it is the very permanence of God which grounds the independence of the triune persons from human personhood. It is the very transitory character of human personhood that grounds its dependence in the triune persons. It is the nature of that "transitoriness" and thereby "dependence" which Scriptures depict with the language of "image." Conversely, the Scriptures use the language of "idolatry" when this peculiar kind of relation-to-God is subverted in religiously significant ways. The idol may be ontologically vacuous, but it is still incredibly powerful. The power of the idol is precisely in the transformation of the idolater into the image of the idol. This is the mirror dynamic at work in the imaging of God. The image-bearer, like the idolator, is re-made in the image of the One she seeks.

The language of "image" argues for a dependence upon an "original."[10] The nature of "dependence" is not manifest until something further is known about the image, the original, and the peculiar relation between them. The earliest account of the *imago dei* (Gen. 1:26-27) is notoriously silent about the character of that concept as such.[11] It is

---

9. It is not my central concern to enter into the theological discussion of the Trinity, which is quite naturally where these themes would need much greater elaboration.

10. Some of what follows finds its genesis in the work of Meredith G. Kline, *Images of the Spirit* (Grand Rapids: Baker Book House, 1980), and in turn from Henri Blocher, *In the Beginning: The Opening Chapters of Genesis,* trans. David G. Preston (Downers Grove, Ill.: InterVarsity Press, 1987).

11. By most reckonings, the language of "image" *(ṣelem)* in the Genesis 1 account is

the witness of the Scriptures as canon which serves as a touchstone for these matters and to which the record of classical Christian theological inquiry continually turns.[12] The shape of the canonical story suggests that the overriding relation of the image (human persons) to the original (triune God) is that of worship, honor, completion, and satisfaction, and conversely suggests that the subverting of that relationship of image to original is that of perversion, corruption, consumption, and possession.[13]

It is a relational dynamic that connects image (person) to original (God), but it is also centrally a relationship of worship/honor that depicts this connection. From the beginning to the end of redemptive history, the image is constituted by its (dis)honoring of God. The image (humankind) finds its *telos* in the honoring relationship to the original (God the creator). This is true at the beginning of the canon and at the end of the canon. Two thematic corollaries highlight this canonical conviction — namely, that of a reflecting/mirroring relationship and, correspondingly, that of light and illumination.

A Peculiar Relationship

The story of redemption begins with the creation of humankind in the image *(ṣelem)* and likeness *(demut)* of its creator with little or no explanation beyond the reality that the origin of human identity lies in the relationship of reflection to the Creator. The image reflects the original.[14] This is merely to say that the image images the original. The

---

rooted in the ancient construct of a concrete form representing an invisible deity. See the related articles under "Image" in *New International Dictionary of New Testament Theology,* ed. Colin Brown, vol. 2 (Grand Rapids: Zondervan, 1976).

12. Grenz provides a paradigmatic hermenuetical discussion of the *imago dei* — moving from Genesis to the remainder of the canon and then returning from the end to the beginning. See *The Social God and the Relational Self,* chap. 7 in particular.

13. Cornelius Plantinga, *Not the Way It's Supposed to Be: A Breviary of Sin* (Grand Rapids: Eerdmans, 1995), argues that "sin" is conceptually messy. So idolatry is never merely "one sort of practice." Rather, it is a large umbrella of concepts all of which subvert the original relationship between image and original.

14. Left unsaid at this point are the content of the reflection, the character of that reflection, the nature in which that reflection occurs. This is not to say that the context, both immediate and more distant across the canon, does not speak to the issue, but

theme of reflection is contextually extended in the emphasis upon light and illumination in the first chapter of Genesis. God governs the temporal character of human existence with the presence of the sun and the moon. They illuminate the earthly existence and they also serve as signs for "seasons and festivals" — religious indicators of human purpose (Gen. 1:14). The Sabbath of Genesis 1 is marked off by the sun and the moon, as will be all of Israel's "religious days." In this sense, God's purposes are reflected in the illumination of human life with the sun and the moon.

The unique character of the human reflection is the relationship that is constituted with the God who speaks creation into being but is peculiarly involved in speaking to and with our human parents. They speak as individuals-in-relationship. They do not speak as equals, but they do nonetheless carry on a speaking which quite clearly denotes a social character to the human/divine interaction. The relational character of the *imago dei* is also apparent in the immediate context of Genesis 1 in the mention of male and female after the initial designation of the *imago dei* (Gen. 1:26-27).[15] At the end of the canon, these two themes of relationality and illumination are again highlighted. In the new heavens and new earth, there is no need for the sun or the moon, for the "glory of God gives it light, and the Lamb is its lamp" (Rev. 21:23). The relationality theme comes out most strongly here in the affirmation that "Now the dwelling of God is with men, and he will live with them. They will be his people, and God himself will be with them and be their God" (Rev. 21:3).

The argument or proposal to follow is that the substance of the reflection is the nature of the relation and the ground of the relation is the character of the reflection. This would further suggest that bare notions of sociality will not sufficiently ground personhood in the ca-

---

rather that we ought not infuse the concept of "image" with meaning extraneous to it. See G. C. Berkouwer, *Man: The Image of God* (Grand Rapids: Eerdmans, 1962), chap. 3, for further elaboration of this hermeneutical point.

15. Grenz's discussion of the Barthian contention that the *imago dei* is constituted by the male/female claim is most helpful. He both affirms the importance of the male/female claim and also places it in the larger construct of "community" themes present in the canon. Without great elaboration here, let me also suggest the later canonical connection between idolatry and adultery. The subversion of the marital relationship intrinsic to the concept of adultery serves as a theological analogy to understand the nature of the subversion intrinsic to idolatry.

nonical soil. The substance of the relationship is defined by God creating, redeeming, and consummating the image. The image stands in a peculiar relationship to a God who speaks and acts in peculiar ways. And it is those "peculiar ways" that serve as the thread that holds the canon together and that thereby hold human identity together. This proposal also claims that the subversion of those "peculiar ways" is the very underside of the canonical witness regarding the *imago dei,* namely, that of idolatry. Idolatry is the conceptual "turning upside down" of the originally intended relationship of image to origin.[16] It is the defining of human life on terms different than those revealed in creation, redemption, and consummation. There is a profoundly religious substance to the relational character of the human person because of the God who creates, redeems, and consummates and thus a profound danger across the canon toward the subverting of that relationship. The distinctive character of divine speech and divine action constitutes the distinctiveness of the image and therefore in turn defines idolatry. To that suggestion I now turn.

Genesis, the *Imago,* and Personhood

The two accounts of creation in Genesis 1-3 have been a point of great discussion over the last one hundred years.[17] Without supposing that those controversies have been settled, research on ancient covenant treaties suggests that the first account/tablet (Gen. 1:1-2:4a) offers a prologue to the story of Israel's history as a covenant people while the second account/tablet (Gen. 2:4b-3:24) is the first story (the first of the *toledots,* "these are the generations") in that covenant history.[18] The first

---

16. G. C. Berkouwer is one of the few theologians in the twentieth century who have drawn the explicit connection between the content of the *imago dei* and idolatry. His treatment is insightful and influential in what follows. See his *Man: The Image of God.*

17. Claus Westermann, *Genesis: An Introduction,* trans. John J. Scullion (Philadelphia: Fortress, 1992), and Victor Hamilton, *The Book of Genesis: Chapters 1-17* (Grand Rapids: Eerdmans 1995), both offer helpful summaries of the critical interpretive tradition of the two tables of Genesis 1-3 in the twentieth century.

18. Hermann Gunkel's commentary on Genesis at the outset of the twentieth century (*Genesis* [Göttingen: Vandenhoeck und Ruprecht, 1910]) effectively framed the discussion of Genesis throughout the twentieth century as a portrayal of a "saga." Gerhard

tablet serves as a kind of overarching preamble to the rest of the Pentateuchal narratives. It is a covenantal preamble that defines the ultimate purpose and destiny of Israel.[19] It is there that the central characters in the drama and the central purposes of the drama are introduced.[20] By all accounts the first table appears as a different literary unit from that which follows, appearing out of place if interpreted as simply the first of the "stories" of Genesis.

The framework of the seven days (in Gen. 1:1–2:4a) embeds the notion that the creation's *telos* is its Creator, who "rests" on the seventh day.[21] God is introduced as *Elohim* (almighty/absolute), who creates by speaking all that is into being (and thereby interpreting all that is). The Spirit of God hovers over the created order, reflecting the presence of God and protecting that presence.[22] In the first table, day 6 appears as climactic in the acts of creation, but it is actually day 7, which never ends, that grants to all of creation its intended purpose — the Sabbath. The Sabbath account of Genesis 2:1-3 argues for the claim that all of creation finds its fulfillment/satisfaction in God.[23] This principle is at stake wherever the Sabbath principle is found across the canon — from

---

Von Rad, *Genesis*, revised ed., Old Testament Library series (Philadelphia: Westminster, 1972), Gunkel's most important interpreter through mid century, accepted the language of "saga" as an appropriate designation but asked how it fit with the language of "faith" which so permeated the account. At mid century (1947) Geerhardus Vos suggested this saga/faith was the relationship between a covenant people and their peculiar covenant history. See his *Biblical Theology* (Grand Rapids: Eerdmans, 1947).

19. Westermann refers to the first table as a "solemn overture" — the first movement in the pentateuchal symphony. Claus Westermann, *Genesis 1–11: A Commentary*, trans. John Scullion (Minneapolis: Augsburg, 1984), p. 129.

20. The recent work by Michael Horton, *Covenant and Eschatology: The Divine Drama* (Louisville: Westminster John Knox, 2002), exploits the metaphor of "drama" as an illuminating theme for a theological description of the covenant relationship between God and his people.

21. The heptadic structure of the days points to the common ancient use of the number 7 as a way to speak of perfection or completion.

22. This is Kline's argument in *Images of the Spirit*. Kline's extended argument linking the presence of the Spirit with the *imago dei* can be found in "Creation in the Image of the Glory Spirit," *Westminster Theological Journal* 39, no. 2 (1977): 250-72.

23. The first account of the decalogue (in Exod. 20:1-17) argues for the routine of 6:1 — six days of work followed or completed by a day of Sabbath. The work of Israel's week found its fulfillment in the worship of their God. Work and worship were to be teleologically related.

Israel's command to rest on the Sabbath (Exod. 20:8-11; Deut. 5:12-15), to the celebration of the festival days and the Sabbath year and climactically the Jubilee year (Lev. 23:32; 25:1-55), to the protection of the Sabbath during the monarchy (2 Kings 11), to the restoration of Sabbath practices after the return from exile (Neh. 13), to Jesus asserting his Lordship over the Sabbath (Luke 6:1-11), to the promise of an eternal Sabbath (Heb. 4:6-11).[24]

The ordering of the "days" is intentional as the themes of "governing" (day 4 governs day 1) and filling (day 5 fills day 2) come together in the relation of day 6 to day 3 (filling and governing).[25] The language of governing is the protection of the created order as reflecting the divine presence, and the language of filling is that of the increase of the divine presence through the created order. The divine presence is both protected and proclaimed, themes that remain central to Israel's well-being throughout redemptive history.

The teleological account of creation in the first tablet suggests that the "image" of verses 26 and 27 reflects the activity of its creator in governing and filling, in protecting and proclaiming the divine presence.[26] The image is not to be equated with this activity but is derivative from its central identifying mark — reflecting God. It is important to note that the language of "governing" implies not only a moral character to human actions, but also an illuminating reflection of the divine activity. On day 4, the sun and the moon are said to "govern" the day and the night (day 1). The imagery here suggests the illumination of these temporal spaces by the sun and the moon, even as they also demarcate the "religious" days of Israel when Israel is called to uniquely worship God. When applied to the "image" in 1:26, the language of "governing"

---

24. See Marva Dawn, *Keeping the Sabbath Wholly: Ceasing, Resting, Embracing, Feasting* (Grand Rapids: Eerdmans, 1989), for an extended discourse on the Sabbath principle. See also Niels-Erik Andreasen, *Rest and Redemption: A Study of the Biblical Sabbath* (Berrien Springs, Mich.: Andrews University Press, 1978).

25. The symmetical structure of the first six days (1-4, 2-5, 3-6) again underscores the asymmetical character of the seventh (Sabbath principle) day.

26. The garden of Genesis 2:4–3:24 is strongly analogous to Israel's later temple where the presence of God is manifest at the center of the temple structure even as the tree of life stands in the middle of the garden. Likewise, the protections accorded the divine presence in the temple bear strong resemblances to the protections around the garden as the means to keep the original couple from the tree of life in the middle of the garden.

argues for the protection of the divine reflection throughout the created order. Humans reflect God's character in their actions. To extend this point of "reflection," the language of "filling" is used, first of the "animal kingdom" (on day 5) but centrally with respect to the image-bearers in verse 28. "To be fruitful and multiply" carries the connotation of increasing/expanding the illumination of the divine reflection throughout the created order.

The relationality of the "image" in Genesis 1 is most emphatically underscored in the immediate context of verses 26 to 27. The plural of divine deliberation ("let us make") in verse 26 is mirrored in the final affirmation of the "image" as male and female. Leaving aside the controversial hermeneutical question as to whether the divine plural of verse 26 is a foreshadowing of the Trinity, it is undoubtedly related to the plurality intrinsic to the creation of humankind as male and female. The ground of humankind's relationality is some kind of plurality in God.[27] At the very least the divine ability to "speak" argues for a God who is personal in some profound sense.[28]

The image reflects the divine being, illuminating the created order with that reflection and thereby manifesting a unique relationship to God. The language of "image" draws attention to this reflection of and relationship to God. It is not without reason historically that theologians have speculated about the substance of the *imago dei* as an alternative means to get clear on the nature of this reflection and this relationship. But we ought to remember that the question of the substance of the *imago dei* is secondary to the teleological claim that the *imago dei* reflects God.

Idolatry and the Loss of *Image* Language

It is often a point of theological curiosity why the language of "image" (*ṣelem*) is used infrequently in the canon though the history of Christian theology has normally allowed the *imago dei* to assume central pro-

---

27. The presence of other divine plurals in the theophanies of Genesis lend further weight to this claim. Cf. Gen 11:7; 18:1-2; 32:28.

28. Cf. Nicholas Wolterstorff, *The Divine Discourse: Philosophical Reflections on the Claim That God Speaks* (Cambridge: Cambridge University Press, 1995).

portions as the defining essence of humankind. Representatively Berkouwer says,

> It is indeed rather striking that the term is not used often at all, and that it is far less "central" in the Bible than it has been in the history of Christian thought. This apparent discrepancy vanishes, however, when we note that Scripture's references to the image of God, whenever there are such, have a special urgency and importance. Furthermore, there is the possibility that Scripture often deals with the concept of the image of God without using those exact words, so that we surely should not a priori limit our investigation of the concept to considering only places where the term itself is used.[29]

The point is important though it probably ought to be nuanced further. That to which the language of the *imago dei* points is most definitely present across the breadth of the canon though the particular language itself changes. And further, without "reading between the lines" too much, it is important to note that the very change of terms across the canon is itself indicative of larger theological points.[30] This becomes clear in at least two ways: first, at the point where the language of "imaging" drops out, the language of idolatry becomes prominent, and, second, the reemergence of the language of "imaging" is most strongly connected to the arrival of Jesus Christ, who is both the restorer of the *imago dei* and the perfect Image of God.

It is to those two concerns I now turn. The image *(ṣelem)* language which appears so important in the first tablet, occurring three times emphatically in the creation act of humankind (vv. 26-27), reoccurs but two more times in the Pentateuch — at Genesis 5:1 and 9:6. At Genesis 5:1 the reference is to Seth being born in the likeness *(demut)* and image *(ṣelem)* of his father, Adam.[31] The larger theology of sonship and inheritance rights is likely in view here as Seth is distinguished

29. Berkouwer, *Man: The Image of God,* p. 67.

30. This important intuition assumes that the canon functions theologically as a covenant document, and thus it is important to understand the interpretive horizons across the canon in which any particular context is embedded. See Horton, *Covenant and Eschatology,* and Richard Lints, *The Fabric of Theology* (Grand Rapids: Eerdmans, 1993).

31. The fact that the word order is reversed in Genesis 5:1 from Genesis 1:26 ("likeness" and then "image") is the primary exegetical argument for the interchangeability of these two terms.

from his older brother Cain, who has forfeited inheritance rights by virtue of the murdering of his other brother, Abel. The connection of "sonship" and "image" here likely connotes a relationship of honor and respect intrinsic to the ancient familial context.[32] The son is the image of the father by virtue of honoring his father, and therefore the son comes to resemble his father. What the son loves and honors, the son becomes like.

At Genesis 9:6 the reference is to the divine prohibition of murder on the grounds that God has made humankind in his image. The protection accorded humanity here is grounded in God's regard for the divine reflection. This protection also is granted as an integral part of the covenant with Noah that mirrors the covenantal administration of the first three chapters of Genesis. And this is the last major section of narrative material prior to the emergence of the covenant of redemption with Abraham in Genesis 12-15. From that point forward the protection accorded is actually the presence of God rather than the reflection of God in humankind. And for the remainder of Israel's history, it was YHWH's promise to be "with his people" that served as the strongest protection against outside threats.

It is also with the advent of the covenant with Abraham that the language of image virtually drops out of use. The particularity of the divine beneficence falls uniquely upon Israel from this point forward, and its most tangible evidence is the theophanic presence of God accompanying Israel out of Egypt, in their journey in the desert wilderness, and in the settlement of the promised land. This "divine presence" is not incidentally related to Israel's well-being but essential to it. To Israel, the divine presence was the source of hope and the source of comfort — if not also the source of fear. God was not to be approached heedlessly nor without due honor accorded.

From the exodus event forward in Israel's history, the greatest danger toward the removing of the divine presence was idolatry amidst the people of Israel. The landmark text in this regard is Exodus 32, which records the golden calf incident. The Israelites were in the wilderness

---

32. In this regard it is significant that in the genealogy at the beginning of the Gospel of Luke, Adam is called the "son of God," as Seth is called the "son of Adam" (Luke 3:38). This genealogy is unique among ancient genealogies for its inclusion of God in the list.

after their release from Egypt. God had brought Israel to Sinai to renew Israel's covenant identity and to (re)establish the terms of the covenant. The mount of Sinai was the place where the theophanic glory was manifest (smoke and fire and earth trembling). Warnings were given to Israel not to come near the mount lest they see God and perish. God's presence was protected. Moses ascended the mountain as the mediator for the people to meet with God face to face. The narrative portrayal of the encounter between Moses and the divine presence remained as the abiding validation of Mosaic authority.

The central challenge to the divine presence was the ritual creation of the golden calf — an idol likely modeled upon the fertility idols of Egypt from whence Israel had recently come. The divine judgment is swift and terrible, the final consequence being the removing of the divine presence from the camp of meeting. The haunting words of God recorded in Exodus 33:3 represent a grave concern to Israel's well-being: "I will not go with you, because you are a stiff-necked people and I might destroy you on the way." God will not dwell in the midst of an idolatrous people.

Upon closer scrutiny, we see that it was not simply any act of disobedience that was the root cause for the removing of the divine presence. Rather, idolatry itself — creating a god in one's own image — was the conceptual undoing of the original act of being created in the image of God. Israel's collective act effected an ironic reversal of Israel's original covenantal metanarrative. Rather than illuminating the created order with the reflection of YHWH, Israel now sought to capture its significance and security from the created order. In due course the Israelites became like the idol they had created: stiff-necked, hard-hearted, with eyes that could not see and ears that could not hear. They became images of an idol.[33] Yet the idol was itself powerless to effect the hoped-for help. The idol was not simply an alternative deity, but a false god — no god at all. The idol was strangely powerful and yet not living! YHWH's insistence that no other gods be worshipped (Exod. 20:3) did not imply that there were in fact other gods, but rather that worship and honor were proper only as directed toward YHWH. All other worship refashioned the worshipper in the image of the inani-

---

33. Cf. Dick Keyes, "The Idol Factory," in *No God but God,* ed. Os Guinness and John Seel (Chicago: Moody, 1992).

mate creation rather than in the image of the personal God. And for this reason, the honoring of the golden calf was the theological turning-upside-down of the original created order.[34]

The canonical echo of the Sinai episode is narratively important for Israel's future relationship to YHWH.[35] Israel's peculiar identity rested in their peculiar honoring of YHWH and in retaining their distance from the gods and idols of the other nations.[36] Their place and security in the land were contingent upon this peculiar honoring. Honoring God was not simply a matter of obedience to the divine commands, but also a covenantal loyalty to the God who granted them significance and purpose. They were to desire the things YHWH desired and to delight in the things YHWH delighted in. The language of marital infidelity was often used as an overlapping explanation of idolatry.[37] "To go whoring after other gods" was to desire the very things YHWH abhorred, which suggested not simply the breaking of laws but also the straying of the heart from the relationship with YHWH, the relationship that would be uniquely satisfying. The language of desire connoted that sense in which the whole person had gone astray, and though momentarily pleasurable, ultimately the alliance with the false gods was destructive of the whole person and the whole community.[38]

34. Cf. Jacques Ellul, *The Humiliation of the Word* (Grand Rapids: Eerdmans, 1985), for a provocative discussion of the relationship between idolatry and the original divine Word in the context of the episode at Sinai. See pp. 86-96.

35. Moses reflects on the long-term impact of the ironic reversal in Deuteronomy 9. The psalmist mentions it as a defining episode in redemptive history in Psalm 106. Allusions to it are found in the indictment which comes upon Samaria during the period following the Babylonian exile (Hosea 6-8). The episode helps to frame the purpose of rebuilding the temple in the restoration of Israel after exile (Nehemiah 9). Finally, mention ought to be made of Luke's recounting (in Stephen's speech) Israel's history, and his description of the golden calf episode as a defining episode in that history (Acts 7).

36. See Walter Brueggemann, *Israel's Praise: Doxology against Idolatry and Ideology* (Philadelphia: Fortress, 1988), for an extended discussion of the relationship of idolatry and the public identity of Israel in the ancient Near East.

37. Cf. Exodus 34:14-15, Leviticus 20:5, Judges 2:17, 1 Chronicles 5:25, Isaiah 1:21, 23:17, Jeremiah 3:8-9, Ezekiel 16:17, Hosea 4:12-13, Micah 1:7. The exegetical trajectory linking idolatry conceptually with adultery likely begins with the original placing of *imago dei* together with the male/female reference in Genesis 1:27.

38. See Raymond C. Ortlund, *Whoredom: God's Unfaithful Wife in Biblical Theology* (Grand Rapids: Eerdmans, 1996), for an extended treatment of these themes.

By way of contrast, Israel's true bridegroom (YHWH) manifested a genuine love for the bride — a love which both was glorious and illuminated the glory of YHWH. In the later prophets (Isaiah, Jeremiah, Ezekiel, Hosea)[39] especially, YHWH's faithful love of Israel stands in stark contrast to Israel's infidelity. The use of marital language to depict YHWH's relationship to Israel hearkens back to the Genesis account where the marriage relationship was an integral part of the created order — and most especially a reflection of the divine image. The sense of "belonging to each other" which marriage affirmed was rooted in the original relationship of *Elohim* to our human parents. They were created in God's image as those who naturally belong to God, not as possessions but as persons-in-relationship. Those created in the *imago dei* were called and privileged to be in a relationship of intimacy with their creator.

With the emergence of Israel's canon, their identity as the people of YHWH was rooted in the original calling to image YHWH. And this "imaging" called them to a relationship of intimacy with their creator and to reflect that relationship in all their relationships. The original image was theologically turned upside down with the idolatrous pursuit of meaning and purpose apart from YHWH. Yet YHWH was resolutely faithful to his people/image. It is God whose fidelity stands in contrast to these people's infidelity. Is this not the primary reason that image language disappears after Genesis 9? The focus of the covenant history from that point forward is upon YHWH's actions in redeeming, restoring, and renewing Israel.

Image and Idol in the New Covenant

The New Testament affirms this inverted relationship between the image and the original, but extends the analysis by suggesting that God takes the form of the image and thereby renews, restores, and redeems it. This is one of the important metaphors through which the notion of the incarnation is elaborated in the New Testament. God has taken on human nature as the very means of reconciling the alienated parties. And so it is not surprising to find the interweaving of canonical

---

39. See, for example, Isaiah 61-62, Jeremiah 25 and 33, Ezekiel 16, and Hosea 3.

themes of reflection and relationship as central to the image language in the New Testament.

All four Gospels depict Jesus against the backdrop of earlier canonical material. Matthew and Luke place Jesus in a genealogical relationship to both David and Abraham. Intriguingly, Luke places Adam in Jesus' genealogy as the "son of God." Mark's Gospel opens with John the Baptist inheriting the vocation of Isaiah as the "one crying in the wilderness, preparing the way of the Lord" (Mark 1:3). John's Gospel begins in the beginning with a virtual rehearsal of Genesis 1 through the person of Jesus.[40] Jesus is the divine presence who is "in the beginning" and has come now to "tabernacle with us."

In each of these accounts the narrative identity of Jesus is rooted in the Old Testament portrayal of YHWH's relationship to Israel. Of particular interest is the argument each makes that Jesus manifested more clearly what it means to be human by fulfilling the original intention of the *imago dei*. As Israel was typologically related to Adam, so Jesus was typologically related both to Adam (as the second/last Adam; see Rom. 5:12-21 and 1 Cor. 15:45) and to Israel (as the son of David; see Acts 2:14-41 and Rev. 22:13-17). Sonship language reflects the relationship of image to original (as representative) as well as that of the one who inherits the blessings and property of the father. These two themes, interwoven together, track the earlier discussions on reflection and relationship at the heart of the *imago dei* construct.

Central to any discussion of the New Testament appropriation of the *imago dei* construct are two Pauline texts, 2 Corinthians 4:4 and Colossians 1:15. In the former, the apostle was arguing for the character of the gospel as formerly veiled but now revealed in the person of Jesus, who is the image/likeness *(eikōn)* of God. The gospel is the glory of Christ whose light illuminates those whose eyes had formerly been blinded by idolatry. The "god of this world" *(theos tou aiōnos)*, like the golden calf, has blinded all those who sought security and purpose at its feet. The idol has refashioned its worshippers after its own image — blind and dumb. Christ, in a virtual act of re-creation, restores the "inner nature" *(esō hēmōn)*, but now, in an ironic reversal, the second cre-

---

40. See Masanobu Endo, *Creation and Christology* (Tübingen: Mohr Siebeck, 2002), for an extended argument linking John's Prologue to the customary early Jewish tradition of commentaries on Genesis 1.

ation is enacted by one who is the very image/likeness of God. This is a re-creation in the image of the Image.

In the larger context of 2 Corinthians 3 and 4, Paul draws his readers' attention to the encounter at Sinai when Moses' face shone because he had been in the presence of God. The glory of God was reflected in the glow of Moses' body — hearkening back to the Genesis claim that humans are the images/reflections of God. Not only does Paul now make the claim that Jesus is the image/likeness of God, but further that those who know him shine with a glory greater than Moses'. The divine presence has now reached a redemptive climax, and the glory of God shines in a qualitatively greater way than it had previously. The *imago dei* is being filled with yet a "greater" reflection of the divine glory than even at Sinai.

Paul complements this claim in Colossians 1:15 by again affirming that Jesus is the image of God *(eikōn tou theou)* but now claiming that in Jesus dwells the fullness of God. Jesus carries the full weight of the divine glory. Yet Jesus, like YHWH, creates all things both visible and invisible — language which reminds the reader that the visible is a reflection of the invisible, as the image is a reflection of the original. Paul (like John) places Jesus in the opening act of creation as a means to argue that he is the *telos* of creation — as God was the *telos* of humankind. In Colossians we read that "In him [Jesus] all things hold together" (1:17), even as Paul affirmed in Acts 17 that "In him [God] we live and move and have our being" (v. 28). As the image of God, Jesus reflects God and, paradoxically, fills all things with that reflection. He is the new creator echoing his role as the original creator. As Paul will argue in Romans 8:28-30, the destiny of those "in Christ" is to be conformed to the image of the Son by the redemptive power of the Spirit. Christ is the new creator as well as the *telos* of the new creation, even as the Spirit is the one who constructs the new temple presence of God through Christ by means of setting up Christ's (and the Father's) residence in the believers' hearts.

The author of the letter to the Hebrews makes the claim that Jesus is the exact representation *(charaktēr)* of God, the one in whom the beginning and the end hold together (Heb. 1:3). John represents Jesus as the *alpha* and *omega* even as he is the visible representation of the invisible God. The *imago dei* finds its fullest theological significance in Jesus, in whom the ironic reversal of the original reversal of sin is begun (and will be consummated).[41] If idolatry is the theological act of honoring the self above the creator, Jesus is the one who reverses that theological move by reconstituting the *imago dei* with the full reflection of the divine glory in his own person. Jesus is the true image in contrast to the false idol.[42]

Conclusion: Images and Possession

The canonical relationship between imaging and idolatry suggests that the *imago dei* is fundamentally a relational term but one with a peculiar relationship in view. It is not merely the sociality of the human person which is at stake in the language of the *imago dei* but rather an honoring of God (and others) above oneself. The *imago dei* is constituted as complete and fulfilled in that reflecting/honoring relation. Idolatry is not simply substituting one's object of worship (from God to the created thing), but also involves the manner in which the object is worshipped. The worship of the living God does not seek to possess God for one's own purposes.[43] In this sense to worship idols *is* to be possessed by the desire to possess. One will become what one worships, but worship itself denigrates the self when its highest good is itself. It is also not merely "giving yourself away" at stake in proper worship, but also "whom you are giving yourself away to and in what manner are you giving yourself up." Martin Buber supposed that idols turned people into objects — and therefore God could be worshipped idolatrously, that is, as an object for one's own purposes.[44] This is

---

41. Grenz's reminder that the image has a significant eschatological component to it, though not explored here, is exactly right and here begs for a fuller treatment. See Grenz, *Social God and the Relational Self,* chap. 6.

42. Notice the language of idolatry used in 1 Corinthians 12 and 2 Corinthians 6 as a way to describe the former state of those who have now come to confess Jesus as Lord.

43. It is intriguing that the secular prophets of the nineteenth century (such as Ludwig Feuerbach, Karl Marx, and Friedrich Nietzsche) leveled the charge of idolatry against Christianity itself, supposing that the god of Christianity had been created in the church's own image as a means to further its own interests. An intended trajectory of this essay is the comparison of the Old Testament prophets' use of the language of idolatry with the secular prophets' use of the same. Cf. Merold Westphal, *Suspicion and Faith: The Religious Uses of Modern Atheism* (Grand Rapids: Eerdmans, 1994).

44. Buber writes, "Whoever has been converted by substitution, now 'has' a phantom that he calls God. God, however, the eternal presence, cannot be had. Woe unto the possessed who fancy they possess God" (*I and Thou* [1922], p. 110).

the difference between the image of reflection and the image/idol of possession.[45]

It is the turn to the subject in recent times, however, which runs the risk of defining the subject-in-relation without due regard for its ultimate purpose — honoring/delighting in the living God.[46] It is a peculiar kind of sociality that the canon of Scripture holds out for our purview and which the Redeemer has come to re-constitute. It is a sociality that resists the idolatrous intentions of possession and consumption and resists them at the cost of our being aliens in our wider culture of consumption. The unleashing of desire for consumptive purposes is near the center of our present cultural story.[47] The turn toward consumption both follows and precipitates the turn to the subject in the wider culture, and it is entirely vulnerable to a peculiar idolatry of possession — an idolatry to which the evangelical movement is peculiarly susceptible given its relationship to modernity.[48]

The divine community (Trinity) is the blueprint of the redeemed ecclesial community as well as the ontological weight of what substantiates the ecclesial community as a redeemed image and not as the original. It is God, by virtue of being God, who grants significance and purpose to the human community and who thereby redeems and

45. There is a lengthy secondary literature which arose from Erving Goffman's sociological study, *The Presentation of Self in Everyday Life* (New York: Doubleday, 1959), owing in some measure to Goffman's provocative insight that human identity in the modern era is accompanied by the pressure to manage an image. "Image management" became an increasingly fruitful construct to speak about the postmodern extension of the modern turn to the subject. It is not difficult to coordinate the preceding canonical account of the *imago dei* to Goffman's insights about the "art of impression management." The best analysis of Goffman's legacy can be found in E. Tseelon, "Is the Presented Self Sincere? Goffman, Impression Management and the Postmodern Self," *Theory, Culture and Society* 9, no. 2 (1992): 115-28.

46. Cf. Craig Gay, *The Way of the (Modern) World* (Grand Rapids: Eerdmans, 1998), for helpful insights into the character of modernity as a technological kind of institution which reshapes human desire in its own image. Gay's final chapter, "Toward a Theology of Personhood," suggests the danger of idolatry in the context of the modern world, though he underscores the tendency toward reductionism whenever idolatry is highlighted as theologically significant.

47. Cf. Mike Featherstone, *Consumer Culture and Postmodernism* (London: Sage, 1991), and George Ritzer, *Explorations in the Sociology of Consumption* (London: Sage, 2001).

48. Robert Wuthnow, *God and Mammon* (New York: Free Press, 1994), and R. Laurence Moore, *Selling God* (New York: Oxford University Press, 1994).

reconciles that community to its proper purpose. It is the *Godness* of God (ontological weight) that serves as the foundational assumption in the redemptive historical account of persons as created, redeemed, and consummated images. It is not just any sociality that defines the human person but a sociality whose *telos* is found in the permanence of God — in the very *Godness* of God.[49]

The very "ordinariness" of biblical language supposes that God's *oneness* is not a theological abstraction from the *threeness* of God.[50] Nor is God's *threeness* a theological abstraction from the oneness of God. The substantiality of divine unity (monotheism) ought not to undermine the sociality of the divine trinity (triunity). But neither should the sociality of the divine trinity undermine the substantiality of the divine unity. If evangelical theology has insufficiently appreciated the sociality of the divine trinity (and it has), it has nonetheless recognized the substantiality of the divine unity. The recent Trinitarian revisioning of the *imago dei* runs the risk of insufficiently appreciating the ontological weight of the classic claim of monotheism — the very weight needed to sustain the divine-human covenant in the face of idolatry.

The evangelical tradition has too frequently embraced the "solitary minds" of modernity as the means to resist the tyranny of corrupting communities. And in doing so, it has left itself open to the danger of reflecting the idolatries of our peculiar age of consumption. The evangelical sense of sociality rests too lightly on its understanding of the Christian faith, and evangelicals' protection of the individual has weighed too heavily in their soteriology. The "Christian life" in evangelical piety has too little space for the "Christian community." Often lost in practice is the sense of being covenantly bound to the people of God as a reflection of the triune God to whom they are covenantly bound.

---

49. To use other words, the economic Trinity and the immanent Trinity are both theologically significant grounds of a fuller conception of the *imago dei*. It is precisely the ontological weight of the immanent Trinity which underlies the relational significance of the economic Trinity for a doctrine of human personhood. This would suggest that collapsing of the immanent Trinity into the economic Trinity in Rahner (and Barth) is flawed. The consensus of the church prior to the twentieth century would also suggest this.

50. For example: Deuteronomy 6:4, "The Lord our God, the Lord is one"; the prophet Malachi ask rhetorically, "Did not one God create us all?" (Mal. 2:10); the epistle of Romans affirms that "There is only one God who will justify" (Rom. 3:30).

But where evangelical theology has mostly gotten it correct is its emphasis upon the uniqueness of the gospel — uniqueness grounded in the claim that there is only one God. The God revealed is the one divine being who requires an experiential encounter, who enacts the grounds of the encounter, and who authorizes the narrating of that encounter on the pages of Scripture. All of this points inextricably to Jesus Christ. It is Jesus Christ in whom the experiential encounter takes place. It is Jesus Christ who enacts that encounter in his incarnation. And it is the narrative of Jesus Christ as the alpha and omega of the canon of Scripture that is the hermeneutical center of the gospel. In each of these ways, the uniqueness of Jesus Christ is the necessary ground for the resistance of idolatry, the very idolatry to which evangelicals, on other grounds, are so susceptible. But it is this resource internal to the evangelical tradition (and the "Great Tradition" of Christianity) which serves as a ground for the hope of exodus from its present cultural captivity and as a route through which personhood might be recovered as "being-in-relation."

With Peter Berger, whom I quoted at the outset of this essay, we affirm that human identity is wrapped up in the dialectical relationship of the community to its constitutive elements — persons. As social creatures we do not exist independent of society, and theologically we do not exist apart from the reflecting relation to the divine community. Human significance rests precisely in what or whom we reflect and the relationships in which that reflection occurs.

Contributors

Stanley J. Grenz, formerly Pioneer McDonald Professor of Theology, Carey Theological College, Vancouver, British Columbia

Michael S. Horton, Professor of Theology, Westminster Theological Seminary, Escondido, California

Stanton L. Jones, Provost and Professor of Psychology, Wheaton College, Wheaton, Illinois

David H. Kelsey, Luther A. Weigle Professor of Theology, Yale Divinity School, New Haven, Connecticut

Richard Lints, Professor of Theology, Gordon-Conwell Theological Seminary, South Hamilton, Massachusetts

Nancey Murphy, Professor of Christian Philosophy, Fuller Theological Seminary, Pasadena, California

Mark R. Talbot, Associate Professor of Philosophy, Wheaton College, Wheaton, Illinois

William C. Weinrich, Academic Dean and Professor of Historical Theology, Concordia Theological Seminary, Fort Wayne, Indiana

Robert Louis Wilken, William R. Kenan Jr. Professor of Early Christian History, University of Virginia, Charlottesville, Virginia

Mark A. Yarhouse, Associate Professor of Clinical Psychology, Regent University, Virginia Beach, Virginia